THE MONEYSPINNERS

The MONEY-SPINNERS

An Intimate Portrait of the Men Who Run Canada's Banks

ROD McQUEEN

Macmillan of Canada
A Division of Gage Publishing Limited
Toronto, Canada

CANADIAN CATALOGUING IN PUBLICATION DATA

McQueen, Rod
The moneyspinners

Includes index.
ISBN 0-7715-9779-7

1. Bankers — Canada — Biography. 2. Banks and banking — Canada. I. Title.

HG2704.M36 332.1'2'0922 C83-098685-5

DESIGN: Brant Cowie/Artplus
Printed in Canada

To Sandy, whose creation this is as much as mine

TABLE OF CONTENTS

Preface and Acknowledgements

WHILE THERE HAVE BEEN many dusty corporate histories, and not a few technical textbooks, no one has ever written extensively about the human side of Canadian banking. That is what this book sets out to do. At once reviled and revered, bankers often feel themselves to be little understood and even less admired. Nor are they particularly talkative. As a result, it took some three hundred interviews to piece together the profiles of the men who run the banks and the system that exists in Canada. While *The Moneyspinners* was not written with the blessing of the institutions or the people described herein, most individuals (with one notable exception) were at least co-operative, although sometimes reluctantly so. For example, Chapter Three would not have been possible without the investigative efforts of the Ontario Securities Commission. In the end, however, one can only press on through such an undertaking for the most ethereal of reasons. Writing a book, in fact, is just the opposite of mountain climbing. You write a book because it's *not* there.

It can only be done with the help of many people. They include Frances McNeely and Maureen Mason-Jamieson, both of whom saw more of this book at various stages than they may care to remember. As well, praise be to three others: my publisher, the ever-cheerful Doug Gibson, who immediately saw the 140,000 words to come after reading a two-page outline; Anne Holloway, Macmillan editor-in-chief, who with endless patience taught me much about writing; and Peter C. Newman, without whose trail-blazing work, little would be possible in Canadian business journalism today.

ROD McQUEEN
JULY 1983

ONE

INTRODUCTION

The History and the Hysteria

ON QUIET WINGS they come, slipping into an awakening nation's capital by a dozen different routes to meet around the same mahogany table where they and their predecessors have gathered for two decades. The conclave occurs in a room with a sombre green rug and green walls, on the third floor of the Bank of Canada offices in Ottawa. The building is only two blocks west of the Parliament buildings on Wellington Street, but light-years from the televised braying and barracking of the Commons cockpit. There, a few petty politicians strut their stuff and have little lasting impact. At this twice-yearly meeting down the street, real power is played out — moneypower.

The twelve men who meet with the governor of the Bank of Canada are the chief executive officers of the country's chartered banks. Among them they oversee $350 billion in assets — about $15,000 for every man, woman, and child in the country. Of the twelve, seven are relatively small institutions; the others, the "Big Five" banks, together account for about 85 per cent of the money in the system. They wield power the way an orator plays with words — easily; they control corporate destinies the way a surgeon makes an incision — clinically; they run the financial lives of all Canadians like master puppeteers — secretly.

The looking-glass walls of the expanded Bank of Canada building are a mute symbol of the mixed signals that the bankers send. The harder you try to see through the looking-glass, the more you see a reflection of the outside world. It is here, behind the looking-glass curtain, that the country's monetary policy is set by the central bank and carried out by its twelve banking disciples.

These unelected governors of our financial system, out of reach of the ballot box and beyond the ken of the common man, are the keepers of the free-enterprise flame. They guard its flickering light as if they were the modern-day inheritors of an ancient religion, today's high priests of materialism. They have the power of life and death over entire communities; they can snuff out a struggling business with a telephone call; they find the funds for take-overs, hostile and friendly alike. These men see themselves as the quintessential capitalists, putting money at risk for any venturesome idea all the way from a new car through a new company to a needy country.

Each of the five major players at the meeting carries the title of chairman and chief executive officer (CEO); it is the only title that matters at their respective institutions. All the rest are mere mortals. The Big Five bosses are Rowland Frazee, chairman and chief executive officer of The Royal Bank of Canada — with $90 billion in assets, the largest bank in the country and the fourth-largest bank in North America. His engaging manner, easy gap-toothed smile, and commanding presence make him the closest thing to a statesman in the group. Russell Harrison heads the number two bank, the Canadian Imperial Bank of Commerce, an institution wracked by internal feuds and struggling corporate clients. He runs his fiefdom like a single-combat warrior — a hangover from his days as a paratrooper. William Mulholland presides over the Bank of Montreal, the only one of the five to come from outside banking to head a Big Five bank; he is arguably the brightest financier in Canada — certainly the one with the biggest ego. Fourth in size at $55 billion is The Bank of Nova Scotia, run by chairman and CEO Cedric Ritchie, a workaholic fuelled by cigarettes and black coffee, a man who is on the run even when he's sitting down. The smallest bank, and in some ways the most aggressive, is The Toronto-Dominion, run by Richard Thomson. The first of the Harvard MBAs to rocket to the top in Canadian banking, Thomson is one of the new breed, overseeing his $45-billion empire with a nationalist posture and all the self-control of a Zen Buddhist in a trance.

These five men are the moneyspinners.

Light streams in from three north-facing windows into the meeting room, which is essentially unchanged since the building opened in 1937. On the walls hang portraits of the central bank's first three governors: Graham Towers, James Coyne, and Louis Rasminsky. Another portrait is of Dr. Clifford Clark, who was deputy finance minister when the bank was created. It was during Rasminsky's time (1961–1973) that these meetings were begun. Gerald Bouey, now nearing the middle of his second seven-year term, has maintained the tradition. The Bank of Canada, as the government's agent, controls the amount of money in the country, prints currency, sets the value of the Canadian dollar, maintains reserves for the chartered banks, stores the nation's gold, keeps voluminous records of financial transactions, and sets interest rates.

The chartered banks take their cue from the Bank of Canada, fix their interest rates accordingly, take in deposits, loan money, and participate in a myriad of other retail and wholesale money activities. The business of banking is simple: gather deposits at one interest rate and loan the money out at a higher rate. The difference, or "spread," is the profit. A simple business, and, on the face of it, a correct and proper pastime, just as correct as the meeting and the lunch that follows, served on Royal Worcester china. There, Bouey will unwind a little, smoke a cigar, and talk about his occasional golf games.

At the two-and-a-half-hour meetings, convened by Bouey, the bankers hear the central bank's views on the economy and offer a few observations of their own. Loan demand in various regions is discussed, inflation expectations are traded, the lie of the land is debated, and measurements on the recovery from the recession are compared. Substantive suggestions are put forward about information that might be gathered that could be of value to all. TD's Richard Thomson once urged the Bank of Canada to collect data from all the banks about loans to foreign nations so that all participants would have an idea of Canada's risk to other powers. Bill Mulholland and Bank of Nova Scotia chairman Ced Ritchie more often than not find themselves in agreement on issues that crop up, for both are well connected with the Ottawa legislators.

In the room where they meet, usually in April and September, they gather as equals, corporate commandos who are part of the most profitable business sector in the country. These institutions will generate at least $2 billion in profit this year through 150,000 employees, more than seven thousand branches in Canada, and operations and loans in some two hundred countries around the world. These men represent the biggest multinationals this country has ever produced, and the Big Five Canadian banks number among the top seventy-five banks in the world. Some 40 per cent of their total assets are held outside Canada in foreign currencies. As well, the banks hold about $35 billion in mortgages (more than twice what they held five years ago) and control two-thirds of Canada's consumer loan market.

In their respective fiduciary fiefdoms, the moneyspinners hold the power of life and death in their canny hands. They can breathe life into a project with an infusion of funds or suffocate it forever by withdrawing the flow of capital. The decision may not be made on a whim, but it can come in a single sentence. All that a customer has struggled to build can be ended as the bankers begin to talk about getting back to the fundamentals, and stalk the country cutting off borrowers at the knees. This book is about their power and how they wield it at the Big Five and throughout Canada. As today's counterparts to the moneylenders Jesus threw out of the temple, they know they are not loved. Their strength comes from elsewhere, their power comes from the idol we have created. Says Henry Stalder, former Toronto representative for the Union Bank of Switzerland and now a first vice-president in Sydney, Australia: "When they dig in two thousand years and discover the banking temples we built, the archeologists of that time will ask, What did they worship? The answer, of course, is *money*. And the bankers are the priests of that society." As Commerce chairman Russ Harrison told his 1983 shareholders' meeting: "When you come into a bank, you come into a confessional in the financial sense." These men are money's guardians, the keepers of the keys. As long as Mammon rules, all must bow down as supplicants.

In the beginning, Canada's banks were tiny, formed by merchants to satisfy their own financial needs and to offer credit for trade deals. As pioneers progressed westward across the country, bank branches sprang up to serve the mines and mills around which communities were built, to arrange export payments and letters of credit, to safeguard payrolls, to fund farming regions. But most of all, the branches existed to look just plain solid. The manager often lived in back or upstairs, where there was a hole in the floor so he could see the vault door at night if strange noises disturbed his sleep. Larger branches were erected with enough steps up from the street to make a customer feel suitably winded, even relieved, to get inside.

The portals were heavy for solemnity as well as security. The façades were tricked out with columns and cornices, balustrades and balconies — any ancient architectural device reminiscent of some past Aegean splendour — to evoke trust, respect, and a little awe. Inside, the floors were marble, the ceilings often vaulted, the tellers (all male) ensconced in cages, the manager nowhere to be seen. The manner was suitably decorous, the aura ever so calm, the atmosphere almost reverential. With the wood and the granite and the quiet, it was hard to tell a bank counter from a church pew. The minister and the bank manager both instilled fear into their flocks, offered few favours, and expected blind trust. Admits Robin Korthals, Toronto-Dominion Bank president: "We're only solvent as long as people think we are." The amount of money loaned out should match the amount on deposit, but a mismatch can occur because it's easier for a customer to take out money on deposit than it is for the bank to get back the full amount owing on a loan. Banking, like religion, remains an institutionalized act of faith.

The first Canadian bank to operate successfully was the Montreal Bank, now the Bank of Montreal, begun in 1817. By 1867 there were thirty-five banks in Canada, most of them small, local businesses in specific regions of the country. By 1967, 163 bank charters had been issued, but only eight were active. Gone were some institutions with bizarre names and even more bizarre histories. In Montreal, Henry's Bank was born and died in 1837. The Bank of the People lasted five years, then merged with the Bank of Montreal in 1840. There was a Colonial Bank, a Consolidated Bank, and six different Commercial Banks in six cities. On Prince Edward Island, the Farmers Bank of Rustico struggled gamely along for thirty years until 1892. Hamilton, Ontario, had the Gore Bank; Cayuga, Ontario, was the proud home of the International Bank of Canada for a year until it failed in 1859. In Chippewa, Ontario, the Niagara Suspension Bridge Bank lasted five years; the bridge hung in longer. The last bank to fail in Canada was the Home Bank; its demise in 1923 swallowed more than half of the $15 million lost by Canadians in bank failures since Confederation. The failure also precipitated the establishment of the Inspector-General's office in Ottawa. During the Depression, when 5,522 banks went out of business in the U.S. (there are still some 14,000 U.S. banks),no Canadian bank failed, although several were kept afloat by the others.

Through the first half of the twentieth century, banks would merge rather than fail, creating a series of ever-larger national institutions. It was government policy to promote bigness; in the U.S., by contrast, banks were limited to operations in a single state. A few railways, a few banks, a small élite—the tactic was to keep Canada's ruling class within limits, perpetuating what Vancouver economist Herschel Hardin has called our "monopoly culture."

After the Second World War, through the go-go days of the 1950s and 1960s, competition among the banks actually decreased. More mergers occurred (the Toronto-Dominion Bank was created in 1955, the Canadian Imperial Bank of Commerce in 1961); the Mercantile, created in 1953, was the only addition to the family. The business had become petrified, a classic oligopoly. The price of admission was too high for any new group; rates charged were identical; new services were few and far between. The banks were like so many soldiers marching to the same command. Most bankers had joined as young men indentured to the service, and received all their training in the bank's systems. The corporate world and the public were relatively unsophisticated. Came the mid-1960s, however, and businesses began to demand more expertise from their bankers. The public began to have access to financial services from a host of other, more aggressive places: credit unions, trust companies, caisses populaires, finance companies. Money suddenly had velocity; credit was as casual as free love; there was no need to kowtow to a stuffy banker any more.

In response, the federal Bank Act revision of 1967, coming at the time of Expo and Centennial Year, made the banks more modern. The major changes in the act were the removal of the 6 per cent ceiling charged on bank loans; a reduction in the cash reserve requirements; and the removal of the prohibition on conventional mortgage lending by banks. For the first time, banks could get into consumer loans and mortgages with a vengeance.

It was a switch in direction that demanded changes within the banks — right from the counter to the executive suites where sleepy management was about to be awakened by the sounds of tomorrow. At the same time it laid the groundwork for the easier entry of new banks and the fifty-five foreign banks that have officially set up shop here. Just as electrification came to farm homes and city streets a few decades earlier, the banks were about to be jolted into the future.

Canadians have long had a love–hate relationship with their bankers. There is, first of all, trust. Canadians save more than twice as much money as Americans, about 13 per cent of take-home pay, compared with 5 per cent in the U.S. In a country where too little is owned by Canadians, there are twelve Canadian chartered banks, each of them more than 90 per cent Canadian-owned. In national terms, it is an efficient system. Daily the banks move some seven million items worth $16 billion through the country-wide clearing system. They lose so few cheques in the process that one could argue that they should run the post office.

They are stable, but they have had a little help. The Unity Bank, founded in 1972, was taken over by the Provincial Bank of Canada in 1977, which in turn merged with the Bank Canadian National in 1979 to become the National Bank of Canada, the sixth-largest bank in the country. It has been struggling ever since. Even under the brilliant Michel Bélanger, National's chief executive officer, the bank lost money until 1982 and only turned the corner the year after. Unity had been in serious trouble. Admits Inspector-General of Banks William Kennett, "There was a liquidity crisis and this office became involved. The commercial depositors lost confidence and stopped putting money in the bank. It was not a shotgun marriage," he claims. Maybe not, but as one chief operating officer at another bank described Provincial's position during the Unity take-over: "They got the short straw." In sum, bank failure is unlikely because the system closes in around a weak member. "It's possible that a bank might fail," says Kennett, "but the tendency would be to merge."

But there is no need to weep for the banks or worry about the deposits.

Industry profits are huge, even during the bad times. In the first quarter of 1983, for example, when many customers were still having trouble paying off loans although the recession appeared to be drawing to a close, the banks posted a 41 per cent increase in profits.

Of no little assistance is the fact that the banks pay little or no income tax, because of various tax-exempt deals they are allowed by law. In 1982, for example, both the Bank of Montreal and the Royal Bank not only escaped paying taxes, they had carry-forward tax *credits* of $22 million and $28 million respectively.

The bankers have become the bad boys of the Western world, replacing OPEC as the cartel least likely to be loved. Bankers argue, of course, that they are a competitive bunch. "I don't think banking is an oligopoly," says Kennett, "although oligopoly and banks working in perfect competition are similar definitions."

But the bankers see themselves as pretty chummy, too. "It's a club," says Scotiabank vice-chairman Peter Godsoe. "We have a mutual set of interests. You know all the members. They're at the Toronto Club, or if they're out in Calgary, you always know." Still, there is more competition now than there once was, particularly among the new boys who have been thrust to the top in the past decade. "There's a new breed now," says Tom Bell, former chairman of forest products giant Abitibi-Price. "The bunch before were real bastards. They thought they were above everything." Part of the change has been a more aggressive atmosphere. "You've got hustlers now," says Stelco chairman Peter Gordon, "not gentleman bankers."

Above all, bankers are powerful. Says Fred Eaton, chairman, president, and chief executive officer of the T. Eaton Co. of Canada, the country's largest privately owned retailer: "They are undoubtedly very powerful men in this society. No question about it. They don't really exercise their power except *in extremis*. Bankers give good advice, give you money, pat you on the back—everything is really neat until you're in trouble. That's when they're tough and powerful, because they have all the jellybeans."

It happened to Eaton's when its catalogue business was losing money. Says Fred McNeil, former Bank of Montreal chairman: "We told them to quit fooling around with that god-damned catalogue and get rid of it, or they'd go broke. They were losing about $18 million a year."

"The most unpleasant part for bankers," says Eaton, "must be to go in and say, 'Sorry, you don't have the money any more.' That's when the power is exercised. They're really much nicer when they're lending you the money than when they come for it back. There's power in the beginning, but it's not the same as the *raw* power at the other end."

Eaton relates how a friend went bankrupt and learned things he'd never been taught in business school. "I had a real education," Eaton quotes his friend. "The banker came in and banged on the table, and all of a sudden we were in a different world."

There was a strange and shuffling quiet to the group of farmers who gathered on John Otto's Palmerston, Ontario, farm one sunny February morning in 1983. It was as if they shared a community secret, a foreknowledge of events to come. If so, it was a well-promoted secret, for mingling with the parka-clad local folk were camera-toting reporters up from the city. The occasion was an auction of a dozen pieces of farm equipment, a sale ordered by the Toronto-Dominion Bank. Otto owed $450,000 to the TD and the federal Farm Credit Corporation.

Like many young farmers, Otto began farming with a little help from his father and a little cash from the bank. A $200,000 loan five years earlier had allowed him to buy cattle, feed, and the two-hundred-acre beef farm thirty miles northwest of Kitchener. Poor prices and sky-rocketing interest rates forced Otto to keep adding to his loan for operating money and interest repayment. By early 1983, the TD had liens against everything and wanted further security from his father — $200,000 in collateral, using property owned by the father in nearby Elmira. The Ottos refused. The bank already had enough, they suggested. The TD then requested the impossible: pay the loan off by June. When the Ottos refused that, too, the bank sent the auctioneer around to sell off the equipment for cash.

The slicks from the city hadn't counted on the guerrilla tactics of the locals. A flotilla of cars and pick-up trucks had deposited members of the Canadian Farm Survival Association at the auction. Association vice-president Thomas Shoebottom confronted one of the representatives of the receiver, Coopers and Lybrand, grabbed the discharge order authorizing the sale, and announced that the Survival Association was running the auction.

What happened next had not been seen in Canada since the Depression. As some three hundred farmers looked on approvingly, a penny auction was held. A $40,000 tractor sold for $2.20; a truck commanded $5.20; hay wagons sold for eight cents each as CFSA members tossed up ridiculous bids to the amusement of onlookers. In the end, $100,000 worth of machinery went for $19.81. As Ontario Provincial Police, summoned to the scene by the receivers, questioned association president Allen Wilford in a cruiser, the bidders hauled away their booty, intending to rent it all back to Otto for a dollar.

"We've just told the banks, 'You can't take a guy out of his house, you can't have the equipment, you can't have the cattle, piss off,' " said

Wilford. "We've got 150 or 200 negotiations on hold, we haven't had a judgement against a farmer in pretty near a year and half now. We'd sooner talk it out, but the banks aren't very intelligent. They're very disheartening to talk to, they aren't very good businessmen. They can't make good decisions."

Wilford is an unlikely crusader. His pinched face and 140-pound frame make him look like an unlikely farmer also, but he has become a rural radical. With his fellows in the Survival Association, he stood off forty OPP officers in a farm-gate defence a few months earlier outside Walkerton, when the sheriff came to seize a man's horses. There was shouting, some shoving, and a flurry of phone calls to bank vice-presidents, attempts to find a judge to gain an injunction, and calls to the office of the farmer's friend, federal agriculture minister Eugene Whelan, who has said that the bankers are "verging on fraud" in dealings with farmers. In the end, Wilford was charged with obstruction, but the sheriff went away — without the horses.

"We haven't lost anybody yet," insists Wilford, who owes the Royal Bank $400,000. "The basis of our whole thing is moral authority. We're standing up for what's right. It's not right to put people out in these economic times because of conditions completely beyond their control. A piece of paper might say that — but there's no justice there."

For their part in the penny auction, Wilford and Shoebottom were charged with theft by the OPP. In jail, Wilford went on a week-long hunger strike, ending it only when a private member's bill that would bring in debt moratoriums received second reading in Parliament. Throughout, the TD's only response was a two-page press release issued from its Toronto tower denouncing the "small group of radicals" and calling the penny auction "illegal." It was a meagre response to a growing problem. A record 410 farmers went broke across Canada in 1982, 60 per cent more than in 1981. Early figures for 1983 suggest the number may double. According to the Ontario Federation of Agriculture, for every farmer who formally declares bankruptcy, ten others simply pack up and leave before reaching that point.

The bankers claim that fewer than 5 per cent of farmers are in trouble; they say they despise the sorry end as much as the farmers and don't want to seize assets or drive families off their land. "What the hell are we going to do," says Bank of Montreal chairman Bill Mulholland, "with a bunch of houses, closed-down factories, or weed-filled farms?" And yet all too often the bankers publicly handle the situations in ways that can only precipitate ill will and another generation of hatred.

The farmer–banker confrontation began in earnest in December 1981, when Bradford, Ontario, farmer Cec Romanelli dumped a dead cow and two calves in front of a Royal Bank branch in North Toronto, charging that the bank — to which he owed more than $1 million — had caused the animals' death by starvation because it wouldn't advance him any more money. Initially, the bank hid behind customer confidentiality rules and did not respond to Romanelli's charges. Two days after the incident, however, the usual policy was thrown out on orders from senior vice-president M. O. P. Morrison. Before Christmas, the Ontario Humane Society took charge of the herd for a time, then the bank hired a herdsman and paid the bills itself. With an impeccable sense of seasonal cheer, there was a push to foreclose on Romanelli on Christmas Eve. Only at the last minute was senior vice-president and general manager Bill Henry convinced that the timing was bad. The cattle were finally seized the next month despite a spirited farmer blockade of cars and blazing bales of hay.

It was an incident that reached right into the executive suite. "I didn't like it," chairman Rowlie Frazee said of the situation a month later, when the topic was brought up at a Detroit news conference. Dumping dead cattle, he maintained, "was completely uncalled for. We were not responsible in any way, shape, or form for the death of those animals. The person concerned should have and did know better, but he went ahead and did it. It certainly attracted a lot of publicity and lot of unfavourable reaction."

It was easy to paint a picture of the black-hearted banker, but it was not quite that simple. Said Frazee later in the year: "We try to work out tough situations and stay away from causing bankruptcies. Bankruptcies are the worst thing from our point of view. We just did one in Winnipeg, Victoria Leather. We've nursed that one along, and along, and along, and finally we just had to do something. I know that account; I saw the picture in the paper of Jim [Mobuty] crying, making the announcement, and I know that was real."

For bankers, the trouble lies with government — that's where interest rates are set, that's where public dislike of banks begins. Says Scotiabank deputy chairman Gordon Bell: "If the Salvation Army was to take the government monetary policy to the people, the Sally Ann would replace the banks in the popularity poll." Still, he knows that bankruptcy is, in the end, destructive for society. "I worry if a guy goes under. Maybe he won't come back again with another idea. Maybe he'll become a drone in society, a net taker, not a giver. That's not the kind of society I'd want to live in. As bankers, if there were no entrepreneurial spirit, we'd just be financing various public operations. We'd be like the post office. There's no dynamic in that."

Such bankerly anguish, however, is soothed by power, pay, and perks. The highest-paid bankers are the Royal's Frazee and the Montreal's

Mulholland, each of whom earns between $500,000 and $550,000 a year. Robin Korthals, president of the Toronto-Dominion Bank, earns about $300,000, as does Grant Reuber, deputy chairman at the Bank of Montreal. At the Commerce the three highest-paid, immediately beneath chairman Harrison, are vice-chairman Don Fullerton and senior executive vice-presidents Warren Moysey and Peter Cole, all in the $200,000 to $250,000 range. At the Bank of Nova Scotia, Ced Ritchie earns $400,000.

Along with club memberships, company cars, and six-figure pension plans — which cost the banks $1 million each to establish — come low-cost loans. For example, Commerce chairman Russ Harrison owed $192,442 on May 31, 1981, at an interest rate of 7.81 per cent; in 1982 TD chairman Dick Thomson owed $290,223 at 5.01 per cent. Former Bank of Montreal chairman Fred McNeil owed $403,917 a year ago, with about half of it at rates of half-prime — 50 per cent below the rates charged best corporate customers. At lower levels in the banking hierarchy, where 3 per cent mortgages and credit at half the usual bank-card rate are available, such perks are called "the golden handcuffs," for their ability to buy loyalty.

Today's banker is restricted as to where he can invest his money. When Jack Mackenzie, now of Elliott and Page, was a broker with Greenshields in the late 1950s, some of his best customers were bankers. "Security laws," says Mackenzie, "were such that until fifteen years ago, bankers could get rich making money on deals they knew about. When I was at Greenshields, bankers would take positions [in stock], big positions. There was a list of bankers to be phoned. I refused. Nowadays, they'd be sent to jail."

As a result, bankers claim they cannot become *really* rich. Most of the Big Five chairmen, however, have a second home and stock options. Most could probably cash out, be millionaires, and live on their healthy pensions. But the bankers maintain that they see more wealth around them than they'll ever have. "I don't know any rich bankers," claims Commerce chairman Russ Harrison. "Most of my customers, the people I see, could buy me out twenty times over." He pauses and thinks for a moment, then adds with a snort: "Most of them ... all of them."

Typical is Fred McNeil, former chairman of the Bank of Montreal, the most recently retired from the top of the Big Five. His salary in his last year as chairman, in 1981, was $500,000. He has retired on a six-figure pension. He denies that he is wealthy or was motivated by money: "What do you want to be wealthy for? You can only eat so much and drink so much. I've got enough freedom of action to take a holiday. Both my wife and I have travelled enough, that's not appealing. Banking gives you such a window on the world. You can't avoid being privy to a lot of very interesting information about trends, what people are like, how people get in trouble. If you are a reflective person, that's the fascination of banking." As for the power: "That's a lot of crap," says McNeil.

For all the power and position of the CEO, causing change within is difficult, simply because banks are huge, ponderous institutions. Says David Lewis, president of Continental Bank, Canada's seventh-largest bank: "It's frustrating running a bank. You want things done, yet you can't do it yourself and the next echelon down can't do it themselves. If you want to cause change, you can't just say, 'I've had a smart idea in the shower this morning,' and call your henchmen in and tell them, and expect it necessarily to happen. You can have the annual report orange and black if you want, but if you want to improve service to customers next year, fifteen thousand people are involved."

Tony Hampson, president and chief executive officer of Canada Development Corporation, a major bank borrower, believes that the inability to cause change has a further detrimental effect. "The banks are like chickens," says Hampson; "they'd go on for quite a long time with their heads cut off, but then it's an equally long time before you resurrect them again. If you chopped off the executive floor of those banks ... it would be a long time before you noticed anybody was missing. Equally, the lack of leadership or the wrong kind of leadership on that executive floor can permeate a whole organization."

There is no need, however, to feel sorry for today's bankers. They are, after all, a crafty bunch, out to make money for their institutions. They make that profit on the spread, which has widened so much recently that it is now twice what it was half a dozen years ago. It's the equivalent of a retailer doubling the mark-up on a pair of jeans — and still selling the same volume.

From 1970 to 1978, the spread averaged about 2.4 per cent (or 240 "basis points"). Then a savings account paid, say, 6 per cent and prime was 8.5. In 1980, the spread increased to 2.9 per cent; in 1981 it widened further, averaging 4 per cent over the year. By 1983, the spread had reached 5 per cent. Royal Bank vice-chairman Bob Utting dismisses the change as "the disassociation of the former historical association of prime and savings rate." Another banker, talking off the record about the change and what it has done for bank profits, says: "The spread between the deposit rate and the prime rate has doubled — and we've gotten away with that. That has been helpful."

The trend gives new meaning to Ogden Nash's quip: "Bankers are just like anybody else — except richer."

The men who ran the banks prior to the current crop were, in the main, tyrants in top hats. With little education except the rigours of moving through many branches, management methods were non-existent. Some, such as William Nicks, who headed the Bank of Nova Scotia until his death in 1972, were austere and unapproachable; others were genteel and polished, like Arnold Hart at the Bank of Montreal. Then there was the affable Sam Paton, former deputy chairman of the Toronto-Dominion, who represented the last of the indentured young men brought from Scotland in the 1920s to people Canada's bank branches.

They ran things with a combination of wham and whim. Nicks, for example, wanted to know both the time and the temperature on his way to work, so a sign flashing each was installed on the exterior of a branch on his morning route. For all of his professed blue blood, however, it was he who propelled the bank into consumer lending, blue-collar borrowing. The Bank of Nova Scotia raided the finance companies for staff in the late 1950s and got off to such a fast start that it still commands the biggest market share in this area, perhaps 23 per cent of the consumer loan business done by banks in Canada.

Not all the bankers were so prescient. Former Royal chairman Jimmy Muir presided over his bank's expansion in the 1950s and completely missed the growth that would come to the West. At the time, new buildings were being built by the bank in both Hamilton, Ontario, and Calgary. Both were to look the same and come from the same architect's cookie-cutter—except for height. In Hamilton, it would rise eleven storeys. For Calgary, Muir said: "You'll never need eleven storeys, cut it off at three."

Muir's successor at the Royal, Earle McLaughlin, was the bank boss in early transition. Although he was university-educated, he didn't broadcast his background; it was not an advantage in his world. His first job in 1936 in Toronto included sweeping out the vault and he was paid a starting salary of $750 a year. He couldn't marry until it reached $1,400, ten years away. "You looked for a transfer," he recalls. "All you had to do when it came was go down to the local laundry, get your other shirt, and catch the train that night."

He became such an imposing figure, not just the head of Canada's largest bank but a perceived spokesman for them all, that when Donald Macdonald, during his time as finance minister, was asked if McLaughlin had yet given Macdonald his views on some topic, Macdonald replied by saying: "We have not yet been summoned to the throne." But in the sneer, there was significance, too, a respect for the power and the clout. "May God love you," McLaughlin would say, "but not too fast."

Arnold Hart, who steered the Bank of Montreal in its downward run through the 1960s, was more polish than performance. He was the last gentleman banker, a man who saw banking as a combination of public relations, receptions, and connections. But for all his old-world nature and quill-pen charm, Hart did see that he needed help. It was he who brought in Fred McNeil in 1966 from Ford, and it was he who agreed to hiring Bill Mulholland in 1974 to save the bank.

Only in private would he forgo the social graces for a little salty gusto. In 1970, Fred McNeil and B of M president Len Walker made the final presentation to Hart urging that the bank install a country-wide computer system. When they told him it would cost $150 million, Hart was flummoxed by both the expenditure and the risk. His first reaction was an expletive: "Jesus Christ." After the afternoon had been worn away with explanations, Hart was a little more sanguine, but no less worried — and no less the boss. "If this works," he said, "we'll all be heroes. If it doesn't, we'll all be fired." Then he added, "You guys first."

At the Commerce, Neil McKinnon started out as a brilliant banker, ready to back a businessman who came with a good idea, just as a bettor might go with a jockey even though he didn't yet know the horse. Bobby Brown was such a one, and in the early 1950s, when he was getting nowhere at the other banks, he turned to McKinnon for the money to start up Home Oil. McKinnon liked the cut of his jib, took a chance, and established the Commerce as a major lender in energy. He went haywire at the end, became reclusive, and could not carry out the single most important function of a chief executive — designating a successor. Every time one got close, McKinnon would beat him back: Larry Greenwood, Gordon Sharwood, Chuck Laidley, Page Wadsworth, Russ Harrison — the list is lengthy of those whom McKinnon would bring close to the flame, offering warmth but giving them burns. In *The Canadian Establishment*, Peter C. Newman vividly tells how McKinnon was finally pushed out by his board in 1973. He died in 1975, leaving bomb-cratered executive offices filled with shell-shocked survivors.

The current crop of chief executives at the Big Five is better educated and more likely to have had broadening experience outside banking. Currently they are presiding over a revolution, as automation is affecting how people deal with banks. At the Toronto-Dominion, for example, 250 self-serve Green Machines process 1.5 million transactions a month. The next sea change will toss up more skilled technocrats and a world of debit cards, electronic funds transfers, and home banking.

That sea change includes a switch in how the banks must do business. In the last half-dozen years, thirty of the top hundred Canadian firms have changed ownership. The great majority of those transactions were financed by the banks. Some of the deals were huge, such as the $2.1-billion Canada Development Corporation take-over of Aquitaine detailed later in this book. That deal was the last of the jumbos, and left the CDC burdened with debt in a time of rising rates. In those heady days, hundreds of millions of dollars were available with a single telephone call. The bankers fell all over each other to finance any deal brought to them — particularly for resource companies. All the banks have now imposed self-restraint to limit loans to individual companies. About time, too, with Dome Petroleum, for example, owing $1.4 billion to the Commerce and $1 billion to the TD.

The fact that bankers are no better at forecasting disaster than anyone else should not be surprising, but they do suffer less than the rest. As companies struggled with repayments through the recession and out the other side, banks became more than just moneylenders; they adopted the role of proprietor as well, ready to move in as owners of companies rather than see them go under. The list of companies partly owned by the banks grows daily. It began with Massey-Ferguson, moved on to Dome Petroleum, through West Coast forest products firms such as Whonnock Industries and Eastern real estate companies like Costain Ltd. The Bank of Nova Scotia, largest single lender to the East Coast fishing industry, with some $400 million in loans at stake, will likely become an owner rather than see more firms go under and more jobs lost.

Their intent may not be to own companies, but the result is the same. These days, rather than lose its investment, a bank will take an equity position, sit on the company's board, watch management and the balance sheet, and wait for recovery. This approach is arguably better than allowing jobs to be lost, but the question remains: Are bankers good proprietors? The simple answer is that some bankers are better than others. This book points to those who run their banks well — and those who don't. The same range in skill may well apply to the management ability that they bring to the companies they are sweeping under their wings. For those Canadians who already fear the power of banks, there will be more in future to be afraid of, as their control over the country and its business grows.

The question is not whether they have the whole world in their hands: they do. The question is whether they are competent.

A banker is not an entrepreneur; he has little marketing or production experience. Too often he is a numbers man with little notion of where the horizon is, let alone what's beyond it. At the top, too many banks are too thin. There are legions of vice-presidents, but too few of them have the stamina, smarts, desire, and vision to go right to the top. Women are widely and wrongly regarded as years away from deserving positions of authority in the banks. It is a regrettable sexist slight, because 75 per cent of all bank employees are women. The men who make up the other 25 per cent do not want the internal competition to grow stiffer, so they perpetuate the fallacy that women are not ready for jobs near the top. Even in the branches, only 10 per cent of the managers are female. In many ways banks suffer from an inbreeding that comes from offices filled with people who have been promoted from within, often beyond their competence. Among the Big Five, only the Royal and the Bank of Montreal have brought much fresh talent in from the outside.

There are other areas where the banks could improve. The bank boards have finally added a few women members in recent years; at the same time they are losing their tendency to rubber-stamp the decisions of management. But they are still watering-holes for the favoured few. Big business is well represented, as is academe. The professions have their lawyer spokesmen, a sprinkling of doctors, and a host of former politicians, but the boards — some of which have as many as fifty members — cannot be said to represent society. They should. Bank chairmen argue that they need business advice to help them run their business, but they have plenty of that from their current directors. As some with business backgrounds retire, they should be replaced by others who can bring to the various boards views of the world that include labour relations, religion, small business, and other social awareness perspectives. The old school tie should go out of fashion.

There are two other areas where the banks should take new tacks. One is to disclose more about their own way of working, and the other is to ensure that they disclose less about individual client accounts. Important strides have been made in the last few years about loan disclosure, but more needs to be done. There is no reason why — particularly on loans to foreign countries — the banks can't supply a complete list of indebted countries and specific amounts. So, too, with salaries.

It is a ticklish issue for bankers, but it is an attitudinal touchstone as well. In the U.S., the Securities and Exchange Commission requires the publication of management salaries of publicly traded companies. Canadian bankers should meet similar criteria, so that shareholders may judge whether they are getting their money's worth. In some cases, they are not. Banks must, however, tighten up on disclosures about individual accounts. Currently, it is all too easy to gain access to confidential data by telephone. Bank branches will readily divulge credit information to unauthorized callers. With accelerating growth in data-base systems, more information will be on file. Greater security must be promised and provided.

Banks and bankers must become better communicators — beginning at the top. The time for hiding behind secret walls has passed. They'll never be loved, but they might be better understood if they took the time to explain. As well, banks must return to their former role as financial counsellors. With the plethora of services available and the increasing consumer demand for advice on money matters, banks — and particularly the individual branch managers — are failing customers by remaining too remote from their clients and being too reluctant to offer advice.

The public has a role here, too. Too few journalists watch the banks closely, and the public is poorly served by most media as a result. The politicians are particularly badly informed. Only a handful of members of Parliament understand banking well enough to ask thoughtful questions when legislation affecting banks is up for study or a banker testifies before a Parliamentary committee. As a result, bankers get away with murder.

For all their apparent whirr-and-click efficiency and the much-vaunted computer systems, banks are not efficient places. There is much wasted effort and not a few wasted lives. Many employees are poorly used by a system that is too hierarchical and rarely open to new ideas. Modern management techniques are only now grafting new thoughts onto old roots.

For all those failings, and after the close scrutiny of three hundred interviews conducted for this book, I like bankers. They are not men equipped with rubber pockets who come to steal the soup. They make mistakes; don't we all? Anyone who has worked at a bank — and there must be more than a million people in Canada who have — knows the strains and the strengths. What few know, however, is how the man at the top of a Big Five bank thinks and works. The intention of this book is to prop open the office doors and peer into their minds.

TWO

STATESMAN WITH A SOCIAL CONSCIENCE

Rowland Frazee

CHAIRMAN, THE ROYAL BANK OF CANADA

THERE USED TO BE a spot on New Brunswick's Highway 1, between Saint John and St. Andrews, where Rowlie Frazee liked to stop. A bridge crossed over the sea-water and the tides made the vista different, yet reassuringly similar, each time. It offered him particular personal joy, a part of the world that was unchanged, a place that brought a certain continuity to his life. No matter how events about him altered, or which way the corporate ladder leaned, here he could always feel peace, replenish his soul, and restore his psyche. Like his boyhood home of St. Stephen nearby, or his birthplace of Halifax, this was a place to feel good about himself as a true Maritimer who forever carried within him the rhythms, sounds, and smells of the sea.

Then it happened. A pulp mill was erected nearby and the putrid stench permeated the landscape. It destroyed the place and the moment that Rowlie Frazee had thought was eternal. "I stop and I think to myself, 'What a shame, what a shame.'" Now, when his Buick Riviera crosses the bridge, he holds his breath, tightens the car windows, and rolls on through, shaking his head and squinting sadly at the place that can never be the same again.

Rowland Cardwell Frazee, president, chief executive officer, and chairman of the board of the Royal Bank of Canada, the banker with a social conscience. For him, banking is not just a career, it is a calling. Banking has been bred into him: he followed his father and led his son into the business; his uncle was in banking, as were his sister and his wife. As honcho of Canada's largest bank and the fourth-largest bank in North America, he is not simply a captive of the endless numbers. He is as much the small-town boy who cares about his heritage as he is the cosmopolitan man with a mission. And it is the constant interplay between the two roles that shapes his existence.

Of all the Big Five bank chairmen, he is the most public-spirited, the most responsive to the external demands placed on him, the most conscious of the need to say something worthwhile. "You try," he said shortly after his appointment as chief executive officer in 1979, "to give responsible, thoughtful speeches on important occasions when you're invited. You have to realize that when you are giving this speech, you're speaking on behalf of the largest bank in Canada. It can't be half-baked. It should address issues that are important to the country, not just the bank."

Frazee will go to any lengths to carry out commitments to promote his bank abroad. In March 1983, Frazee took a four-day holiday in the Bahamas. As he walked alone along a sea-wall, headed for a swim, a fisherman out of sight below was casting into the ocean. Suddenly the line came flashing in front of Frazee's face. He instinctively ducked out of the way, stepping backward off the wall. He plunged twelve feet onto concrete, landed on his heel, and broke it. He spent the weekend in pain and was flown to Montreal for an operation Monday. The following week he was scheduled to speak in Los Angeles; on Wednesday he decided he would keep the commitment—even with his cumbersome cast. A jerry-rigged podium and stool were set up, and he began by cracking a few jokes about his condition. The injury, he quipped, was not sustained in the stampede for cheap Air Canada seats to California; the crutches were not made of Canadian softwood subject to import duty. The audience was in his hands; Frazee gave the best speech of his life.

On the same trip, he paid a visit to the editorial board of the *Los Angeles Times*, where he spread the word about stability in the Canadian banking system after the slaughter that business had seen in the previous year. The cast did not prevent him from making two more trips into the U.S. in the next few weeks, visits that included further editorial board sessions with *Fortune* and *Business Week*. And he worked in a few speeches as well. "It's important for the bank and for the country that I do that sort of thing," Frazee says.

He is a key member of the Business Council on National Issues and gives hundreds of hours as chairman of Junior Achievement, an organization dedicated to teaching young people about business. He spends about half his time travelling away from Montreal, leaving little time for social life. In one typical month last year, he visited twelve cities (twice to Ottawa and Toronto). He attended meetings in New York, Arizona, Florida, and the Bahamas and gave three speeches during that time. "Each man reflects his setting," says Inspector-General of Banks William Kennett, of the senior men in the Big Five banks. "Frazee grew up within and took over a consistently strong and well-oiled machine. When Frazee is abroad, he's very statesman-like, almost a spokesman for the Canadian private sector. By the time you get to be CEO of the Royal, you're no longer running the bank on a day-to-day basis, you *are* a statesman." Most in the industry agree. Says Mike Gausden, for a decade on the staff of the Canadian Bankers' Association: "If I had to choose Mr. Banker, for integrity and foresight, it would be Frazee."

As both a statesman and a banker with power, Frazee is beset at the bank's annual meetings by environmentalists and other activists demanding that the bank cease funding projects that foul the air or requesting that he halt loans to repressive countries. While the Royal has responded by not giving any new loans to the South African government or its agencies for six years, he dismisses any suggestion that he has the single-handed power to make a difference. He cannot call a loan and close the New Brunswick pulp mill that so riles him, because the company is not a bank customer. He does not say he would close it, but he is, on the other hand, on the board of Frasers, a firm based in Edmundston, New Brunswick, that owns pulp mills. "Their mill isn't near as bad," he says. "If it was, I'd tell them." He sees the point of view of the employees and knows his environmentalist view is not always welcome. "People in these communities, in places like Rumford, Maine — God, *there's* a smell — say, 'You come through here once a year and try to tell us what to do. We're used to it. We need the jobs.'"

And yet.... You can't swim in the St. Croix River in St. Stephen any more, where Frazee swam as a boy. He winces when he talks about the mill built upstream from St. Stephen a decade ago and the effluent that suddenly began to flow. Then there was the trip he made up the Saint John River Valley a few years back with his wife, Marie. He shakes his head in bewilderment, recalling the stench from another new mill en route.

New Brunswick sets the bells of his conscience ringing because it is in his blood and in his future. In 1981, he bought a ninety-year-old house in St. Andrews, his first "second" home. In 1986, when he reaches the bank's mandatory retirement age of sixty-five, he will step down as chairman to live there, at the edge of a golf course, half a mile from the rustic Algonquin Hotel. The house now serves as a summer place, with its southern exposure, picture windows overlooking the Bay of Fundy, market garden, rose garden, and surrounding cedar hedge. His wife was born in Marysville, New Brunswick (now part of Fredericton), and with both sets of parents living in the province, they have spent many vacations with their own two children, Stephen and Catherine, sharing with the family and soaking up the joys of the land.

Vacations these days, with the children grown and gone, are quiet times in St. Andrews or a winter week at the bank-owned condominium in Nassau. The rest of his spare time is spent with family friends or with family, or listening to the stereo he set up at home. An occasional drinker, he unsuccessfully tried to give up smoking twenty years ago, although he would like the outside world to believe that he has quit. At work, he may smoke half a dozen in a day, leaving in the midst of a meeting to find one if he cannot bum a cigarette from a colleague.

Like many Maritimers, Frazee cherishes both the sea and the soil, although he left the Maritimes in 1950 to work in the Montreal head office. Even when he is in his two-storey home in the Mount Royal area of Montreal, he will often disappear suddenly, but there is no mystery about where he has gone. In fact, it's a family joke that in the middle of a meal or a visit with friends, he will step out to admire his two dozen varieties of roses. His other outdoor pride is his market garden.

In spite of his position in the highest echelon of Canadian banking, Frazee is rarely comfortable with the accompanying pomp, nor could he ever measure his life by the bottom line alone. He is a man who may never become accustomed to his public persona as a corporate leader. At receptions, he is an uncomfortable guest of honour. He will contrive to arrive late, then stand at the edge of the crowd, speaking when spoken to, greeting each person in turn only as introductions are made. Two or three times a minute, he will rise up on his toes, then rock back on his heels, like a cop on the corner who knows he has been posted there for a time and is striving to prevent stiffness in the limbs. He laughs a little too heartily, his head and upper torso shaking. He knows that he is meant to be having fun, lending his name or his presence to some affair, but his manner shows that it is a duty, something to be suffered. He worries that people will not know him and wonder what he is doing at the centre of things. When the new Royal building on Ottawa's Sparks Street Mall opened, he was photographed with Rough Rider football star Tony Gabriel. When the photo was put on the bulletin board, along with several others, the most common comment from the staff was: "Who's the guy with Tony Gabriel?" He laughed when he was told, but the incident stayed in his mind. When he was having his picture taken in the Montreal main branch for an article in *Forbes* magazine, he confided to the photographer, "I always worry that people won't recognize me; they may wonder why I'm having my picture taken here."

His commanding presence comes from his position, not any high-profile looks. His head appears almost hairless from the front, his balding dome only covered at the sides and back where the hair is a tad too long and going a little wispy. The effect is to make him appear like some British lord, a duke perhaps, walking the hedgerows with his hands clasped behind his back, Corgis scuttling at his feet, looking earnestly at the world as if to see it clearly and thus assure any watchful tenants of his sincerity and interest.

His blue, flinty eyes are set well apart in a round face. They are eyes that can grow dark and hooded when the conversation heads into uncharted waters where decisions are expected. Next to the eyes, the second most noticeable aspect of his face is the mouth, always ready to split into an easy smile showing slightly gapped front teeth that give him an engaging, almost boyish look even when he is at his most serious. At five-foot-ten and 170 pounds, his build has changed little since his hockey-playing youth. While he is no physical fitness freak, in summer he does swim thirty lengths of his backyard pool twice a day, and in winter he pedals five miles at a time on an exercycle to stay in shape. When he became chairman of the Royal, collecting the last of the three titles he now holds, the Montreal *Gazette* featured him in a profile. For accompanying pictures, they wanted to shoot him swimming in his pool. "No way," he said. "Fifty-nine-year-old men do not appear in public in bathing suits." Not even *in* the water? "Nope," he replied, wise to the sneaky ways of photographers; "when I rise, dripping, from the pool, you'll take that shot." In fact, he carries himself with loose-limbed grace, like the former athlete he is. His is a happy bouncing step that signals a man both at ease with life and in tune with his success.

The Renaissance Center rises above the Detroit skyline like the space shuttle poised for launch. It is here, to this seven-hundred-foot-high hotel, surrounded by four thirty-nine-storey office buildings, that Frazee came in February 1982 to speak to four hundred people gathered for lunch at the prestigious Economics Club of Detroit. The topic was foreign investment in Canada, a follow-up to another speech in Winnipeg three months earlier. Both were written by staff speech-writer Rob Parker, a former member of Parliament and an actor in television commercials (including one for American Express where he loses his wallet on the beach). Both were important occasions for Frazee and, as usual, he honed and rehearsed the speech under the watchful eyes of both Parker and a videotape camera. A cigarette calmed his nerves; a final run-through in the hotel room smoothed his delivery.

In Winnipeg he had told members of the Canadian Club, "We are losing friends internationally at a very rapid rate. We are being called economic pirates and worse." He mentioned five "burrs under the saddle" for foreign investors in Canada and worried about the negative impact those factors would bring to economic performance. Unlike a lot of Canadian businessmen who blindly welcome anyone's money, his is a decidedly pro-Canadian stance. "Canadians want and need foreign investment," he said, "but on our own terms, and in a proportion we choose."

While the speech in Detroit was geared to an American audience, he did not tone down his nationalist views in any pandering way. He quoted everybody from John F. Kennedy through Michigan's favourite president, Gerald Ford, to actor Peter Finch in *Network*: "We're mad as hell and we're not going to take it any more." While it would have been easy to take the usual hands-across-the-border approach, he instead defended the Canadian view, arguing for wider Canadian ownership and Canadian management of U.S. subsidiaries. He called for more co-operation and pragmatism, including more joint ventures between the two countries. "Shooting ourselves in the foot can't happen," he concluded, "if we don't reach for the gun in the first place."

The speech was read into the Congressional Record and gained continental attention and accolades. His office received thirty-six letters after Winnipeg, twenty following Detroit, from businessmen, U.S. senators, diplomats, a former provincial premier, and cabinet ministers — a high response level that would impress any politician running for office.

Frazee bemoans the unwillingness of Canadian businessmen to express their views publicly. "If businessmen don't speak out, then all you get are the views of politicians," he says. "I read the reports of [Bank of Montreal chairman] Bill Mulholland's speech to the Canadian Club, and I phoned him up and congratulated him. I didn't agree with everything he said, but I think it's great he spoke out. If you're not prepared to speak up and speak out, then you shouldn't bellyache about how things are. I don't understand why [TD chairman] Dick Thomson doesn't speak out, for example. He's a bright man, has things to say. I feel a sense of obligation. It's a tradition in our bank." Referring to his predecessors, he says: "Muir did it. McLaughlin did it. I do it."

The pilot's voice, resonant with reassurance, fills the cabin: "There's some pretty nice real estate coming up." Rowland Frazee perks up from his morning paper and the scattered remains of corn flakes and a Danish on the breakfast tray in front of him. "Well, it's either St. Andrews or St. Stephen," he says and scoots excitedly up the aisle of the bank's eleven-year-old Lockheed Jetstar to the cockpit to find out. He lopes back, ducking in a pose worthy of Groucho Marx, to avoid a low ceiling. "It's St. Andrews," he announces and presses his nose against the window for a long and languid look.

The peninsula juts out into Passamaquoddy Bay with the Bay of Fundy beyond and the town of St. Andrews clearly visible and bathed in sun, spotlit and warmed. Rowland Frazee falls silent, almost reverential. His eyes soften and his mouth forms a smile as if, just for a minute, he wished himself down there instead of en route to the Royal's Montreal head office in Place Ville Marie. There his $90-billion bank waits with its thirty-eight thousand employees in 1,500 branches in Canada, 200 operating units and offices in 45 countries around the world, loans in 195 countries, connections with 3,400 correspondent banks, and the clout that comes when corporations and governments come looking for cash and credit.

High above St. Stephen, his boyhood home and the place his banking career began, he recalls the early days and the distance he has travelled. At first, banking was just a job, a place to turn in 1939 after a year at King's College in Halifax. The family ran out of money, so he returned to St. Stephen, where his father was manager of the Royal Bank branch and his mother, a Toronto Conservatory of Music grad, directed the church choir. There were three banks with branches in the town, and they took turns each year, after appropriate interviews at the school and with the principal, choosing the brightest boy from the graduating class. The top scholar in Frazee's year had won a Beaverbrook scholarship and gone on to the University of New Brunswick, so it fell to the second-place Frazee to go into the Royal.

Under his father's watchful eye Frazee wrote the two-hour bank entry exam sent out from Montreal and was hired as a $400-a-year teller. The bank, beginning to be less stringent about some rules, allowed him to work in his father's branch for a year—family members were not supposed to work together—because the salary was not large enough to enable him to live away from home. After a year, his salary was hiked to $600 and he was ordered to move forty-five miles to Harvey Station, a small railway junction near Fredericton.

There he was the junior who posted the ledger, served as teller and janitor—and became the local hockey hero. His agile limbs and scrappy frame offered the perfect build for the dips and doodles of small-town hockey. One Saturday night in particular has stuck in his mind. Harvey Station was playing a team from McAdam, another railway town, but Frazee was cloistered at the branch. The bank inspectors had swooped in that afternoon for one of their regular audits, and no employee was allowed to leave until everything was checked. The team sorely missed the young defenceman, so a group of the town's most substantial businessmen was dispatched to hammer on the branch door and demand that Frazee be allowed to play or they'd pull their business out and go to other banks. The inspectors finally relented, and Frazee arrived at the beginning of the second period to pilot Harvey Station to a 9–8 come-from-behind win.

After a lifetime of working within the bank's rules and constraints, he tells this story, a favourite anecdote, not to draw attention to his past hockey prowess, but to show the restrictions placed upon hidebound inspectors, who had to lock up everything while he was gone and cool their heels until his return. "The bank was just so god-damned inflexible in those days." Harvey Station also gave him the first inkling that one man can make a difference, that the right presence does inspire. A man can lead by example and push others to their limit, but only with their consent and the necessary inherent talent — a lesson forever branded on his mind by the Second World War.

Maturity and the full flowering of an attachment to an institution — in this case, his regiment — were both to come in the hills of Sicily and on the bloody coast of Italy. As a teenager, he had been a member of the Second Militia Battalion. He tried and failed to make aircrew, so the young man who had already shown himself eager to do his duty enlisted in the army in 1941, donned the khaki summer drill uniform of the Carleton and York regiment, and headed overseas. He joined his regiment in England, where he suffered the first and least honourable of the wounds he was to receive: a few bored recruits, using live ammunition against orders, wounded him in the leg. He still carries the shrapnel. It was there, lying in an English hospital in 1942, that he discovered the writings of desert warrior T. E. Lawrence and immediately devoured all his works. Lawrence's views forever set his own style of command. One quote in particular that he recalls captures the essence of his view of management: "You must live with the men, share their food, their hardships, and their dangers. And yet, while being one of them, you must always possess that extra something that identifies you as their leader."

Forty years later, speaking to a group of army cadets at the Gagetown, New Brunswick, Combat Training Centre, he readily admitted to them that the infantry and the war developed "a pretty green, naive kid from St. Stephen into a man in pretty short order." He also learned the benefit of knowledge, experience, and self-discipline as well as the need to communicate. "After forty years," he told the students, "I have to confess to you that I'm not exactly sure I know what makes a leader. I think I know when I see it. Leadership is like sex appeal. It's easier to recognize in action than it is to describe in the abstract." Like three of the five men who run the Big Five banks, Frazee formed his management style during the war. His views of human nature and his organizational methods flow from his military background. Further, his need for order in his life and in his work stems from the discipline that comes when the line between life and death can be snapped by one thoughtless move.

It was life and death the Gagetown cadets wanted to hear about, particularly how they would react when first fired upon. Questions on the topic dominated the afternoon session following his speech and continued through dinner in the mess. "Your concerns are predictable," he said and told them that he had thought of little else than his response under first fire as he waited the eighteen months after enlisting for his European posting. "First, know your job. Second, know your weapons. Beyond that, remember that 98 per cent of you will react well." But the questions rolled on, for each cadet secretly feared that he would number among the 2 per cent who wouldn't react well. "They were worried," he recalled, "about disgracing themselves." So Frazee told them over and over again how they were likely to react when fired upon, how, as officer cadets, to lead men into battle, and how (harder still) to *send* men into battle. They moved outside after dinner and the drinks flowed that warm July evening, as they sat while Rowlie Frazee patiently explained and reassured and counselled until the sun had long gone.

When Frazee started as a platoon commander, a lieutenant, it didn't take long to find out how *he* would react to fire. He and a corporal were climbing a slight rise on reconnaissance in Sicily after sailing from Britain for the push through Italy, when suddenly they heard the sound of shells whistling toward them. "We hit the ground and we hit it hard. When it was over, we looked at each other and realized that we had both split our lower lips when we hit the ground. It just broke me up. After that, I didn't think about it." Others responded less well. "I saw the toughest sergeant on the parade square, the heavyweight champ of the regiment, go bonkers when fired at for the first time," said Frazee. "He just started to cry. It was not a pleasant sight."

He also watched another man crack under the pressure of battle. The man had been the only lieutenant not wounded at Ortona, a battle that took the lives of hundreds of Canadians whose carefully tended graves overlook the Adriatic Sea. They died amid the endless ravines that scar the Italian coast, pinned down and helpless under fire. After, as the survivors sat around reliving the battle over drinks, the general hove into sight. The lieutenant tackled him head-on: "You didn't fight that battle properly." Rather than pass off the lieutenant's comments as the false bravado that wells from a bottle, the general pressed him for an explanation. Then he cancelled the lieutenant's leave and promotion. Two weeks later, the same pressured lieutenant was being briefed by the general for a mission. After the lengthy instructions had been given, the lieutenant responded simply, "I can't go." There was a moment of tension as Frazee and others watched their comrade on the brink of collapse. "What did you say?" barked the general. A medical officer happened to have heard the exchange, rushed over and checked the man's pupils and his pulse, made a few other rudimentary observations, and said: "General, I'm evacuating this man." When the general protested, the medical officer pointed out that even the rank of general was no match for his diagnosis. Two weeks of convalescence brought full recovery.

For Frazee, the retold memories of war are not of death and carnage. Those scenes are carefully kept in the dark corners of his mind, meant to be brought out and relived only with the utmost of care and reverence. Instead, for him, the war and the times like Ortona were a period to celebrate life, an opportunity to learn about people as well as to understand himself. Frazee did not shun the man who cracked after Ortona. In fact, he remained a close friend after the war. The incident became another of life's lessons embraced, more warp and woof in the fabric of experience that Frazee took with him into the corporate world.

Of course, there are differences between the ravines of Italy and the corridors of banking. Bankers are not shoulder-to-shoulder for days on end; they have private offices to which they can retreat. Frazee, having seen what too much pressure can do, knows how much push men do need — along with the right situation — to bring out the best. He watches his colleagues closely with the worried eyes of a man who knows the danger signs, rather than pouring on the coals to burn someone out, then pressing on with fresh troops from the second line.

His second wound, an instructive brush with death, came in Rimini. Struck in the head and bleeding profusely, he was taken to the first-aid post, where a medical officer asked the whereabouts of his steel helmet. When Frazee said he had not been wearing one, they inspected his beret. A German .88 shell had struck the regimental badge pinned on the beret and had been safely deflected across his scalp. The scar remains on his forehead, a reminder of the close call. After he recovered and returned to his regiment, he was welcomed royally. "The way I was received and greeted by those men, that was all the satisfaction I ever needed in life."

He made major by war's end and returned to Canada with confidence in himself, in his ability to lead, and with an appreciation of loyalty and friendship. He also brought back the knowledge that he worked best with others. Today, he has difficulty explaining his views on the war to his pacifist offspring. It was just something you did. Since the war he has not fired a gun. Unlike many other former soldiers, he is no armchair strategist. In April 1982, as Britain and Argentina were sitting on the brink of hostilities — the British fleet three days away from the Falklands and the British home secretary negotiating in Washington — Frazee shook his head when he heard the latest reports from the South Atlantic and said, "God, who could have believed this would happen in this day and age."

Even so, more than thirty years after the war, his strongest sentimental feelings belong to the regiment. The pull is so strong that among the first things he did after he was made president of the Royal was to attend a regimental reunion in St. Stephen. There he staged a walk down Memory Lane that left few dry eyes among the old sweats in the hall. The tape recorder rolled with the rousing sounds of Tchaikovsky's 1812 Overture, followed by Vera Lynn warbling "The White Cliffs of Dover." There was some memorable Churchillian rhetoric, Edward R. Murrow's stirring reportage on the fall of France, and, to close, the regimental march. After the nine-minute show, Frazee spoke warmly and at length.

He had pieced the speech together himself, doggedly going through the regimental diary stored in Ottawa. During a six-month period, every time he went there on bank business or in his capacity as president of the Canadian Bankers' Association (he served from 1976 to 1978), he would steal a couple of hours and pore over the diary, in which a series of soldiers had recorded every day's events from the moment the regiment was first mustered in 1939 to the end of the war in 1945. He would sit there, one eye failing (he has since had a cataract removed from the right eye), slender fingers laboriously copying the excitement and the boredom, the victory and the death, of thirty-five years earlier, stopping every once in a while to ponder something or shake his head in bewilderment or disbelief.

An older and wiser Frazee returned from the war to enrol at King's College in Halifax, this time with the financial help of the Department of Veterans Affairs, to finish the university education interrupted by lack of funds before the war. He studied commerce, was captain of the rugby team, and played varsity hockey. It was here he finally gave up hockey in favour of grander plans. Frazee was a hard-hitting defenceman on the Dalhousie Tigers, a team that featured Thomas (Windy) O'Neill, who had been with the Toronto Maple Leafs in 1944 and made the league finals, losing to a team from St. Francis Xavier University in overtime. In the final, frantic seconds, both Frazee and O'Neill were slashed by a skate — O'Neill on the head, Frazee on the arm. Frazee took six stitches. As a man who had been wounded in the war and survived never to fire a gun again, he now hung up his skates.

After graduation there were job offers at more money than the Royal had offered, but he rejoined the bank with the humble hope that maybe he would one day make manager of the Fredericton branch. The reality far outstripped the dream. He was promoted rapidly through the system and by 1965 was working in Winnipeg, responsible for all of the bank's Manitoba operations. He tested himself in the field and began to flower, away from the suffocation of head office.

Winnipeg, however, brought more than job status and the cachet of a bank car and driver. There he met Culver Riley, a former Olympic rower, later chairman of Canadian Indemnity and a member of the Royal Bank board. Riley became Frazee's mentor. The two men would go for long walks in Assiniboia Park, even at temperatures well below zero, to talk about business. Culver, a practical man with profound ethics, at one point resigned from the board of Great-West Life on a matter of principle. His moral outlook forever influenced Frazee.

He returned to Montreal in 1968 as general manager of Canadian districts and in 1970 was sent to run things in Toronto, the last hurdle before the top. The title was a problem. "I had been general manager, Canada," he laughed; "they didn't know how to handle my ego needs." So they named him vice-president, the first in the bank below the rank of chief general manager — then the number two man — to hold the title.

In 1977 the time came to pick a president and heir to the throne of chairman and chief executive officer Earle McLaughlin, who had been running the bank since 1960 and running off at the mouth as well. McLaughlin had single-handedly changed the institution from the one-man band led by his predecessor, Scots-born Jimmy Muir, into at least a small choir. He had presided over a tenfold increase in assets, from $4 billion to $40 billion, and had seen the introduction of mortgages and consumer credit. He had also shaken up the country with his peppery prose. Canadian nationalism was "the banana republic syndrome." Rent controls, he claimed, were "matched only by the atom bomb in their capacity to destroy cities." And: "If the government had designed the Edsel, they'd still be producing it." He had pitted fully half the country against him in 1976 when he said he could not find a competent woman to join his board. Of the last ten federal budget-bearers, he said: "Some finance ministers were greater failures than others."

McLaughlin was the king whom the Royal sought to replace. Out of the half-dozen candidates during the mid-1970s, the choice came down to two: Frazee and Jock Finlayson. Even though the Royal is three deep in people at all senior positions, succession has often depended in the past on extraneous factors. After McLaughlin himself was chosen over Arthur Mayne in 1960, Mayne always blamed his Catholicism for keeping him from the chairmanship. A similarly personal aspect of Finlayson's life prevented him from reaching the top job, and Frazee was the beneficiary.

Jock Kinghorn Finlayson was born in May 1921, as was Frazee. A handsome man, he has a full head of white hair and a wide smile that embraces an entire room. Around the bank he is called "the man from Central Casting." A native of Nanaimo, British Columbia, he joined the bank the same year as Frazee, 1939, also served in the Second World

War, and returned to scramble on the same corporate ladder. By 1969, he was chief general manager.

It looked as if Finlayson were being groomed for the top. His career path and Frazee's were almost parallel, with Frazee running one step behind until 1972, when he replaced Finlayson as chief general manager (in effect, the chief operating officer); Finlayson became deputy chairman and executive vice-president, promoted and shelved all in the same deft stroke. McLaughlin was not yet ready for a successor and gave up none of his three titles: president, chief executive officer, and chairman. Finlayson languished in corporate limbo, as neither the chief executive officer nor the chief operating officer. McLaughlin had suffered a heart attack and Finlayson ran the bank, but he had been sidetracked. It was the first indication that the succession might take another route.

In the conservative world of banking, where mores and tradition are made of marble as impervious as the branch countertops, an executive's wife is considered a corporate appendage. It did not help Finlayson that McLaughlin's wife, Ethel, did not approve of Finlayson's first wife, Jean, who suffered severe migraines that affected her personality. A designer and a piano player, Jean "would just go to pieces with some of those headaches," according to a colleague. "She had a very bitter tongue when she was not feeling herself. My wife, who had been exposed to her quite a bit and had felt her wrath as much as anyone, probably, had great sympathy for her. Finlayson had problems with his marriage and he made the decision. He didn't really withdraw, but it became obvious that he wasn't going to be able to do this job. So they got Rowlie into it."

Finlayson's subsequent divorce and remarriage to his secretary, Maddy, a Belgian-born woman in her fifties, was more than some of the directors as well as others in the bank could stomach. "There was a scandal," says one senior banker. "Well, I call it a scandal. Let's say some of the more fastidious members of the board were upset over his divorce and subsequent marriage to a younger, attractive woman."

A Royal Bank director, one who served during that period and is still on the board, said of McLaughlin's choice of Frazee as president in 1977: "He was smart enough to get a feel of the consensus before he proceeded." Of Finlayson's personal life, the director admitted: "It wasn't a plus."

Finlayson was named president in 1980 when Frazee shed the title; he took early retirement three years later at sixty-three. He claims his divorce and remarriage were irrelevant to his corporate success. Refusing to admit what is obvious to others, he maintains, "I don't think it's had any [effect]. In fact, I'm sure it hasn't. I have never had any indication from anyone in the bank or on the board that that was the case. I don't think it is an issue." A moment later he adds with finality: "Even if it was, I would have done it anyhow."

For Frazee, the moment of triumph — whatever the combination of events and circumstances — is something still to be savoured. "I would assume and I would hope that Jock Finlayson was disappointed when I was appointed chief executive and he wasn't."

And so it was that on Friday night, June 4, 1977, Rowlie and Marie Frazee celebrated their son Stephen's birthday and Rowlie's ascendancy with their friends Syd and Terry Whiteman, over dinner and several bottles of Dom Perignon. For Frazee, it was an intimate and entirely appropriate group. Not for him the grand occasion with fifty cronies and much congratulatory rhetoric. Instead, he confined the guest list to family and Syd, whom he'd met in Montreal in 1952. He'd made Whiteman a car loan, then begged a regular ride to work, and they became lifelong friends. The location for the celebration was equally appropriate, the lush Le Mascaron, in Toronto's Royal Bank Plaza, with its motif of masks leering at the patrons from the walls and glassed-in boxes. The restaurant, of course, was a bank customer. *His* customer. If you are going to blow some money on bubbly, might as well do it where it'll do some good for the bank. *His* bank.

During the first two years, Frazee operated very much in the shadow of Earle McLaughlin, who was out in his own spotlit world, filling his days with meetings of the more than two dozen corporate boards on which he served. Frazee, meanwhile, quietly ran the Royal from within, chafing on the short leash on which McLaughlin kept him. McLaughlin orchestrated the board meetings, retained the ultimate decision-making responsibility, and was still seen far and wide as major-domo. Frazee, meanwhile, was preparing the place for his rule. His first step as president was to look into the future through the vehicle of the President's Task Force, a two-year study that was to set the bank's direction for the next five years.

Two years later, in January 1979, he picked up the next of the three titles and became chief executive officer as well. While he occupied the same office space he had as president, power was beginning to flow into his hands. He revelled in the change. "The ultimate responsibility for the bank is now in my hands, and it *wasn't* before," Frazee said at the time, "it was in Mr. McLaughlin's. No matter how much he delegated — and he was excellent at that — the ultimate responsibility in a crisis was on his desk." Frazee also became the principal liaison between the board of directors and the bank and directly responsible to the board. "Before, I was responsible to him."

Although McLaughlin remained chairman and ran the board meetings, the change in Frazee's reporting relationship was meaningful. He could now begin to mould the institution in his own image. He saw his principal responsibilities as threefold: strategic planning, good management continuity, and external relations. Like a young prince raised from the cradle to ascend the throne, he was certain about his capacity: "I've been conditioned for this sort of thing. I'm not afraid to make a decision and be responsible for it. I prefer not to make mistakes, but I know I'm going to make some because I've made them before.

"I sometimes wonder," he continued, "if the general public has the mistaken perception that a guy sits in his office all day long and he has all the knowledge up here" — his slender finger tapped his temple — "that he needs to make those decisions, and if he's good enough he'll make right decisions and make the odd wrong one. But the kind of decisions you are making are based on firm recommendations that come from many people."

The area in which he initially felt the least confident was external relations. McLaughlin had been such a well-known spokesman that Frazee felt almost voiceless by comparison in the role, although some of McLaughlin's bursts had made Frazee wince. "He was always willing to meet the press. Every once in a while he came out with some little gems — once in a while gems that you could have lived without — but he was quotable and he was a damn good banker."

In January 1980, when Frazee inherited the title of chairman, the final jewel from the McLaughlin crown, and moved to a new office on the executive floor, he was remade in other ways as well. A year earlier, even though he was chief executive officer, he would sit quietly during any conversation in his office, his hands laced together on his lap as if they had been placed there by someone else before anyone entered the room. The feet were quiet, too, and while the style was relaxed, and he was comfortable within his own skin, he was undemonstrative. He may have been confident of his capacity, but he did not reveal much of himself. He acted like a subdued, slightly leery person who had stepped into a room wearing new shoes that might squeak and draw undue attention.

By the end of the year it took to claim the chairman's job in addition to the titles of president and chief executive officer, the change was remarkable. He could barely contain his exuberance: his slender hands and arms took on an almost Gallic expressiveness and a crossed leg would bob with impatient enthusiasm. Every gesture expressed the desire to get on with the next item on life's agenda.

The reason for his previous restraint was simple. Explained Frazee: "Mr. McLaughlin was still *here*," using both hands to indicate McLaughlin's physical presence not just at his side but within the very room. "Mr. McLaughlin was still in this office," he said, spitting out every word with the emphasis that can only come from an exasperation too long contained. "This is where the traffic was. The ultimate responsibility rests in this office. Well," he paused, "things are different now. We've had a pretty good year in tough circumstances. We have momentum. I'm quite pleased."

With the final departure of McLaughlin, the executive floor and the forty-first-floor dining room area underwent a $3-million redesign by a New York firm. In English manor-house style, brass wall sconces and chandeliers were hung everywhere, wainscoting was placed half-way up the wall, padded cloth covered the rest. Behind Frazee's desk was hung a Jack Gray oil that, symbolically, shows a lone Nova Scotia fisherman heading out to sea in a dory; in the sitting area, a painting by Montagu Dawson of a ship with all sails set.

At the top of Place Ville Marie, his dining room, called the Merchants' Room, has a southeast panoramic view of the refineries, the docks, and the St. Lawrence. There is a box with a lighted map to name the sights, an eighteenth-century grandfather clock manufactured by John Russell of Falkirk, Scotland, and a table that seats six or eight for lunch. It is one of a dozen rooms on the dining and entertaining floor, most of them decorated and named after different geographic areas of the country. (The Royal's best dining room, however, may well be the president's in Toronto, where a ten-foot-high lemon tree bears real fruit.)

Frazee's pride and joy is a $25,000 Bidjar rug in his office. One hundred years old, it is unusually large — twenty-six by fifteen feet — and was hand-knotted in the province of Kurdistan in Iran, close to the Iraqi border. In the centre there is a large, rose-coloured medallion on a ground of dark blue, all overlaid with a crab pattern. Amid the stylized and small animal figures, flowers, leaves, and frogs, there are three tiny human figures just in front of Frazee's desk. One of them is headless, a harsh reminder amid the discreet symbols that not every decision augurs well for those caught in its widening swath.

By 1981 there were freedoms won and freedoms yet to be won in Frazee's growing role. First, there were some changes to be implemented within, before he could move into the wider world, for none of the other senior bankers had yet claimed McLaughlin's mantle as chief spokesman for the banking community.

Frazee was now able to put in place the plans he'd made since becoming president four years earlier. First, he set up a new group in Toronto, the world trade and merchant banking division, under Geoff Styles, who had been previously based in London, England. Then the Royal bought

London-based Orion Bank, a merchant bank with $3 billion in assets. With its contacts in other banks around the world (and the 350 banks in London), Orion gave the Royal a leg up on syndicated loans and other international deals.

Frazee also reorganized the board of directors, changing it from the cloistered coterie under McLaughlin to an expanded, more open group. Recommendations came from a committee chaired by director John Tory, president of International Thomson, and were accepted by Frazee. The results were more work distributed away from the main board to board committees, a higher ceiling ($50 million) than previously existed for loans needing board approval, and new powers given to the executive committee for approving other loans.

While these changes meant that the few loans that now reached the board were examined with more discussion and disclosure, perhaps the most dramatic change in the Royal's operations came when Frazee substantially increased the number of directors attending the meetings. In McLaughlin's day, only a dozen of the forty-seven directors would attend — usually six bank officers and six outside directors from firms in Montreal. "The board would meet fifty-two times a year," said Frazee, "and decisions were made by half a dozen people. I couldn't believe it." Other directors were discouraged from attending. Once a month, the board would move out of Montreal and meet in Toronto — meaning that Toronto-based directors would attend — but McLaughlin would ensure that his Montreal cronies also attended in force by paying their travelling expenses. But Toronto directors were not reimbursed for expenses if they came to Montreal — and Vancouver directors, for example, had to pay their own way to meetings in either city. Under Frazee, all directors were paid for travel expenses.

The changes Frazee made, in international banking and to the board, were coupled with market studies that showed that the United States would be a major area of market growth. He ordered that additional offices be opened there and staff added to snag a larger share of the growing corporate business. Growth in the petroleum business was also targeted, and staff was buttressed with the addition of Jack Stabback, former chairman of the National Energy Board, as a vice-president based in Calgary.

Frazee moved to hire other non-bankers and put them in at senior levels. Ed Neufeld, a former senior civil servant, was recruited to become chief economist. John Abell, a corporate finance specialist from the underwriting firm Wood Gundy, became vice-chairman and chief executive of Orion.

The appointments showed Frazee's recognition of the wider world beyond banking. While a background in the branches or the credit department had been sufficient in the past to prepare a man for a major role, the upper echelons of the bank could no longer be manned only from within. It was a tough decision to take, one that caused resentment from long-time bankers and colleagues, but a move that Frazee knew needed to be made.

Having picked the areas for action and the people he wanted around him, Frazee also chose not to spread himself as thin with other corporate connections as McLaughlin had done. Says Frazee: "I'm more of a hands-on chairman than Earle was." He rises up, his elbows perched on the chair arms for added height to emphasize his next statement: "I'm not on twenty-five outside boards."

McLaughlin, of course, was, and would simply inform his directors when he was accepting the prestige and pressure on his time of yet another seat. Until last year, Frazee limited his outside boards to two: Frasers in New Brunswick and Continental in New York. In 1982, two more were added: Imasco and Power Corporation, both in Montreal. Both were put before the Royal's board for approval, with discussion encouraged, at the April 1982 board meeting in Nassau. Four, he told the board, was his limit.

In addition to placing his own thumb-print on the Royal board and expanding management strength with an eye on growing markets, Frazee's main goal is to keep the Royal number one in Canada. One aspect of this leadership comes in setting the prime interest rate, the rate that the chartered banks charge their best corporate customers and the rate that, in turn, establishes the basis for other loan rates. Each Tuesday, a view begins to develop at the Royal management meeting of what the Bank of Canada might do, and how the Royal might respond, but a final decision is not taken until the central bank sets its rate at 2:00 P.M. Thursday. The decision is a private preserve, jealously guarded by Frazee, because of its impact on prices and profits.

"Recently," he says, "I was caught at the head table of some interminable lunch and didn't get back until three. We had talked [about action] earlier, but no one else had moved. The Bank of Canada rate had been sneaking up the previous few weeks, but that's not the only force at play. The cost of funds on deposit matters, too, and if they are moving up, so will rates."

That day, Frazee considered hiking the Royal's rate by three-quarters of one per cent — in order to send a rocket at the Bank of Canada and signal the Royal's disagreement with the central bank's activity — but settled for a one-half point increase. Within an hour, all the other banks moved their rates a similar amount. Having the others jump on his bandwagon gave Frazee some pleasure, for along with price and profit considerations, there is also the matter of pride. "We're not followers. We like to think of ourselves as leaders."

The event is an alumni fund-raising for Acadia University, a dinner at the staid old Lord Nelson Hotel in Halifax, and guest of honour Rowland Frazee is in his element. If his ease in the bank comes from power and the capacity to wield it, his comfort at the podium springs from knowing people nation-wide and being able to speak about things that are honestly on his mind or in his heart. Halifax is his home town, to be sure, but half of the audience seems to know him from somewhere else—his time in Saint John, or Winnipeg, or Montreal. He begins his speech doggedly dealing with the economy but then turns his tongue to the topic at hand, the role of the university. It is not an easy subject, but one that he tackles with more understanding — and more lyricism — than most in commerce.

"I, as a businessman, plead with the universities that you're preparing young people not for a life in business but for the business of life. Somebody said there are three questions that we should ask over and over again in our lives. Is it good or bad, is it true or false, is it beautiful or ugly? And if education at the university or elsewhere can prepare us at all to answer those questions, it will have served a tremendous purpose." A person, he points out, must develop both the mind and some skills, "and it's the role of the university to find the proper balance between the two." He approvingly quotes management guru Peter Drucker (with whom Frazee has spent some time; Drucker has heavily influenced his management style) as saying that society's knowledge gap is most prominent in raising children, in management skills, and in the impact of technology. The university can have a positive effect on the last two. On child-rearing, he says simply, "You have to search your own conscience for that."

His own conscience is clear on that score, for he enjoys a close and loving relationship with his two children, Catherine and Stephen. Within the family he draws daily strength and his conscience is regularly tested. Life, for him, has been a combination of fiscal diplomacy and family dinners. United by a lifetime of experiences, the Frazees love to retell the story of what happened when the four of them — and the family dachshund — set out from a family Christmas in St. Stephen in 1962 to drive back to Montreal. Off to a 7:00 A.M. start, they were just riding nicely along the roller-coaster highway known as the Airline, between Calais and Bangor, Maine, when a snowstorm struck. As they turned south to pick up U.S. Route 1, the storm worsened and they suddenly skidded into the ditch. Fortunately, a plough happened by and hauled the car out, and they followed the plough down Highway 193 towards the Atlantic Ocean and the town of Cherryfield. The plan was to meet another plough coming the other way. Progress was painful; they covered six miles in four hours. Finally, even the plough became stuck. Frazee urged his car on a further hundred yards until it became stuck, too. After driving all day they had made less than seventy miles.

With dark approaching, the wind howling and whipping the snow around the car, Frazee and the two men from the plough slogged ahead on foot for help. A hermit named Dan Sullivan was found to shelter the Frazees in his ramshackle place with windows covered in plastic. The few sticks of furniture included no beds, so Marie and the two children slept on a sofa. Rowlie pulled two chairs together, with his head resting in the wood box and one eye cocked at the ceiling, for all through the night the hermit ranged about upstairs, hooting and screaming along with the storm. With every step it sounded as if he might come through the plaster with a crazed look in his eye and a hatchet in his hand, ready to kill them all.

Catherine, now twenty-eight, was born with muscular atrophy, a form of muscular dystrophy. She has never walked and has only limited use of her hands, although she can write slowly or hold a glass of wine. Since a recent spinal fusion she has needed a neck brace to keep her head from lolling over. Now she can operate her own electric wheelchair, but during the first seventeen years of her life, she needed constant attention and was fed in a high-chair contraption. If her hand fell off the edge, she would need help getting it back in place. The family is protective, fearing that she might be a target for ransom demands. While all the bank's senior officers know and admire the family's courage and capacity, his daughter's condition is spoken of in whispers, out of respect for Frazee, lest he think they were extending sympathy.

Catherine is off-limits to interviews. That is unfortunate, because those who know her agree that contained inside the uncontrollable body is a brilliant mind, an articulate tongue, and a heart as big as the world. She has taught her father more than he has learned at the bank. She left home at seventeen and attended Ottawa's Carleton University, accompanied by a companion (who was helped financially by her father), and lived both in the university residence and later in an apartment. Now on the staff of an oil company in Toronto, after three years with the same firm in Halifax, she translates the mumbo-jumbo of technical documents into readable prose for use by the sales staff. In 1981, she and her companion (her fourth in a dozen years) toured Japan in a van, taking in the sights and recording the sounds for CBC use. She is a ham-radio operator, plays bridge and chess, is fluently bilingual, and harangues her father regularly about social issues such as the environment and nuclear disarmament.

Stephen also has forced his father to wrap his mind around issues that normally do not come up in the office. Recently when Stephen, who has worked in the branches and at Royal's main office in Toronto, talked of a bank problem, his father said, surprised, "I didn't know about that." "How could you," retorted Stephen, "sitting up in the ivory tower."

Not for him the perfect family with straight teeth, healthy minds, and proper table manners right from birth. Unlike many others in the business world, he has not turned his back on the home or put up a front at the office.

Rowland Frazee is both a statesman with a mission and a small-town boy with a mansion. Even as he moves on the spectrum between and establishes his final image at the top, he becomes less tolerant. It's something that only a few people notice at first; his wife has spotted it, and so has his secretary. For example, a message to be mailed to shareholders was recently sent to him for signature. "No style, no flair, no humanity," he wailed. "I don't think they're teaching English in the schools any more. I look at some of the people who I know can write well in this bank, and every one of them is well over fifty. The young people now are technical to the extreme, full of business-school jargon."

He looks at himself with the same insight. "I've reconfirmed the fact that I can be tough when I *want* to be. I guess I first learned that during the war. I read those profiles of CEOs that say what tough sons-of-bitches they are. Well," he says with some pride, "nobody's ever said that about me. I'm more inclined to be friendly—not outgoing or gregarious—but no tough nut." Just in case anyone should misunderstand, he adds with a slight squint of recrimination in his eyes: "But I'm no patsy, either."

For the most part he is content with his image and his continued growth, although he remains a man in transition, moving his position towards the full-blown power it will one day contain. In spite of his awesome influence, he knows he can only partially change how business and society interrelate. In fact, he may be unique in a hard-nosed world where softness of heart is suspect. He personally ended new loans by the bank to apartheid-plagued South Africa, and during the International Year of the Disabled, he ordered that two hundred Royal branches be made wheelchair-accessible. Those weren't just corporate public relations gestures, they were professional commitments buttressed by personal concern.

There's no doubt that some of Frazee's sensitivity comes from his relationship with his daughter, whose handicap appears to have given her special insight. Once, after Rowlie attended a performance of a modern symphony in Montreal, he complained to her that it seemed to be nothing but individual sounds, instruments battling each other with no unity of purpose, no orchestral flow. She responded that she'd just been to a similar performance in Halifax. Her reaction was to tip her head back and let the cacophony wash over her while she feasted on the ceiling's random jumble of wires and lighting. By themselves, neither made sense. Together, they did. "The music," she explained to her father, "was playing the ceiling." Harmony even in disharmony. Beauty where others miss it. The universe as one.

He understands, even if he cannot see. He knows, although he cannot always act. He is the first wave signalling a sea change within the banks. Just as history is a pontoon bridge where each man works at the building end, Frazee is in the forefront of progress in banking, progress away from mere bottom-line performance to full-blown corporate responsibility. He has led the banks into fuller disclosure of loans and loan losses, at the same time setting a style for more open management, a style that during the next decade will spread to the other banks. The current crop of managers, the bank chairmen of the future, will bring to their roles higher professional profiles and hold ever more profound personal views—and not be afraid to state them publicly. When that signal from the top is clearly seen, others from within will clamour to be heard without as well. The days of the conservative and anonymous banker are not just numbered, they are over. And it is Rowlie Frazee who has led them to the triumph of the other shore.

THREE

The Club Closes Ranks

The Friends of Royal Trust

When Robert Campeau decided he wanted to own Royal Trustco Ltd., the firm decided to fight back. Inextricably involved in the whole affair were senior bankers exercising their clout behind the scenes.

HE IS A DAPPER MAN, given to striped tab shirts and the brusque bearing of an officer eternally ready to take the march-past salute. His hair, stretched over from the right side of his head to hide the unhidable, is the only outward indication of vanity or, for that matter, any other human failing.

Lieutenant-Colonel Kenneth Alan White, university dropout, was sixty-six in 1980, and supposed to be at the close of his career as chairman of Royal Trustco, the parent holding company of Canada's largest trust company and largest broker of residential real estate. As different from the average financial adviser as custom tailoring is from off-the-rack slacks, he conducted the fiduciary function, looking after other people's money, often the funds of people long since dead. Pensions, investments, counselling, trustee activity, he marshalled a phalanx of 9,300 employees in a company with income that passed the magic $1-billion level that year. His manner was genteel, even courtly, until he was attacked. Then, the discreet distance of the officer became the muddy trench tactics of the enlisted man. And no battle was muddier than his last, when the enemy came rolling in with the morning fog on August 27, 1980, for take-over talk with tea.

The interloper was Robert Campeau, an upstart real estate developer and former Inco machinist. With his own firm's assets a mere $866 million, he must have known what a reach it would be to buy Royal Trustco, with more than $26 billion under its administration. His hope, however, was to achieve the kind of corporate coup that would forever place Campeau Corporation in the Canadian business firmament and secure his position as a worthy member of that cloistered world. But the little fighter who had gone up against such indomitable foes as former Ottawa mayor Charlotte Whitton, the man who could walk the tightropes of political Ottawa without a mishap, had rolled a game against an opponent whose biggest guns and best tactics were as invisible as nerve gas. While the intruder was initially forced to flee, he kept up his obstreperous attack, forcing a defensive action unparalleled in Canadian business history and a revolution in Canadian banking methods. In the end, the old colonel would win, but the victory would be an ironic mixture of defiance and defeat.

The take-over plan hatched by Campeau was in some ways absurd. As the owner of two race-tracks, Toronto's Harbour Castle Hilton hotel, and another hostelry in Hull, Quebec, and as a builder of government offices, he had little apparent kinship with Royal Trust. After he had lined up $413 million in financing from his bankers, the Bank of Nova Scotia, he also called at the St. James Street office of the Bank of Montreal's Bill Mulholland. Mulholland told Campeau that the Bank of Montreal would retain the 10 per cent of Royal Trust it held in its investment portfolio rather than sell to Campeau. Recalled Mulholland: "I told him if he was serious about achieving what he wanted, he should go see [White] personally."

Campeau took the banker's advice, flew to the Sherbrooke, Quebec, airport the next day, a Wednesday, and took a limo to White's summer residence near Bromont in the verdant Eastern Townships, where many of Montreal's élite (including Mulholland) have escape houses. Campeau put his case that his construction and commercial real estate business would fit well with Royal Trust's, assured White of a continuing role running the place, and mentioned $21 a share as a possible purchase price.

According to testimony Campeau later gave before the Ontario Securities Commission, White launched into a rambling attack. "I don't see why you don't go and take over something else! Really," he said with the offended dignity of a small-store proprietor, "this is my company. I'm telling you right now I won't work for you, and if this bid is successful I'm going to quit.... I really don't like you, Campeau, and I don't like Paul Desmarais and I don't like Conrad Black and I don't like Edgar Bronsman," he concluded, mispronouncing the name of another of Montreal's well-known business families, the Bronfmans. By that point, White was spitting with rage and widened his attack: "I don't like all these guys making bids for public corporations, and I wish to hell you would stay where you are and don't bother us. This is really going to complicate the Bank Act and is really not helping the French-Canadian and English-Canadian situation."

White then indicated his preferred method of keeping Campeau out by saying: "I'm going to call my friends and I am going to lock up 51 per cent of this stock before you can turn around. I'm telling you that I have got ways to persuade these friends of mine to go along with me, and they will."

White abruptly indicated that the conversation was over, grabbed Campeau by the arm, and escorted him like some petty trespasser to the gate of his property, advising him to "pull that bid." Campeau demurred, saying he was going ahead. As Campeau was about to climb into the limo, kept waiting for longer than the perfunctory few minutes he had planned, White walked towards the house, stopped, turned, and said: "I'm getting on the phone now, and I'm getting my team together and we are going to stop you."

The battle lines were drawn in a war that would rage on through September into October. That forty-five-minute conversation set off a chain of events that would show not only how small the world of Canadian business is, but also the lengths to which its members will go to control the circle. It also led to four agonizingly honest days of hearings before the Ontario Securities Commission, days that brought every private act in high places under public scrutiny.

Both White and Campeau called on Mulholland in his St. James Street offices in old Montreal in the afternoon of their conversation at Bromont. Neither visitor was particularly cheerful. Campeau told Mulholland that his morning call had not gone well.

"I gathered that," said Mulholland.

"I guess," said Campeau, "he is going to fight us."

Replied Mulholland: "There is no two ways about that. He is going to fight you all the way."

In a last-ditch effort to secure Mulholland's support, Campeau offered to switch half of the $413-million take-over financing from the Bank of Nova Scotia to the Bank of Montreal. Mulholland declined, pointing to his bank's policy of not financing unfriendly take-overs. The discussions were to continue through several evening meetings over the next two weeks as Mulholland tried vainly to convince Campeau that he should go for only 25 per cent of Royal Trust, not total control.

As Campeau and White drew sides, upstart French Canadian versus Establishment WASP, behind the mahogany doors the bankers responded to old loyalties and new hopes. In fact, the main warriors were in close enough physical proximity to walk to windows in their respective office towers, face King and Bay streets in downtown Toronto, and make conciliatory waves or rude gestures at each other. Urban geography may have made them neighbours, corporate history might have made them competitors, but the small size and inbred nature of Canada's business community were about to create new foes from old friends. Although his firm was based in Ottawa, Campeau operated from the Bank of Nova Scotia building on the northeast corner of King and Bay; White, also headquartered in Ottawa, would work from the Royal Trust Tower in the TD Centre on the intersection's southwest corner. As for the bankers, who became involved up to their elbows, the TD offices of chairman Dick Thomson were next door to Royal Trust, and chairman Bill Mulholland of the Bank of Montreal was often north across King Street at First Canadian Place. Royal Trust's master strategist and broker, Austin Taylor, chairman of McLeod Young Weir, was encamped in the shortest of the three black pokers that make up the TD Centre.

At 325 pounds, Austin Taylor is the size of a four-man combat tent. Affectionately known as "Firpo" or "the Incredible Hulk," he was born into a wealthy Vancouver mining family and raised by a domineering father. Taylor didn't finish university, choosing instead to plunge headfirst into finance at Mulholland's Alma Mater, Morgan Stanley, the New York investment banker. He then spent five years looking for oil for the wealthy Buckley family in the Philippines, joining McLeod Young Weir in 1964. While at the MYW Vancouver offices, he was a fund-raiser for Social Credit premier Bill Bennett. He rolled east to Toronto in 1978. It was this horseman, free-enterpriser, and *bon vivant* whom Royal Trust hired for strategy and troop recruitment in the battle against Campeau.

Robert Campeau borrowed his first $50,000 as a young builder from a banker—Tom Boyles, later chairman of the Bank of Nova Scotia. Campeau rewarded Boyles's early faith by appointing him to the Campeau board, where he served until his death at seventy-four in 1980. Boyles returned the favour like a father, treating Campeau sometimes with affection and at other times with authoritarian disdain. It was not surprising, then, that Campeau would turn to the Bank of Nova Scotia for his $413-million take-over financing. Nor was it unusual to sound out a second banker, Bank of Montreal chairman Bill Mulholland. During the early stages of a take-over, the banker becomes both midwife and father confessor.

The Montreal was an appropriate adviser. Royal Trust first opened for business on November 24, 1899, with a borrowed desk and a staff of one, Albert E. Holt, tucked away in a corner of the Bank of Montreal's savings department on Place d'Armes in Montreal. The bank did not *own*

Royal Trust, but the president and board of directors were identical. President of both was Lord Strathcona, who had driven the CPR's last spike. The bank's regular directors' meeting and the Royal Trust meeting were held on the same day each month. When the bank meeting was ended, the president and directors, according to Royal Trust lore, "went through a hole in the wall" into the trust company's premises to reassemble around another table as the Royal Trust executive. With such a cosy arrangement, there was no need for ownership (the bank was not allowed to own the trust company anyway), and it was not until the 1967 Bank Act revisions that the Bank of Montreal purchased the maximum 10 per cent of Royal Trust permitted by law.

As the years passed, Royal Trust, which was the largest source of brokerage commissions in the country and the largest source of private-sector deposits at the banks, gained clout. The colonel had troops to summon and some IOUs to call. The day after their confrontation, White announced publicly, "I will not work for Robert Campeau," arguing that no one individual corporation should control a trust company. Meanwhile, on the afternoon of Campeau's visit, a phone call had gone to TD president Ben Boyle from Royal Trust's executive vice-president, Ewart Wickens. Boyle turned Wickens over to Ernest Mercier, vice-president and general manager of national accounts, and a meeting was set for Mercier's office, Friday morning. There Wickens outlined their displeasure with the take-over bid and discussed general techniques of fighting take-overs. Wickens asked if the TD could supply after-tax financing for those interested in purchasing Royal Trust shares, but Mercier pointed out that TD had no after-tax financing available. Wickens also made them aware that the Bank of Montreal held 10 per cent.

After the meeting, TD equity portfolio manager Timothy Hale, Boyle, and Mercier met with chairman Dick Thomson to tell him of Wickens's request that the bank buy shares. On Sunday, Thomson cut short a Labour Day dinner with his mother so that Austin Taylor could come around to Thomson's house. Also at the meeting from TD were Alan B. Hockin, TD executive vice-president for investments, and Timothy Hale. By then the TD response was beginning to form. Thomson was cool to Taylor's suggestion that TD should join "Plan A"—later described by OSC staff as "a syndicate ... which would purchase all of the common shares of Royal Trustco," effectively keeping Campeau out. At the end of the ninety-minute meeting, however, Thomson agreed to a further meeting next day in Taylor's brokerage offices.

Taylor left and the three TD officers discussed the bid, worrying that Taylor's proposal could not be put into action fast enough to take advantage of trading on Tuesday when markets re-opened after the Labour

Day weekend. Thomson proposed that TD buy 10 per cent of Royal Trust. Then he telephoned Donald Love, president and chairman of Edmonton's Oxford Development Group Limited. Said Thomson later: "In any transaction [of this nature], you better get a feel of what the public reaction will be. If you are going to make an enemy of Campeau, you had better make damn sure you are not going to make an enemy of the real estate industry." Oxford had recently gone private in a transaction financed by the TD, a deal that left the TD owning 40 per cent of Oxford. Thomson and Love discussed the bid as well as the general proposition of developers' holdings in trust companies. They agreed Royal Trust should remain widely held, and Love said he would likely be buying 10 per cent. Thomson told him TD would very likely be buying 10 per cent also. While Love did not take his decision to buy immediately, it looked sure enough that Thomson made a pitch for the TD to finance the transaction, saying, "If you are buying, don't forget the TD."

To Love, the purchase seemed like a good investment, and he said that the Campeau bid "sparked my imagination." Thomson's motives were likely many and varied. Perhaps he saw the opportunity for more business from Royal Trust by taking on an activist role; or he may have sincerely believed ownership should not go to Campeau; or, thirdly, he may have simply seen this as a time to gain influence within Royal Trust by making a judicious investment. To this day, Thomson refuses to be interviewed on the take-over, responding to any and all questions with a gentle "no comment." Whatever the explanation, it was an interventionist role no other banker sought.

A three-hour meeting in Taylor's office the next day, Labour Day Monday, confirmed the TD's decision. For Taylor and Royal Trust, Thomson's action in buying $40 million in shares — while he maintained it was taken to make a profit — had the same effect as if the bank had joined Plan A: more shares were moving into friendly hands. There was even a commission on the purchase, although at Taylor's request the Oxford purchase was carried out by a competitor, Burns, Fry. Taylor said he didn't want the appearance of TD and Oxford "acting in concert." For his part, Thomson did not see himself as in league with anyone. In fact, the bank kept itself ready to tender, or sell, its shares throughout, particularly as the month passed and the TD became nervous about being a minority shareholder in a Campeau-controlled Royal Trust.

The day after his meeting with White, Campeau, the man who'd started his building business with a single house in 1949, was holding forth at a press conference in an eighteenth-floor meeting room of the Bank of Nova Scotia. Unaware of the juggernaut beginning to roll, he tried to put the best face on it: "I have known Ken White for over twenty years and we had a pretty good conversation. In the end," he said cockily, "it won't be the colour of my eyes, or Ken White's eyes, that will make up the shareholders' minds. It's how good the offer is." Under pressure, however, he did admit, "White told me that he wasn't happy and that he was going to think the matter over and try to oppose the take-over."

The Royal Trust pension fund had already begun to lock up loose shares by purchasing on the open market — 250,000 shares Thursday alone. At the same time the Taylor strategy began, Royal Trust began a more visible public barrage, too, before the Ontario Supreme Court, the Ontario Securities Commission, the U.S. District Court for the Southern District of Florida (where Royal Trust had offices), the federal Department of Consumer and Corporate Affairs, the U.S. Federal Reserve Board — any governing body that might delay the bid's progress.

But these actions were just so much flak and diversion. Throughout, the real action showed on the stock exchanges, as the market churned delightedly every day, with 12.5 million shares — fully two-thirds of the 19.4 million outstanding — changing hands during September. It was Fraser Elliott, a Toronto lawyer and Royal Trust shareholder since the 1960s, who captured the real mood, a week after the Campeau–White meeting, when he commented on the battle between "Mr. Campeau and the Establishment." Observed Elliott: "It remains to be seen if they will, or can, close ranks to keep him out."

Elliott had put his finger on Taylor's strategy, Plan A, meant to ensure that large shareholders would not tender their stock to Campeau's offer. In addition to the TD's involvement, among the first to commit was the Bank of Montreal. Mulholland assured White, in his rather quaint phrase: "I am not now minded to tender the stock." Other assurances that significant blocks would not be sold, or that Royal Trust would be informed before they were, were reported to a Royal Trust board meeting Tuesday, September 2. These came from Stelco, Commercial Union, Guardian Insurance, Manufacturers Life, Standard Life, Ontario Hydro, Sun Life, and McGill University.

But that was just the holding operation. Also under way was an aggressive buy campaign, urged on by Ken White and Royal Trust. On September 3, Commercial Union bought a further 110,000 shares; after a September 7 conversation between White and Noranda chairman Alf Powis, Noranda bought 500,000 shares between September 8 and 11; the Canadian Imperial Bank of Commerce bought 516,000 shares between September 15 and 19 — as chairman Russ Harrison, a friend of White for fifteen years, put it, "to protect the business relationship" the bank had with Royal Trust. And by September 16 it was also clear to Royal Trust that the 3.3 million shares (about 15 per cent of the total) held in its trust accounts were also secure. Telephone calls to shareholders had discovered that only 24,000 of the 3.3 million would be tendered to the Campeau offer.

For its part, the Bank of Nova Scotia was supporting Campeau on the financing, but took no other action. The Royal stayed out of it; the Commerce bought shares but made no other move. Next to Thomson, Mulholland was the most active. For example, he discovered that his outside pension managers had been selling Royal Trust shares without his knowledge. "We thought we owned just under 10 per cent, then we found we only owned just over 8 per cent. I was told, 'I think the pension fund sold them,' and I said, 'Buy them back.'"

He did not, however, take the same aggressive course as Thomson, wary of what did eventually take place, an investigation by the Ontario Securities Commission. "You could smell that one coming a long way off, that there would be trouble in convincing people to become active in those shares." Did Mulholland consider following Thomson's lead? "The process is not that clear-cut, of considering or rejecting. You just don't entertain it very long." He did, however, as he put it, play "unsuccessful Cupid" between Campeau and White.

On September 10, White, after discussion with Mulholland, agreed to consult his board on Mulholland's compromise idea that Campeau would buy 25 per cent and nominate three directors. Mulholland also warned White of Campeau's solid support from the federal government. Campeau, a long-time builder of federal offices, was known to be a Liberal and a supporter of Prime Minister Pierre Trudeau. The federal government was still angry that Royal Trust had moved its headquarters out of Quebec, and many observers felt that Campeau's bid was made with federal government backing. "Royal might win the battle but could lose the war," Mulholland said, adding that "federal authorities might become more severe in regulating the affairs of Royal." Nevertheless, the next day Royal Trust rejected the compromise.

One final strategy, to be financed by the ever-interested Bank of Montreal, was unveiled about the same time. Izzy Asper's CanWest Investment Corporation had purchased Crown Trust from Conrad Black in 1979 and was looking to expand its Toronto base. It offered to buy 100 per cent of Royal Trust, but a September 18 board meeting resolved to thank CanWest for their interest but "advise them that at this time, it is considered inappropriate to proceed further with their proposal."

By September 17, Royal Trust was confident of success, and White met with Thomson for an hour. During the meeting, White estimated that 60 per cent of the shareholders would not tender, ensuring that the Campeau bid would fail, but there was a vagueness about it all. Recalled

Thomson: "After he left, we commented he never even mentioned that the Bank of Montreal had 10 per cent, and that bothered us, you know, it showed how vague he was."

While it may have seemed vague, counsel to the Ontario Securities Commission later described the presentation by White to Thomson in his office that morning as "an enthusiastic, emotional one." That same afternoon, an optimistic White met with Mulholland at two o'clock to deliver formally his board's rejection of the compromise Campeau position. It was now two days before the expiry of Campeau's $21 offer, but White felt confident enough to call Sun Life chairman Thomas Galt to tell him the bid would likely fail, because he had concluded that insufficient shares would be tendered. Recalled Galt, whose firm held at least one million shares after authorizing the purchase of up to two million shares (10 per cent) at a Sun Life board meeting September 3, "He said he thought I would like to know." When Noranda's Powis called White that day, he too was assured the bid would fail; a visit by Royal Trust's Wickens to the Bank of Commerce vice-president of investments, Peter Cole, passed along the same information. The word was being spread to the friends of Royal Trust: the Campeau bid was dead.

Robert Campeau was baffled. His $21 offer brought only 30 per cent of the outstanding shares, even with the 5.4 per cent holding he'd lined up in the beginning from George Mann, president of Unicorp Financial. Campeau announced that he would extend the bid from September 19 to October 2, raise it to $23 (a total value of $453 million), and see if the group he kept reading about could "stand the heat of another $2." At the same time, Campeau called Mulholland and told him that the OSC was investigating and urged him to tender the bank's shares "to avoid embarrassment." Said Mulholland: "I didn't see what I had to be embarrassed about."

The second round had begun. White was on the telephone to Dick Thomson on September 22. Thomson again confirmed that the TD had not tendered. Replied White: "I hope you won't [tender] at $23." Just to be safe in the face of the increased bid, MYW decided the same day to approach Paul Reichmann, vice-president and secretary of Olympia & York, the largest private empire of commercial buildings in the world. The move, made with the approval of White and the others at Royal Trust, put another irony in the fire. For years, Leonard Ellen and Reuben Cohen of Central Trust Co. had been trying for a Toronto trust company foothold, a place for Jews at the Establishment table. Regularly rebuffed, probably because of anti-Semitism, they had been restricted to their Moncton base. Now the Reichmann brothers were being sought out by the Establishment to be partners, even saviours. Albert, Paul, and

Ralph Reichmann, Orthodox Jews who had fled Europe and started a tile company in Toronto in 1955, had come into the public eye in 1979 — when they bought into Trizec with Peter and Edward Bronfman and began participating in a public company for the first time. They had gained wide respect as men of their word, as owners of a company that built office towers on time and under budget — including, in 1977, the seventy-two-storey First Canadian Place owned by the Bank of Montreal.

The significance of the approach by MYW's Howard Beck to the Reichmanns — calling on Orthodox Jews to beat back the French Canadian — was not lost on the bigots of Bay Street. Reichmann, with office buildings in five countries (including, it is projected, 10 per cent of all the office space in Manhattan by 1985), responded with more interest than anyone planned. He would be happy, he allowed, to come in for 50 per cent of Royal Trust. The suggestion was politely rebuffed; he countered by saying he would buy 10 per cent immediately, looking to build to 20 per cent — if seats on the board went with it. Assured they would, Reichmann also wanted Beck's word that dividend inccreases would continue as they had in previous years. Olympia & York then bought about 9 per cent before the end of September.

Meanwhile, on September 23, Royal Trust was stating, from the unusual podium of full-page newspaper ads: "It is our profound belief that no single person should be entrusted with $26 billion worth of the wealth, the hopes and the expectations of more than a million of us."

In fact, there was no need for such grandstanding or any search for super saviours; the battle was over. When the second bid expired on October 2, Campeau had received only 25 per cent of the shares — 5 per cent less than during the first offer at $2 a share lower. Commented Campeau vice-president W. J. Carroll ruefully: "Maybe we should have tried dropping the price instead of raising it to $23."

Down the street a bit, the victorious Ken White celebrated with a shot of "good old-fashioned Scotch." His toast might well have been to those companies who had just spent some $200 million on 55 per cent of Royal Trust, thereby shutting out Campeau: Canadian Imperial Bank of Commerce; Bank of Montreal; Toronto-Dominion Bank; Deutsche Bank of Frankfurt, West Germany; Hong Kong and Shanghai Banking; Sun Life; Oxford Development; National Trust; Noranda; Midlantic National Bank, of Newark, New Jersey; Olympia & York; Canadian Pacific; Commercial Union.

It was this group on which the Ontario Securities Commission later focused when it investigated the difference between the information given to the shareholders and that known to the general public. OSC lawyer Thomas Lockwood argued that Royal Trust "knew at all times how many shares were in the hands of friends." It was a costly friendship, not just for the embarrassment of the public hearing, but in the other place it hurts — the stock market. The day after the second bid expired the share price fell by $1.12 to $18.25. It had been a frenzied September, with a volume of trading that would normally take place over a three-and-a-half-year period. Campeau exercised his option to buy the 5.4 per cent Royal Trust block owned by George Mann, whose own real estate firm had been bought out by Royal Trust.

But the fight to keep Campeau out had taken a bizarre turn; Royal Trust was letting others in. And the Reichmann incursion wasn't the only one. In fact, by the time the dust had settled and the lawyers and investment advisers were paid their fees (Campeau paid Greenshields $500,000 for losing investment counsel, while Royal Trust's 1980 annual report notes that legal fees and miscellaneous costs jumped by $5 million that year), Royal Trust was 40 per cent owned — and had accepted the boardroom representation that such holdings bring — by two new corporate faces. The Bank of Montreal's Mulholland was willing to admit later the irony in that, too, but he never shared this irony with White. In fact, after the battle was over, White and Mulholland did not speak of it again. Said Mulholland: "I let sleeping dogs lie."

As one war ended, another was born of the first. The Ontario Securities Commission had already begun to visit the offices of McLeod Young Weir and some of the newer shareholders. Hearings in January 1981 led in March to a call by Ontario Securities Commission staff for sanctions against White and senior executive vice-president and chief operating officer John Scholes for actions that "fall far below the standards of conduct expected of senior officers and directors of a corporation whose shares are publicly held." (Scholes, in a show of internal corporate support, was promoted to president two days later.)

Meanwhile, ownership was still tossing about in an unsettled sea. Olympia & York increased its total holdings in Royal Trust to 23.3 per cent, including the chunk that Campeau had managed to acquire, giving him a profit of $2 million on the abortive bid after legal costs of $3.1 million. Even though it was a larger chunk than O & Y had originally sought, White continued bravely to welcome the Reichmanns. "Besides," he said after the annual meeting on March 12, 1981, "we like them. They're all right." In an announcement two weeks later, on March 25, Brascan said it had bought Oxford's 9.8 per cent. Again, it turned out to have been a wise investment for the first buyer, Don Love, who pocketed $2 million. Brascan, 49 per cent owned by Edward and Peter Bronfman, also bought a 5.1 per cent piece of Royal Trust from the other Bronfmans, Charles and Edgar. Again, welcoming noises were voiced by Royal Trust, and Brascan pressed on, upping its stake to 17.4 per cent by June 30.

And so it was that Ken White gained his Pyrrhic victory. Less than ten months after he marched Campeau off his property, Royal Trust had gone from a widely held company with 6,600 shareholders to one owned 40 per cent by the Reichmanns and the Bronfmans. As for the banks, inextricably involved throughout, there were embarrassing moments and repercussions. One had come September 19, when an error in the securities department at the Bank of Montreal caused some of the bank's shares to be inadvertently tendered to Campeau. "That," says Mulholland, "is a very painful subject for me." It was a minor blunder, however, compared with the TD's miscalculation of exactly how much it could legally own. From a position of holding no shares before the Campeau bid, TD raised its stake to nearly 10 per cent in lightning purchases from September 2 to September 8. But TD had a wholly owned subsidiary in California; Royal Trust had a group of Florida banks. In the U.S., a bank holding company that owns a bank in one state can't own more than 5 per cent of a bank in another state. Therefore TD was forced by the U.S. Federal Reserve Board, which regulates U.S. banks, to sell half of its 10 per cent holding in November. It went at fire-sale prices to Cemp Investments and was later resold to Brascan. The bank lost $650,000 in the deal. Said TD president Robin Korthals: "That was not our best chapter."

The hearings conducted by the Ontario Securities Commission in January 1981 were unprecedented in Canadian business history. Never before had the inner members of Canada's business élite been forced to reveal such minute-by-minute detail in public. They scurried in and out of the commission's hearing room for four days, summoned by OSC counsel Thomas Lockwood and Richard Lococo, as the elaborate knot of friends was untangled and held up to the closest possible public scrutiny. Royal Trust produced no evidence itself, arguing through its lawyer that the OSC was offering just "guesses, no facts at all." Claimed Royal Trust lawyer Ronald Robertson: "We very flatly deny that we have anything to hide. We saw no reason to produce further evidence." The OSC deliberated and on October 8, 1981, ruled that trading by Ken White on the Toronto Stock Exchange should be suspended for sixty consecutive days following October 18, 1981. For John Scholes, said the OSC, the suspension would run thirty days. The suspensions were appealed, but in June 1983 the Divisional Court of the Supreme Court of Ontario rejected an application to have the commission's decision reversed. White and Scholes did not launch a further appeal and the OSC imposed the trading suspensions announced more than eighteen months earlier.

In the end, any sanctions were almost secondary. The hearings themselves may have been punishment enough. The OSC had acted as a newly built dam on the river of commerce, halting the water's normal flow, passing each gallon through the sluiceway slowly for inspection. Above the dam, where the waters backed up and collected, the ever-widening pool created new shorelines and threatened to flood property long held and much loved. Below the dam, where the river had once run unimpeded, the muddy bottom was bared, yielding up an unaccustomed smell and unwelcome view.

After a time, when the dam's work was done, the gates were opened to allow the returning water to rush through with a sound that spoke relief, refilling the old channel, hiding the spotty bottom. As the months passed, the healing flow made both participants and observers forget. Robert Campeau, in a speech to La Chambre de Commerce du District de Montréal, would claim that bigotry played no part in the resistance to his bid. "I don't believe," he told the group, "the question of French and English was involved at all." And there was business forgiveness, too. Greenshields, the brokerage firm that had acted for and advised Campeau, getting cut off by Royal Trust for its efforts, was reinstated. "Business as usual," said Roger Otley, a Royal Trust vice-president.

Perhaps. But business, and especially the business of banking, had gone through a change as marked as the ownership make-up of Royal Trust, the storm centre around which the issues were fought. Royal Trust won, but it lost by taking on new owners; Robert Campeau lost, but he won by rising unscathed from the battle. And as for the bankers, their small triumphs and larger tragedies revealed, the discreet doings and careful confidences of take-overs would never be quite the same again. Their fiefdom had been forever changed. The strict world where every conversation was confidential, that protected environment every banker had grown up in, was gone. Regulating bodies, government agencies, and snooping journalists all found themselves peering through newly discovered keyholes, listening in on telephone conversations, and sitting in on strategy sessions. The curtains in the dimly lit bank chairman's office had been parted, then left slightly open. And for the bankers, that damn sunshine will just keep shining in.

FOUR

THE SINGLE-COMBAT WARRIOR

Russell Harrison

CHAIRMAN, THE CANADIAN IMPERIAL BANK OF COMMERCE

RUSS HARRISON was giving pesky questioners every drop of the disdain he felt they deserved. He had been rejecting persistent requests for information throughout the summer of 1982. No wonder. When the Dome bail-out package was finally unveiled in September, the stock's value plunged immediately to $2.50 from $5. Dome shareholders, thus far lulled along by reassuring sounds from market analysts, screamed foul. All those little owners had thought — because the market analysts had told them — that a government rescue would shore up their investment in the company, with its $7.4 billion in debt. There were even some who argued that such support might send the stock sky-rocketing in one of those runs for which Dome founder and chairman Jack Gallagher was so famous. Instead, the stock slumped and the murmurings became Canada-wide rumblings as shareholders beat their briefcases and whimpered about their losses. It wasn't the end of free enterprise that they mourned; rather, they were devastated because state intervention had not increased their personal worth.

In October some shareholders launched a class-action suit claiming Ottawa and the banks had caused them $5 billion in damages. The noise of other angry shareholders and the lamentations of mistaken analysts rose heavenward until the cacophony finally reached the fifty-sixth-floor aerie of the banker most inextricably involved — Russell E. Harrison, chairman and chief executive officer of the Canadian Imperial Bank of Commerce. With Gallagher not only on his board as a director but a member of the bank's international advisory committee as well, Harrison cared deeply about Dome. And he cared deeply about retrieving the $1.4 billion Dome owed the bank. After all, hadn't he dispatched his vice-chairman, Don Fullerton, to get a bail-out? Hadn't the Commerce fought with the Toronto-Dominion Bank and its chairman, Dick Thomson, who wanted no government intervention? Hadn't he, Russell E. Harrison, himself participated in the self-congratulatory secret signing ceremonies? Hadn't he saved not just Dome, but the integrity of the country? Who *were* these rabble saying the deal was no good?

The world needed to be told a few things, Harrison decreed, and he summoned as his chosen instrument Paul Taylor, an earnest young reporter for the *Globe and Mail* "Report on Business." For an hour that Monday afternoon, they sat opposite each other at one end of Harrison's plush office, with a coffee table between them. Harrison played coy about the actual negotiations, but he was clear on one count: the shareholders should be ecstatic about the bail-out, in which Ottawa and the four banks had agreed to buy up to $1 billion in Dome debentures. He was even clearer about where their praise should be directed. "The common shareholders should get down on their knees and thank God that we came to an agreement," Harrison told Taylor. "If we hadn't done this, their shares would have been worthless now. The shareholders would have been out of their minds not to go along with it. Their only hope rests with us controlling the company." He pointed out that bankruptcy would have meant that shareholders had nothing, although he admitted that the Canadian banks as a group had made a mistake by lending Dome more than half of its $7.4-billion debt. "Do you realize what bankruptcy would have done to Canada? The credit of the Canadian banking system —and the Canadian government itself—would have been in question."

At one point during the interview, Harrison left his office and returned with an eight-by-ten-inch black-and-white glossy photograph showing himself and the other bankers signing the deal with energy minister Jean Chrétien. He displayed it proudly to Taylor, as if this visual proof confirmed that his intentions towards the shareholders were sound and sensible. Taylor asked to borrow the photo so the newspaper could run it. Harrison was taken aback and refused, saying, "This is a memento. This is for our records."

Throughout the interview, Harrison was jovial, even jubilant, but Taylor was uncomfortable, surprised by Harrison's comments. "To me," says Taylor, until then a Commerce account-holder, "he seemed removed from the realities. I decided if that's the way the chairman is, I wanted out." Since the *Globe* deposited his pay directly into a Commerce account, he couldn't pull out entirely, but he did decide to withdraw the full amount each pay-day and transfer his business to the Royal. Taylor returned to the office about five that afternoon, too late to write his bombshell story for Tuesday's editions.

Meanwhile *Toronto Star* financial reporter Diane Francis had also been phoning Harrison regularly with interview requests. At one o'clock on

Tuesday, October 5, she gave up on the polite route through the public relations department and spoke to Harrison's secretary, saying that she just had one pointed question for Harrison: "What was the bank's internal per-share value for Dome?" Harrison, who must have wondered what had happened when the story he gave Taylor the day before failed to appear, seized upon Francis as his new mouthpiece. Within three minutes after she'd hung up the phone, she was the surprised recipient of a call from Harrison. Their telephone conversation lasted twenty-five minutes. Harrison was in a snit, and the quotes he gave to her were even juicier than those he'd given Taylor the day before.

"Shareholders had absolutely nothing," he said. "They shouldn't be suing me, they should be sending me flowers. As for 'poor old Dome' being under pressure, 'poor old Dome' held a gun to our heads. There's never been a company that's done as much harm to our country and its credit rating internationally as this company." He charged that Dome was adept at playing one bank off against another for loans and, as a result, competition for the company's business got out of hand. "There was a queue. It was a disease; everybody thought it was Christmas."

Harrison reserved his toughest shot, however, for the U.S. banks, which held most of the $3.7 billion owed by Dome to foreign lenders. "A pile of loans out of all this mess were unsecured. I don't think we were too bright in getting in so deeply, but they were downright stupid."

The bickering between Harrison and the U.S. banking community had its beginnings in 1979 when the Commerce backed Brascan Ltd.'s take-over offer for the U.S.-based F. W. Woolworth Co. Ltd. with $700 million. By law, no single U.S. bank could loan that much, and the Americans couldn't understand how the Commerce could, either. They also wondered how the Commerce could keep its loyalties separate, since it acted as bankers for both Brascan and Woolworth in Canada. Those views irked Harrison. Even two years later, in May 1981, he told the Toronto Society of Financial Analysts: "I won't likely forget that easily. They couldn't understand that one bank could put up $700 million." Then his voice turned into a mocking sneer as he parroted the U.S. line: "It was immoral."

Both newspapers carried the stories the following day, Wednesday, October 6, and Harrison immediately telephoned Francis. He began the conversation by blustering: "I don't want a retraction printed because that would do more harm than good." As if he could just phone and get one, thought Francis, as she pressed for details. He remarked on the story's accuracy, except for the comments about U.S. bankers. Countered Francis: "I have it in my notes." "Just because you have it in your notes doesn't mean I said it," he shot back. He went on to say that someone at the bank was phoning all the major U.S. banks to tell them that he had been misquoted. In at least one case, that just piqued their interest. The person phoned at Manufacturers Hanover in New York, for example, rushed to obtain a copy of the *Star* to see what was was being disavowed.

For all Harrison's denials, his friends said that the quotes sounded an awful lot like him. Still, bank analysts at the brokerage houses were stunned at the baldness of his comments and Harrison became the butt of editorial cartoons. Other bankers, even months later, would close their eyes in despair. Typical was Glenn Bumstead, secretary of the Toronto-Dominion Bank, Dome's second-largest Canadian creditor, at $1 billion. "It was," agreed Bumstead, "the shareholders' fault. After all, they shouldn't have bid the price up so high. The essence of what Harrison said was right. If Dome had gone into receivership, the shareholders wouldn't have gotten one sou. If the shareholders thought that the banks — and the TD was the best secured — were going to stand back and lose their money, they were crazy. The shareholders were the last in line. Harrison had a chance to make some yards but he buggered it." Then Bumstead stopped, thought for a few seconds, and snorted: "He is an outspoken and intemperate man."

The bankers were irked that Harrison's comments came while the Canadian banks were involved in trying to buy time for Dome to repay its debts to the U.S. banks. After the Canadian banks had rejected Dome's request for additional funds in 1981, Dome had turned to a consortium of banks led by Citicorp for a (U.S.) $1.8-billion loan. That group had to be brought into the fold now because the Canadian bail-out would not work if the foreign bankers suddenly demanded repayment. Bill Bateman, executive vice-president and general manager of the corporate and government banking group at the Bank of Montreal and the bank's man in charge of the U.S. talks, describes Harrison's outburst as "not useful." While the remarks did not block negotiations, because Harrison was not at the negotiating table, Bateman says, "If someone said that about me, I'd think he was a son of a bitch."

There were those in the Commerce who might agree. They were still smarting from what Harrison had said about *them* in a 1981 interview with Jacquie McNish of the *Financial Times*: "The whole problem this bank has had has been management. Collectively we didn't get our act together. It has been the most agonizing problem I've had here." For that piece of corporate exhibitionism, he received the *Canadian Business* magazine "Agony and Ecstasy Award for Straight Talk in High Places." Once again with Dome, Russ Harrison was oblivious to the fact that he'd parked his sturdy black lace-ups firmly in his mouth. As far as his public relations department was concerned, however, the message that had amazed most observers and shaken the confidence of others had been precisely what Harrison had wanted to say.

Poor Russ Harrison. Unlike most businessmen, he doesn't want to be wealthy. He wants to be worshipped. As the most reactionary and right-wing of the Big Five chairmen, Harrison can barely stomach questions from shareholders at the annual meeting. He presents himself as the beleaguered loner, defending free enterprise, fending off critics, feuding with governments, and fighting for his life. There's hardly time left to build a bigger bank all on his own. At annual meetings with hundreds of shareholders ranged before him, it is typical of Harrison to refer briefly to the bank's secretary for procedural information and necessary voting results, but never to the rest of his high-paid executive help arrayed on stage. Similarly, when he appeared before the parliamentary committee looking into bank profits in 1982, he fielded all questions himself. Although he was accompanied by vice-chairman John Hilliker and executive vice-president Peter Cole, Harrison turned but one question over to Cole — and interrupted the only sentence Cole was able to squeeze in.

Harrison runs the bank the same way, like a single-combat warrior, taking advice from few fronts. The most notable exception is board member and lawyer A. J. MacIntosh of Blake, Cassels & Graydon in Toronto. "When Harrison and MacIntosh sit down," says one insider, "the Commerce sits down." Most of the other directors, except for some chosen souls on the executive committee, can barely retain interest in the happenings at the monthly meetings. Claims one director: "Out of the hour-and-a-half board meeting, maybe five minutes is interesting. Although I wouldn't call him autocratic, Harrison is getting more like [former chairman Neil] McKinnon all the time."

Russ Harrison is a solid five-foot-ten and sports swept-back silver-grey hair. At sixty-two, his public face is uncomplicated and wreathed in a perpetual smile. He can be an awesome sight, this old sweat, draped in his pin-stripe suit. Only the canny brown eyes betray the banker's heart beneath. Woe to the politician or Ottawa mandarin who tells Harrison what the bank's public interest should be. Harrison has been known to blow up in private and curse the "group of asshole politicians and bureaucrats" who think they know how he should run his business. He is tough enough to have beaten his way to the top, yet he is no workaholic. In the office from eight-thirty to six, he rarely takes work home, although he will often make an appearance at a business-related cocktail party. Most noon-hours are taken up with business lunches outside the office or in the executive dining room, with its expansive view of Lake Ontario and the city. In addition to the usual offerings, he serves a liquid concoction that harks back to Prohibition days, when the Commerce chef was ordered to invent a non-alcoholic drink to replace the champagne served after board meetings. The pitcherfuls of apple juice, ginger ale, and bitters have been a staple of the Commerce dining room ever since.

Harrison entertains little in the evenings, preferring free time for escapist books or television: "I don't watch the educational programmes. The moment they start to instruct me, I'm onto something else." He has, however, studied French, and he and his wife have taken month-long vacations in France. When he really wants to flee, he leaves his Toronto home in swanky Forest Hill and heads to his farm near Peterborough, about two hours' drive east of Toronto, to put his feet up for a weekend, chop some wood, or cross-country ski.

Russell Edward Harrison was born in Grandview, Manitoba, on May 31, 1921. A fifth-generation Canadian, he grew up in The Pas, Manitoba, some 350 miles northwest of Winnipeg at the end of the railway line. In a tough town with a large Indian population, the Harrisons were pillars of the community. His father, a member of the merchant class, ran a hardware store. Young Russell received a boost given no one else in his school year when he was sent to the University of Manitoba. There he studied actuarial science until the Second World War broke out and he joined the First Canadian Parachute Battalion. "That had a lot more importance to me than university," he told the *Toronto Sun*'s Joan Sutton in June 1982. "It got me out of my little town into the big world, and I came back with a lot more confidence. I didn't enjoy the parade grounds or the barracks part of it, but I liked the action. I was scared skinny a good part of the time, but even then I enjoyed it."

He met and married his wife, Nancy, an Englishwoman, and brought her to Canada after the war. His father had died and his mother was ill, so he accepted a job offer from the Bank of Commerce because it would pay his way to Winnipeg while another potential employer, Canada Life, would not. At first, he had no intention of staying with the bank, and he looks back on his first five years at low pay as a difficult time. He became assistant manager in Hamilton, Ontario, in 1953, was transferred to Toronto in 1956, and quickly became chief inspector of the bank, then Quebec regional superintendent, living in Montreal, later that same year. "I certainly became very pro a French-Canadian Quebec. I don't know whether I am now. I think they've gone too far." He also made a name for himself as a bit of a maverick in the ranks and was known for not always following the branch operations manuals.

He spent the next fourteen years in Quebec, where he achieved two things. The first, and most important, was that he stayed out of the squabbling at head office in Toronto. Second, he forged lifelong loyalties with a number of colleagues, all of whom he has since rewarded. It was there he first came in contact with Warren Moysey, now senior executive vice-president and Harrison's current choice as his successor; Jack Griffiths, now executive vice-president for corporate and merchant banking; Griffiths' number two man, Larry Hivon; the most recently appointed executive vice-president, Marcel Casavant; and the current heads of the bank's Atlantic and European operations.

While Harrison was able to side-step most of the bitter feuding, the Commerce did not escape unscathed. If the Commerce was a military theatre, Harrison was aloof and alone, just as he was in wartime when he learned to deal with the terror of jumping from aircraft into battle, of being alone when he landed and fighting for personal survival in hostile surroundings where he couldn't always count on help. That background (he rose quickly to officer rank and was decorated for bravery) forever firmed his attitude towards life and death. You fight hard—perhaps for a cause, but for your own skin, too—and you play hard as well. Says David Lewis, who worked with Harrison for twenty years at the Commerce, "I'll bet his men hated him with a vengeance at times, but loved him. He's never lost the feeling of fighting and returning to the mess for a party."

He is, all agree, a guy who likes good times. Peter Gordon, chairman of Stelco and a Bank of Montreal director, points to Bill Mulholland as the best man to run a bank, but cites Harrison for other qualities. "I guess if I were going to choose somebody to run something for me, to bring it all together, I would choose Mulholland. But if I was going to choose somebody to spend a lot of time with, I might choose Harrison." At international gatherings on the road, Harrison will down a few drinks with his counterparts at the other Canadian banks. Ced Ritchie is a favourite drinking buddy, as was Fred McNeil when he was chairman of the Bank of Montreal. In 1982, when Harrison attended a meeting of reserve bankers in Phoenix, he and Scotiabank deputy chairman Gordon Bell stole a few hours from the endless sessions and walked around at the Arizona Biltmore where the meetings were being held. They eyed the lovelies around the swimming pool, inspected some classy condominiums nearby, tried to imagine retiring there with their wives, and speculated on how long it would take before marital fighting broke out. They decided, the two of them, warmed by the relentless sun of the southwest desert, that banking wasn't as much fun as it had been ten years earlier. Being a messenger for the government's monetary policy and high interest rates was no picnic, they agreed. On such occasions, Harrison can be reflective good company. Claims Bell: "Russ likes to portray himself as the individualistic former paratrooper, but he's not really like that."

And yet, in 1980, when long-time colleague and chief operating officer Don Fullerton asked to share in a little more of the bank's power, Harrison took away Fullerton's title and many of his duties and kicked him upstairs, as the saying goes, to the exalted but less exciting role of vice-chairman. So much for team spirit. If ever a business was wracked by internecine warfare, it is the Commerce. Its denizens at head office remain battle-fatigued; its performance in recent years has been the worst of the Big Five; those bailing out or being driven from the top ranks are the talk of the town. The Commerce is the Beirut of Canadian business.

The bank that Harrison heads is the second-largest in total assets in the country, behind the Royal, and the largest in terms of domestic assets. Most of its strength is in Ontario and the West. In addition to the 1,662 branches (the largest and most expensive branch network in the country), it has the biggest number of corporate accounts and, as a result, the largest number of huge loans to individual companies—some twenty-two loans of more than $400 million each. The numerous branches and the bank's gargantuan domestic size had their beginnings in the 1961 merger between the Canadian Bank of Commerce and the Imperial Bank of Canada. Also in that merger were the seeds of the persistent internal animosity, for there are still those in the bank who refer to themselves as "Imperial Bankers," even after more than two decades, while those from the Commerce have gained the upper hand. The Imperial's main strength lay in the Niagara region of Ontario, in northern Ontario, and with the mining companies.

The Imperial chairman was Stuart Mackersy. Born in Scotland, Mackersy was known as the "Bull Moose." A crusty man with a photographic memory, he had made his name when he was assistant manager of the Edmonton branch from 1929 to 1936. It was the Depression, the province was broke, and Mackersy would receive wires from head office telling him not to loan the Alberta government any more money. He and the provincial treasurer would hop in a car together, drive around to provincial liquor outlets, and gather enough cash for deposit in the bank so the government could meet its payroll. To this day, Alberta returns the favour by retaining the Commerce as its main banker.

Mackersy was drawn to a merger for two reasons. First, the Imperial was heavily oriented towards resource-based corporate customers. Those companies were growing rapidly in the 1950s, and the Imperial was having difficulty coming up with the money that was needed to finance further expansion. The Commerce, with assets of $3 billion, was three times larger and could supply the funds. Second, Mackersy was approaching retirement and was worried about succession. Mackersy wanted his general manager, Harold Thomson (father of Dick Thomson, current TD chairman), to succeed him. The board was leaning towards avid tennis player and president John Proctor. Rather than make a decision, and because of the need for access to more funds, Mackersy talked to Neil McKinnon at the Commerce, and a merger was arranged. Elsewhere in the industry it was viewed as more of a take-over by the Commerce than a merger.

Mackersy thus dumped the succession problem onto McKinnon as president and chief executive officer of the new, merged bank. For his part, Mackersy all but retired. He had lunch at the Toronto Club every day, then returned to the office for a one-hour nap, during which his secretary was under strict instructions to fend off any and all callers, including McKinnon. McKinnon, who had joined the Commerce in his home town of Cobalt, Ontario, in 1925, had no greater success picking a successor than Mackersy. Thomson was out of the running because he developed heart trouble; McKinnon and Proctor did not get along, and Proctor resigned as executive vice-president less than a year after the merger. He joined the Bank of Nova Scotia across the street, an unheard-of defection in an era of lifelong institutional loyalties.

McKinnon was still hunting for a successor ten years later. He would hand out responsibilities, then stick his nose in or take duties back. One typical casualty was chief general manager Gordon Sharwood, who had joined the bank in 1956 and came to be viewed as McKinnon's heir. He had piloted the bank to the point in the spring of 1969 when, for a time, the Commerce passed the Royal in assets and was briefly the largest bank in the country. None of this was good enough for McKinnon, however, and without notice he turned on Sharwood. Even McKinnon's protective father–daughter relationship with Sharwood's wife (they were both from Cobalt) didn't help Sharwood.

Sharwood first learned what was happening one August morning in 1969 when he was reading the paper over breakfast at home. There in the *Globe and Mail* was a brief news story saying that Russell Harrison, then regional general manager in Quebec, was being transferred to Toronto to become the bank's first executive vice-president. His responsibility: day-to-day operations of the bank. Until that moment, those had been Sharwood's duties. He telephoned his wife, Sandy, who was at a summer cottage near Prescott, in eastern Ontario. "Take the train home," he told her, "I'm going to resign." He went in to the office, but McKinnon refused to see him. As to Sharwood's relayed question about why he hadn't been consulted concerning the executive reshuffling, McKinnon sent back a message: "I didn't consult the people Sharwood was brought in over." Sharwood cleared out his desk and left.

Among the reasons McKinnon had gone sour on Sharwood was Sharwood's sustained campaign the previous year to have the Massey-Ferguson account split with the Royal. He could see that it was getting too big for the Commerce; the Royal had agreed to take half. "I lost that battle," said Sharwood. "It would have made a tremendous difference if they'd listened to me. The account was in reasonably good shape then." Even so, the Commerce, as the largest domestic bank in the country, was beginning to slip. In the 1960s the Royal, for example, stole away half of the Commerce's oil and gas production loan business. In the early 1970s the Bank of Montreal was wrestling with the computer installation that would give it an edge in branch network capability even though it had some four hundred fewer branches than the Commerce. The slide had begun.

This was the faltering behemoth that Harrison was to inherit. Succession would remain muddled; troublesome corporate accounts were not dealt with swiftly; the ranks at the top, continually depopulated by McKinnon, stayed thin through the 1970s because there was no outside recruitment. After McKinnon was finally turfed out by the board of directors in 1973, it was as if a war had taken the best of a generation. There was simply no one to turn to except Page Wadsworth. Appointed chairman at sixty-two, Wadsworth had been bounced around by McKinnon and had been CEO since 1971. The hope was that his appointment would be a healing operation.

Scion of a prominent Toronto family, Page Wadsworth was just the ticket to settle down a Bay Street still abuzz with the eccentricities of McKinnon in his last years. Comments Sydney Hermant, chairman and chief executive officer of Imperial Optical Co. Ltd. and a bank director since 1960, "Page Wadsworth is a gentleman. After the appointment, I think he got up every morning, looked in the mirror and said: 'Holy smoke, is it really me?' I don't think he ever in his wildest imagination thought he would be chairman. He was a good caretaker. He was there. He was safe. Everything came together by accident for him." Wadsworth, in the words of another member of the executive committee, was "the Gerry Ford of the Commerce."

With Wadsworth a surprised, if pleasant, captain at the helm, Harrison was named president and chief operating officer, with Don Fullerton taking over Harrison's former title of executive vice-president and chief general manager. When Wadsworth retired in 1976, Harrison became chairman and CEO, with Fullerton as president and chief operating officer. McKinnon remained on the board until his death in 1975, and his cronies stayed on beyond. As a result, even after the healing hands of Wadsworth, there was still acrimony and divisiveness in the boardroom and the executive hallways.

There were board members who felt McKinnon had been done wrong, and there were many others who did not want to place authority in any *one* man. The board, made cumbersome by the 1961 merger, was rendered cautious in the wake of McKinnon. As a result, the directors tied Harrison down, fashioning a two-headed management beast with Fullerton as chief operating officer. Fullerton often did things without Harrison's consent and the ruling "duumvirate" thus created the further problem of a delicate political balance that discouraged change. Recalled one director: "There were real limits on the authority Harrison had. There was support for Fullerton."

While Harrison shuffled his management about a bit, he really could make no serious attempt in the first few years to put his stamp on the place. Harrison brought in no new blood from outside, although many — even his competitors — urged him to do so. Bank of Montreal chairman Fred McNeil recalls Harrison's "snide" remarks about B of M's outside recruiting. Harrison would kid McNeil: "Christ, isn't there anybody in that bank of yours?" Said McNeil: "Poor old Russ hasn't got enough sense to go out and get [help]." Finally, in 1980, McNeil ran into Harrison at the International Monetary Conference meeting, and Harrison admitted: "I'm afraid you were right. I gotta do more." During Harrison's early years in charge, any changes carried out seemed to be no more than a riffle through the same deck of cards. Operations were tightened under four new executive vice-presidents, replacing the arrangement that had seen seven senior vice-presidents reporting to Fullerton. In the main, however, responsibilities altered little.

Publicly, Harrison defended the status quo and claimed that it fit his view of how things should run. "Reorganization is very disruptive," he said in a 1979 interview with me. "Even changing someone's title is perceived to be changing the job." He did make some tentative steps by raising loan limits and moving towards decentralization of loan decisions, because of increasing volumes of business ("the sheer inability to flip the paper," as he put it) as well as the "growing regional nationalism in Canada."

But the changes were slight and after three years at the top, Harrison seemed to find difficulty in making his bank hum. "Making it function can be particularly difficult in the face of a hundred-year-old tradition. Lifelong careers of people are involved. We're not at the end of our job as far as having it work. I'm not suggesting it's not working," he added quickly, "but we're not finished." His final thought on the topic that day said more about his attitude towards the people under him than he realized. "It's a helluva lot easier to give the authority than have someone take it or the accountability that goes with it."

Harrison was faced with a weakened shop when he took over. Management ranks "were pretty thin," he admitted in that 1979 interview. "We're still thin, but we're not as thin as we were." Yet he had added no one new at the top to beef up senior management, seeming to blame the ghosts of the past for the goblins of the day. After three years as boss, he also seemed troubled by the bank's rigid traditionalism, as if he couldn't cause change even if he wanted. "There's a lot of thinking that goes, 'This is the way we do it, this is the way we've always done it.' "

In 1979 he was also struggling with the size and expense of the branch network, trying to see how to make it profitable, rather than following the route taken by the other banks, which had closed excess offices, thus saving on growing overhead costs. Further, he still seemed to be wrestling with himself, trying to adapt to his role at the top, not quite accustomed to giving orders rather than carrying them out. "I've got to give up some of the joys," he said sadly, "stop dealing with Customer X if someone else [in the bank] is closer. It's no longer possible for someone in an organization this size to have that kind of one-on-one relationship. It's harder to get somebody else to do things than to do it yourself, but that's my job," he concluded.

He spoke out of frustration, as if he hadn't finished the training required for the top job. Because there was no mentor to turn to, so little time to plan, he spent most of his days putting out brushfires in the valley, too busy to climb the hill and size up the lie of the land. No one knew what he had in mind — either for individuals or for the institution — because there was no expressed strategy. Lack of planning frustrated senior management personnel. David Lewis, who in 1981 left his vice-president's role at the Commerce to become president of the much smaller Continental Bank, said in 1980 that planning seemed impossible to accomplish at the Commerce. "We've never been successful," he said. "We've taken about five cracks at it." Says Chuck Laidley, who fled from his vice-chairman's post in 1981: "It is apparent that Harrison can look ahead. He *thinks* about next year, but I'm not sure that an awful lot is done to *prepare* for next year. The real problem I had was a lack of clear, definitive resolution coming from senior officers about 'where we are going.' There wasn't any real prioritizing, or even, 'Here are some of things we *aren't* going to do.' " Nor did Harrison warmly welcome the suggestions of others. "He was more apt to sit blue-skying his ideas than blue-sky other people's. There wasn't too much laying the problem on the table and saying, 'Let's find a solution.' Presenting a problem and asking for solutions when you already have a solution in your mind tends to suffocate things."

No one felt that professional suffocation more than Don Fullerton, yoked as he was to Harrison in an unwieldy duumvirate. A more innovative thinker and less authoritarian delegater than Harrison, Fullerton was champing for more power. He had joined the bank immediately after graduation from the University of Toronto in 1953 and worked his way up through the branch and operations side. As chief general manager by

1973, he was a single step behind Harrison and, in his own mind at least, a candidate for the top job in 1976 when Wadsworth retired. Fullerton is ten years younger than Harrison, and his management style is a full generation advanced. Harrison had treated him like a son after Fullerton's first wife died, and he had spent much time at Harrison's home.

At the office, however, Harrison would regularly delegate duties to Fullerton — and just as regularly take them back. "Russ and Don never really came to an agreement as to who was to do what," recalls Laidley. "There were all sorts of nice things said about how they operated as a team, but that only works if the members of the team know what each of them is to do." After the 1980 shuffle, Laidley would refer matters beyond his authority (any credit over $10 million) to either Harrison or Fullerton, depending on who was available. If Harrison were away and Fullerton approved, Harrison would sometimes not be told upon his return. He would find out about it and say to Laidley: "What the hell happened here?" "I referred it to Don," Laidley would reply. "I thought he'd tell you." Harrison didn't like to be caught out like that, and particularly did not know how to handle a situation at a cocktail party where someone would sidle up to him and thank him for a loan approval. Rather than nod a "You're welcome" and pretend full knowledge, Harrison would be embarrassed, return to the office, and go back to his old ways of demanding more detail on all kinds of deals.

At the same time, Harrison and the Commerce were saddled with the fiasco of Massey-Ferguson, the first of many corporate Canadian giants to lose massive amounts of money and fall upon bad times with their bankers. As Massey's main banker, the Commerce had to write off $100 million in losses. The $715-million refinancing that included two hundred banks took inordinate amounts of Harrison's time. A lot of observers wondered why the Commerce hadn't forced Massey into a self-rescue earlier.

By 1980, Harrison had too much on his plate. External image and internal morale had hit all-time lows. Harrison was overseeing a bank with a cumbersome and outdated branch system. There was still a gaggle of directors left over from the McKinnon era who didn't approve of him. Massey was a public basket-case, and the bank itself had just gone through a year of terrible operating results. Along with the rest of the industry, the Commerce had rolled mindlessly along in the 1970s in a reasonable profitable position. After-tax profits, on a scale where the industry average was 100, were 106 in the early 1970s. By 1980, however, they had slumped to 65. Even the Bank of Montreal at its most moribund in the mid-1970s had only declined to 71. Not even the long-running and high-priced ad campaign using pop singer Anne Murray could paper over the problems. Nor did the campaign seem to be having an effect. Said Harrison: "I don't know how to measure it and neither does our ad agency." In the 1980 fiscal year, net income at the Commerce actually declined at a time when the other Big Five banks reported solid gains. Analysts looking at the Commerce numbers were baffled by the apparent inability of the Commerce to match assets and liabilities.

Banks make money on the spread, by taking in deposits and lending them out at higher rates. Under ideal circumstances, the length of the term on both sides matches. A deposit taken in at 10 per cent guaranteed for five years and loaned out in a mortgage at 12 per cent for five years is a banker's happiest chore. Then everything is secure, rates won't change, and there is built-in profit. At the Commerce, however, Harrison let things get topsy-turvy. When prime-rate loans were down around 8 or 8.5 per cent, the Commerce turned its attention to consumer loans at 13 per cent and mortgages at 10, taking business away from the other banks in the process. Trouble was that the Commerce wasn't taking in the five-year money at the right rates to fund those areas. Penalties assessed by the Commerce when long-term deposits were cashed in early were too low. As a result, the bank was locked into long-term loans at fixed rates while long-term depositors were withdrawing at minimal costs in order to take advantage of ever-higher deposit rates. The mismatch of assets and liabilities grew to between $5 billion and $6 billion.

Frustrated by these problems and fed up with his own lack of authority, Fullerton decided that "life with Father" was finished; he wanted the title of chief executive officer. Such a promotion would signal that he had moved up from his role overseeing day-to-day operations as chief operating officer to the more strategy-oriented post of CEO. More important, the world would see him as Harrison's designated successor and would expect Harrison to take on increasingly honorific duties until he gracefully retired. It was precisely the wrong moment for such a manoeuvre. Harrison himself was feeling the heat of the industry criticism and the pressure on profits. Fullerton's declaration of war offered Harrison a focal point for a fight. He was going to turn the Commerce around and take the credit for any good results he achieved — or go down trying. Suddenly, Fullerton was a threat. "Harrison was concerned," said Laidley, "that Fullerton was going to be number one before Harrison was through being number one."

To fight Fullerton, Harrison told executive committee member Jack Leitch to phone board members and round up their support. Harrison approached each of the eighteen people on the executive committee himself. According to one, Harrison's message went like this: "The division [of duties] between him and Don was not working. While their relations were cordial, it was putting some strain on that, not because there was any natural antipathy between them but just because it was a division that was not working administratively." The choice Harrison put was simple: make Fullerton chief executive officer, replacing Harrison, or strip away Fullerton's chief operating officer title and make him a vice-chairman responsible for international.

"We have to put an end to the schism," Harrison told each director. "I'd be happy to hand it over to Don or happy to accept the mandate." Too smart to let himself be fired, Harrison had lined up his board support, support he'd been carefully building since he took over. The board chose Harrison. Explains a director: "There had been a season of lassitude. It got to the point of '*Le roi s'amuse.*' Chairmen play these games, you know. He went from being a co-equal with Fullerton to being the great emperor."

Deeply hurt by Fullerton's lunge for the top, Harrison had taught a lesson to the man he had treated like a son. In public, the result was an August 7, 1980, announcement that Fullerton would continue as president and become vice-chairman responsible for international business — but he lost his title as chief operating officer, although the press release making the announcement failed to mention that important change. In order to give the reorganization a convincing ring, John Hilliker and Chuck Laidley were also promoted to the position of vice-chairman. Now Harrison had three people reporting to him, not just the president. It was a more hands-on operation. For the Commerce, the authoritarian days of McKinnon followed by a more co-operative framework under Harrison had both proven to be failures. Within the executive hierarchy there was confusion and flagging morale. Shortly after, David Lewis left, then Chuck Laidley. All the while, Hilliker was saying to his colleagues: "You know how this will end? Someone will come in from the outside." But in 1982, Hilliker left, too, after supervising the shutdown of a hundred branches. Hilliker, one of the bright stars, became chief executive officer of Canada Permanent Trust, a job that had been vacant for a year and that paid him a reputed $500,000 annually — about twice his compensation package at the bank. He took with him Thomas Hodgson, a Commerce policy and planning vice-president.

All that mattered to Harrison in 1980, however, was that he was in control — once again the single-combat warrior. Harrison assumed all Fullerton's functions at meetings of the board. Fullerton, once a strong number two, had been reduced to the role of a yes-man. According to one director who joined the board after the corporate carnage: "The blood was still on the floor when I came in." Says another, more seasoned, member of the board who watched the change: "Fullerton has been going around with his tail between his legs ever since." The old paratrooper had landed on his feet at last.

Control at the top did not, however, show up immediately on the bottom line. Bank performance since Harrison's consolidation of control in 1980 has remained mixed. In 1981, net income jumped 61 per cent; it then slumped by 12 per cent in 1982. The Commerce did, however, begin to take the lead in offering some new services. In 1981 it was the first with variable-rate mortgages, and in 1983 the first to announce a drop in credit-card interest rates from 24 per cent to 21 per cent. While such firsts don't punch much profit into annual statements, they do signal a shift. That kind of leadership in an industry such as banking has some internal morale value, if nothing else, and makes employees feel that a corner has been reached, if not yet turned. In 1981 the bank recorded its largest earnings ever. In 1982 with loan losses also at record levels, earnings remained high — second-highest in the institution's history. The mismatch was gone, branch computer installations were completed, and non-interest expenses were up by only 11 per cent, compared with 20 per cent at the Royal.

Even so, by one of the standard measurements accepted in the industry — return on average total assets — the Commerce was still struggling. Because of loan losses, domestic performance in 1982 was half the 1978 level. When both domestic and foreign business are taken into account, each of the years from 1979 to 1982 was worse than the 1978 results. The imbalance in the mortgage portfolio grew to desperate proportions. By 1981, the average yield was 11.2 per cent; the cost of funds was almost twice as much, at 20 per cent. By 1982, the bank had lost $1.25 billion on its mortgage portfolio during the previous five years.

The Commerce had been saddled with the old-fashioned view that each branch was an inexpensive vacuum cleaner sucking deposits in from hundreds of domestic locations. When the realization hit Harrison that he had to cut overhead costs, it was a decision taken five years too late.

As someone who worked his way up in the bank, Harrison had found it personally difficult to cut back on the number of branches. It was a reluctance that an outsider like Mulholland, for example, did not face at the Bank of Montreal. Commented Scotiabank chairman Ced Ritchie: "Mulholland would have closed branches sooner. The Commerce has a huge number and may have found for a time that it was cheaper to keep two open than build a new one." It wasn't until 1981 that the process of closing branches and cutting staff was under way.

The Commerce's record and Harrison's management difficulties have made bank-watchers and depositors particularly twitchy. In July 1982, while the Dome bail-out was being negotiated, Gary Lauk, the NDP member of the British Columbia legislature from Vancouver Centre and a former minister in the Dave Barrett government, stood in his place and charged that the Canadian Imperial Bank of Commerce would be virtually bankrupt by October. The cause would be bad loans, especially the $1.4-billion loan to Dome on which, Lauk said, no interest was being paid. Lauk may not have been a household word, but he quickly became a boardroom expletive. Nervous investors stampeded. On the Toronto Stock Exchange, Commerce share value dropped by $1.25, touching a low for the year. That morning, Harrison was in Ottawa, Fullerton was running a board meeting, and Peter Cole was in conference with representatives of Standard & Poor's, an investor information service.

Cole first heard about the statement and the effect it was having on the value of Commerce shares during the meeting. "Gentlemen," he said, "I can't keep this from you any longer. You are going to read about this in the papers. We've got an emergency on our hands." Cole charged up to the fifty-sixth floor, pulled Fullerton out of the meeting, and briefed him. A statement was drawn up and taken to the Toronto Stock Exchange. Officials at Dome were also called and asked to issue reassuring words as well.

That done, the Commerce turned its attention to the branch network, where counter staff, hit with increased demands for withdrawals, were following the rules all too avidly. They were refusing requests for sizeable withdrawals, demanding forty-eight hours' notice. It may have been proper procedure, but it wasn't politic. Facing such refusals, customers were telling others that the Commerce was not allowing them to take all their money out. In the banking world, where so much depends on trust and confidence, such word of mouth—even if ill-informed—can be enough to start a run. The order was issued to waive notice requirements and let people take out any amount on deposit. Normally, interest penalties result if a term deposit is removed early, but branches were instructed to refund the full amount with full interest — and work out any penalty later. Depositors hastened to withdraw the amounts that would reduce their holdings to the $20,000 level then guaranteed by the Canadian Deposit Insurance Corporation. The Bank of Montreal and the Royal were called, and both agreed to back the Commerce to the hilt with funds if a real run developed.

Another telephone call went to Lauk in order to explain the impact of his comments. At a hastily called news conference, Lauk changed his view. "I am concerned that my statement had the reaction that it's had," he said. "I did not foresee that it would have such a wide reaction."

Lauk's charges, huffed Harrison in a statement of his own amid the flurry of comments, were "completely without foundation and reflect a total lack of understanding of the Canadian banking system in general and the position of the Commerce in particular."

The verdict, however, of a jittery public had been swift, the damage severe. By November the Commerce calculated it had lost $500 million in deposits that were withdrawn, moved elsewhere, and never found their way back. And the fragility of the Commerce's hold on the public trust was forever recorded.

With all the bank's problems, it's no wonder Russ Harrison runs the place with a certain gallows humour. Conrad Black likes to tell the story about his brother, TD director Monte Black, during the time when the Commerce was up to its armpits in trouble with Massey. Monte's home is in Harrison's neighbourhood, and as he sat on the porch one Sunday morning, he spied a middle-aged couple coming down the street on foot. As they passed, Monte exclaimed, to no one in particular, "Holy Jesus, that's Russell E. Harrison." "Who," said one of his two children, "is Russell E. Harrison?" "He's the chairman of the Bank of Commerce, and unless they're getting a flying start at lunch, they're going to church. My God," he continued, "if that ringtail is going to church, that bank *must* be in trouble." When Conrad told Harrison of Monte's sighting and comments, Harrison laughed and said: "Indeed, I was on my way to church, and it *is* something I don't regularly do. And when I got there, I found Galen Weston, so maybe he's in trouble, too."

Harrison may try to jest about his bank's difficulties, but they so preoccupy him that it shows in the simplest of social exchanges. Another bank's CEO sat beside him recently at a head table and asked as a conversation-starter: "What's new and exciting?" Harrison replied grimly: "Nothing too drastic this morning, but I don't know about tomorrow."

As a result of this bleak view, Harrison often lays down the law after insufficient consultation. A close observer in the investment community puts it this way: "Russ runs the place on fear. He is a good credit man, but he is crotchety and antediluvian beyond belief. Russ wants to go out as someone who brought the bank around. His attitude is, 'If I'm going to get hung with it, I'm going to go out trying it on my own. And if it doesn't work — so what? I'm going to get hung anyway.' "

At one time, he may have been prepared to be collegial, but Fullerton's eagerness and the thin ranks changed his mind. Now, although the vice-chairmen are supposed to be independent policy gurus, none will make a major move without knowing where Harrison stands. "But the chairman," notes the observer, "often has trigger answers that may not always be right."

The plain fact is that Harrison has less than three years until the normal retirement age—and that may not be enough time to effect any change he does conceptualize. The fact that he has hung on as long as he has is a surprise to many of his peers. "I'm surprised he's still in the chair," says the chief executive officer of one of the foreign banks in Canada. "The board should replace him."

A self-described right-wing conservative, Harrison is outspoken in his criticism of government and the lack of political leadership. While his views may not be uncommon among businessmen, few would put them quite so vocally. Business knows it has to deal with government and is more likely to don the cloak of hypocrisy. Harrison scoffed at the parliamentary investigation into bank profits conducted by the Standing Committee on Finance, Trade and Economic Affairs in 1982. Although he appeared and testified, he told his board later that he thought the whole thing was a waste of time: "The politicians just made political hay," was his judgement. If he does nothing else, Harrison lets people know what he thinks of them. Like many who fought in the Second World War, he dislikes Germans to this day. As for residents of the Middle East—he has been known to refer to some of them as "rug-riders."

On other modern-day topics such as women and unions in the bank, Harrison is all but dismissive. In 1979, as the union drive spluttered, Harrison knew it was doomed. "I honestly think we'll be rid of it," he said. "We had the most branches certified; now we have the fewest." Women have made little progress in the Commerce hierarchy. Harrison seems to see them chiefly in the role of the banker's wife, uncomplaining when career shifts and corporate shake-ups disrupt their lives.

He was quoted in 1982 as saying: "The worst question you can ask an up-and-coming young man is, 'Would you like to go to a certain city?' If you do that, then he has to ask his wife. Then if he takes it and the family doesn't like it, they natter at him. If he doesn't take it, he worries about whether he's ruined his career. Better to tell him, 'You are going. If you don't want to go, tell me.' I don't remember ever asking my wife. I phoned her and told her we were moving. I don't remember her ever expecting to be asked. It was part of our business and I don't think there's anything wrong with that."

Harrison holds equally traditional views about public disclosure of the bank's loans. While the bank's 1982 annual report did reveal loans to selected foreign countries, the Commerce has not been a disclosure leader. He regards journalists with scorn and puts up with investment analysts as a game fish might withstand a lamprey eel, as a parasite to be endured. As far as Harrison is concerned, banks should be trusted without question. At the end of my interview with him in 1979, he moved behind his desk, took a speaker's pose, and gave an impromptu diatribe that rattled through trust, disclosure, and published salaries. With barely a pause for breath, he could have been a fire-and-brimstone preacher spieling out the gospel to sin-filled parishioners huddled in the pews below. Peppered with rhetorical questions, bald statements, and flat-out assertions, it was Harrison in full flight.

"Banks have an aura about them, like a church. I don't know anybody who doesn't trust a bank, do you? I mean, you put your money in, and you know it's safe. Even during the Depression when the banks were *bankrupt* — they said there were hidden reserves, but there weren't — I mean, we loaned money to the Royal. I can't prove that, but I've been told that. The system hung together. Would it have served the Canadian people to know there were no reserves? I don't think so. Disclosure, as an issue, is the same. The government's going to push and push and push. And we — I don't mean the Commerce, but the industry — are going to resist, resist, resist. I mean, no one knows my name, but they know the chairman of the Bank of Commerce. If disclosure could hurt my wife or my grandchildren . . ." He shuddered and did not finish the thought. "Ritchie's had threatening calls, a lot of them — and his kids, too. Thomson's wife was tied up four or five years ago. What purpose would it serve to publish our salaries? If Canadian banks loan hundreds of millions in a country, does it do any good for anyone to know? We'll survive. Our salaries are comparable to the U.S. — two to four hundred thousand — *but* there is a difference. We've got a 62 per cent tax bracket. [It fell to 50 per cent in 1982.] Our books should be open, but to responsible people."

For all his toughness, Harrison lacks self-confidence. At one point, the Commerce was offered a deal to become involved in a New York-based operation that had, as other partners, members of the Rockefeller and Mellon families. His predecessor, McKinnon, would have joined such esteemed ranks in a wink. Harrison, however, turned down the opportunity to associate with the monied Americans. His explanation? "I don't *know* any of those people."

Some of Harrison's apparent paralysis, his sheer incapacity to change the bank, may be caused by the constant carping he hears from outside. He spends too much time as a staunch defender rather than a visionary strategist. For example, he receives the worst roasting of any bank chairman, living or dead, at annual meeting time. The 1982 meeting set longevity records, dragging on for two and a half hours through the verbal assaults of half a dozen questioners. At a time when consumer loan rates hovered near 20 per cent, Harrison's own loan ($166,136 at

6.25 per cent) also came up for assault. The final indignity came from a woman who rose to suggest: "One way to catch bank robbers is to put surveillance cameras in the executive suites."

The 1983 annual meeting wasn't much better. Harrison had little but bad news for the packed hall. Loan losses had tripled to reach $488 million and non-productive loans (where no interest was being collected) totalled $1.6 billion. The main attack came from the United Church of Canada and the Jesuit Fathers of Upper Canada (owners between them of about a hundred thousand Commerce shares). They had picked the Commerce as the target for a motion to make public more information about foreign loans. The motion asked the Commerce to identify the countries where the bank had loans over $100 million. At the meeting, Jesuit Father James Webb complained that some shareholders who had voted for the motion and mailed in their ballots had been phoned by the bank and asked if they were sure they wanted their vote cast that way. "There was some confusion," explained Harrison. "A form of pressure," countered Webb. The bank won the vote, 22,752,646 to 525,284.

The slanging match continued as Webb and others in the audience pushed Harrison to say that the bank would give no more loans to South Africa. Harrison refused to comply but pointed out: "Please don't assume, because we don't say we don't, that we do." When pressed for clarification, he said, "By refusing to say we won't, it certainly doesn't mean we are. This is why our conversations with the churches have come on rough ground. What we say there comes out differently." The church questioner expressed some confusion with what he was hearing. "I know you're confused," Harrison retorted, his voice tinged with sarcasm. "I don't know why." He then went on to do what he said he wouldn't and admitted that the bank did have loans with South Africa by saying: "We have thousands of clients that owe us a lot more than South Africa."

After the meeting the testy debate started up again in the hall outside. Harrison and United Church treasurer Bill Davis were arguing about morality — who has it and who doesn't. Each denied he was setting himself up as a moralist on the question of loans. Speaking of the other banks and their position on the issue of loans to South Africa, Harrison said: "They're not all that moral, I'm not all that moral. The trouble with you," he said, addressing Davis, "is that you're trying to make this a political issue." Harrison's face was reddening and his right hand was making chopping motions on his open left palm as he continued. "We've gone further than the other banks in disclosure in this annual report," he said, waving towards the booklets being handed out. Davis was left to whine, "Why didn't you tell us *before* the meeting? There I was making a speech that you hadn't arrived in the 1980s and you're there." Harrison paused before replying, his head bobbing and lips curled back to show long and glistening white teeth: "There was no need to tell *you*," he said. Having reduced Davis to what he regarded as the appropriate state — silent — Harrison stalked off.

It was not the best moment to ask another question, but it was the first direct opportunity I'd had after requesting an interview with Harrison almost two years earlier and finally getting a no the previous month. I had even submitted, on request, a list of a hundred questions on his upbringing, his war record, and his professional life. When I introduced myself, before I could say anything else, Harrison jumped on the one question that had apparently stuck in his craw: "I *know* who you are. You want to know how many Germans I shot." I pointed out to him that he was the only Big Five chairman to refuse an interview for this book. He agreed to reconsider, but did not change his mind.

Harrison's swipe at Davis and his refusal to be interviewed are not untypical. At the Commerce, public relations is all but non-existent. It used to be worse, according to one director. "When I say to people that the bank's PR is terrible, they say that it has improved since McKinnon's time." Maybe so. But of all the Big Five, the Commerce is the one about which bankers and the community they serve least want to be quoted. It is at once a measure of the low esteem in which they hold the institution and of the fear they have that honest comment will bring retribution. Even the black sheep of the banking family has the power to avenge slights and slams from both inside and outside the fold.

In many ways, Russ Harrison cannot move into the future because he is forever stuck in the past. He talks often and with much fondness about his days as regional general manager for Quebec. It is not that he thinks he can go back, but he exudes the notion that maybe, just maybe, the world is not much changed. As a result of that pull to the regions, a decentralized credit system with delegated decision-making existed at precisely the wrong time — when the economy went sour and loans needed experienced massaging and monitoring. Russ Harrison's vision of the Commerce has yet to be conjured. He is the magician, on stage, without benefit of a top hat, let alone the hidden rabbit.

Equally worrisome, in this institution where the top man continually cites thin ranks, is the growing ownership position that the Commerce is taking in other enterprises. With its 24 per cent interest in Massey-Ferguson, as well as potential holdings in Maislin Industries, Dome, and Turbo Resources Ltd. (where unpaid interest owed the Commerce was running at $8 million a month at the beginning of 1983), the Commerce is no longer just a moneylender, but likely a manager as well.

As a proprietor, Russ Harrison already has a busy desk at the bank. Is there time, too, to step in and help run four more companies that are $10 billion in debt? If past performance is any criterion, the answer may be no. On the other hand, maybe he has never really been in charge. "The Commerce," claims former chief general manager Gordon Sharwood, "is still run by McKinnon's ghost."

FIVE

A DAY IN THE LIFE OF THE BAD NEWS BEARS

Inside a Bank Branch

The most familiar face that Canada's chartered banks put forward to consumers can be seen in the 7,400 branches across the country. However, the world looks different from behind the counter, as this day in the life of a typical branch indicates.

THE EARLY-MORNING sun paints its thin colour, like some pale mustard wash, on the brick and stone occupants of the intersection. At seven o'clock, the only noise is the whirr and click of the traffic signal box changing the stop-lights even though there are no vehicles, obedient or otherwise. Only two things are in motion. The first is a revolving sign atop a yellow-brick and glass single-storey building. It winks in the sun at every half-turn, its green square repeating the white letters "TD" as it surveys the scene. In view, three street-corner companions at King and Francis streets in Kitchener, Ontario: a small mall, the Corkscrew Restaurant, and the Kaufman Footwear factory. A block away, the skyline is punctuated by a brick chimney thrust upward from the B. F. Goodrich plant. Three thousand workers within walking distance of the bank branch located at this intersection for more than fifty years. At the moment, none of them is in sight.

The other moving object that morning amid the quiet tableau is Ric Knapp, senior accounting officer at the Toronto-Dominion branch on the corner. As he approaches the double front doors, he takes a final searching look around the empty street, slides his key quietly into the lock, and quickly lets himself in. Carefully locking the door behind him, he begins his slow walk around the branch, for no other employee can enter until he, as the first, is sure no one has broken in during the night to lie in wait for someone who can open the safe.

His thin face and neck poke out of a shirt collar that looks a full size too large, as he doffs and folds his grey sportscoat and lays it on his desk in the middle of the office, making sure that the carnation boutonnière faces up. Rolling up his sleeves, he gazes around the five-thousand-square-foot main floor of the branch with its fifteen-foot ceiling. With the fluorescent lights now on, Knapp's tour begins at the front door, where he peers into an office on the right, newly built for personal loans officer Neil McMillan. He walks behind the long tellers' counter towards the back door and the cash room, where currency is counted and money kept during the day. Retracing his steps past the desks where current and chequing accounts are monitored, he pauses at the Diebold vault. Its wall-mounted needle gauge registers in the black portion of the dial, showing that the safe is still armed and unable to be opened, the time mechanism on for another thirty minutes. He proceeds towards the centre of the room, past the stairs leading to the basement, looking under desks as he goes.

Next, a glance into the office of manager Bill Ellis, to the left of the front door, then a stroll past the six offices that stretch along the back wall. One is empty; the others are occupied by five credit officers, for this branch splits its banking business between personal and commercial. As the TD begins to organize its branches more around function, rather than trying to offer all services everywhere, this is one of four branches with business clients among the seven TD branches in this southern Ontario manufacturing city of two hundred thousand people. He heads downstairs to the lunch room, turns on the coffee-maker for the first of many pots, and looks around the room containing tables, chairs, a counter, soft drink machine, and toaster oven.

Next, both washrooms, the men's pasted with scores of pin-ups, the women's plain by comparison. He checks the training room, where amid some ancient machinery sits a word processor, recently seized from a defaulting client. Finally, he checks the locks on the mail room, furnace room, and three rooms where old files are stored. All in order. He returns upstairs, walks towards the front door, and props open one of an inside set of double doors, a signal to any arriving employees that all is safe. Without that door signal (or some other visible sign, which is regularly changed), other colleagues carrying keys won't enter, even if they see the lights on and people inside.

As Knapp returns to his desk, the doorbell rings; Rose Traplin, the accounting officer for mortgages, waits outside. Branch procedure requires him to go out on the street in order to show her, as the second person to arrive, that he is free to leave, that no interloper is inside. There has been no trouble recently, however, and he simply swings the door open for her. The first customer will not be admitted for almost three hours.

This is a long way from head office in Toronto, where the pace is fast and the promotions are even quicker. Here, the *real* work gets done, with customers whose bad behaviour runs the gamut from ignorance through impatience to connivance. Here staff is often called upon to defend a system they don't agree with, work within procedures that seem archaic, and explain how loans to Poland can be endlessly rescheduled while a car loan payment cannot be a day late. Even with the life-support systems of data centres, newsletters, operations manuals, and higher-ups on call, the branch can feel a little lonely. That distance in time and space between head office and the branch causes an employee camaraderie that is further fuelled by a shared fear of robbers or ransom demands. While the entire system is structured to prevent fraud from within or theft from without, fear is always nibbling at a corner of the mind, or lurking in the unknown darkness just beyond branch doors.

The branch is an island between two worlds. In one world exists the demanding customer who may have evil intent; in the other, a faraway hierarchy that may not pay much heed. The effect of both influences is to isolate the branch and render it unable to satisfy either side fully. It is this isolation that forms and frames the identity of each branch of each of the Big Five banks. Just as the human brain needs each individual cell, so too does head office need each branch. But, sometimes, not very much.

7:30 A.M. A yellow Loomis courier van pulls up to the rear door and bangs a bag into a lockbox protruding into the branch. Ric unlocks the box from inside and spills out the bag's contents. Computer print-out sheets from the Toronto data centre showing account information, loan amounts owing, cheques drawn on this branch at other branches, mail and circulars from head office. Other employees are beginning to arrive. The manager, Bill Ellis, in a burgundy sportscoat with a slick puff handkerchief, enters, waving a cheery hello at everyone, and heads for his office. Moustachioed John Doerffer, assistant manager for administration, pulls out a wad of files. Senior assistant manager Ron Cotnam, a bearded big bear of a man, goes through overdrafts and other problems. He begins the day by reviewing with each of the five senior credit officers their accounts with various businesses, for these are bad times. Many companies are operating at or over their credit lines with interest payments overdue.

7:40 A.M. The time lock is off the Diebold vault. Ric Knapp and John Doerffer pull out their wallets to look at the four-digit number entrusted to them, one man assigned to each of the two combination numbers required to open the vault. The door is swung ajar and the eight carts that were stuffed in the night before rolled out. On them, loan information, chequing account statements, the Protectograph machines for cheques, any information about customer accounts, safe even from the uninterested eyes of the cleaning staff.

8:15 A.M. The men — there are no female loan officers — meet in the manager's office, each reporting on accounts in trouble. There is heckling and jeering about mistakes made, but for the most part, this is serious business. The first involves a company with an operating line of credit of $700,000. By the end of June, it had gone beyond that ceiling and owed $850,000, largely because the company wasn't collecting amounts owing from its own customers quickly enough. There were too many accounts receivable that had been owing for more than ninety days. A search of those accounts by banker and businessman, it is reported, turned up $50,000 that could be collected readily by the company and turned over to the bank. That still left the company needing $100,000. To lend this much and add it to the allowed debt, Ellis told the company, the bank needed more security. There was nothing more in the business that could be offered as collateral since everything was already pledged to loans, so the two partners were each forced to take out $50,000 mortgages on their homes. "The wives will have to sign, too," Ellis points out, knowing that the wives will urge their husbands to collect on overdue accounts. "The wife is a great way to put pressure on those ninety-day accounts. The firm is getting pressure to pay its own suppliers after thirty days, but they are reluctant to push even after ninety for what they're owed." There is very little new business discussed. As Dave Gibson, one of the assistant credit managers, put it: "If anybody's shopping for loans, they're likely in trouble with their present banker."

The second company in trouble has been massaged by the branch for four months, since the last time the business reported its financial affairs to the bank. The company disregarded repeated written requests for information updates and has only come forward now because it wants more money. Ellis reconstructs the conversation, for this early-morning meeting with his colleagues is a learning session, too. "It needs more equity. You have personal assets, you put them into the company," Ellis told them. They responded: "No, we've got orders on the books. You should finance us, we're a viable company." Demanded Ellis: "Show me in writing; I've been looking since March. I'll put more money in your company if you will." "I know the banks are nervous," the businessmen had told Ellis, "but it's Dome that's causing you the trouble, not us little guys." Mere weeks before Dome was finally bailed out, Ellis can only protest: "There's shoring up going on there that we aren't aware of." He admits that the small-business view that Dome was receiving preferential treatment is a hard argument to answer. He sums up for the group: "I suspect we'll see some equity come in later today."

As the staff, totalling twenty-seven, assembles at various work stations around the branch, the meeting drags on through a final thorny item. A small local firm employing sixty people has been scrambling almost since the day it opened. Financed in 1975 by a venture capital outfit, it had manufacturing problems and quality problems, and after the tough start-up years, it discovered that the product wasn't as popular as it had hoped. Now, after an amalgamation with another firm in the hopes of strengthening both, along with funds from the venture capital company (and four local businessmen who had invested and pulled out), there is money owing to three chartered banks, a term lender, and three government agencies. Debt is $2 million on annual sales of only $1 million. The venture capital company, after two months of not receiving interest payments, has decided it wants out and has asked the firm for the $200,000 still owing. With the TD already in for about $80,000, Ellis is nervous. "Great potential. Great idea. But they couldn't get production under control. By the time they did, they had such a debt load." He shakes his head in dismay. "I might have to pick up a receiver and go out there and change the locks today."

The company is calling for an orderly wind-up, and wants the banks to step in. That way, points out Ellis, the owner can say the banks have precipitated the closing. On the other hand, if the wind-up is not orderly, the inventory will only be worth about one-tenth its value. Play the bad guys, step in, and maybe all of the debt will be paid. Laments Ellis: "If you have to go to court, with banks just going through a profit period, it's not hard to figure out which way the ruling will go." The one last hope is a European investor who might put additional money in. His local representative has $85,000 ready and is awaiting word from Europe about a further $450,000. With that infusion, the venture capital company probably will not call its loan and the firm will survive. The TD decides to wait out the day. "I've never," says Ellis, "just walked in and said, 'This is it.' "

The bad news over, the six men "knobble" (pronouncing the "k") for coffee. Each puts up to three coins in his closed hand, and tries to guess the total number of the coins hidden by the six men. Closest guess each time drops out and the last man buys.

8:45 A.M. Ric Knapp and Lynn McConnell, the first teller, head downstairs to the vault in the women's washroom where the night deposit bags fall when put in the chute outside. Again, as with opening the vault, two people must be on hand for this operation. The bags are opened with individual keys (100 of them on a plywood board kept in the vault at night and in the cash room during the day), then emptied, and the deposits are counted. Amounts ranging from several hundred dollars to $26,000 are credited to respective accounts, and the empty bags tossed into a cardboard box in the corner for pick-up throughout the day by customers.

8:55 A.M. Kim Ruge, a ledger officer, begins the laborious manual process of "ticking back" all the items drawn on the branch that were sent out to the data centre the night before. Every transaction yesterday that affected accounts in that branch — deposits, withdrawals, money orders, automatic items — is printed on long computer sheets in Toronto. All the original paper has been returned, too, put in order by branch staff before being sent out yesterday. "Ticking back" proves that the entry had been made and returns the item to the branch so that it can be passed back to the customer. Ruge looks for items over $1,000 — "the guys like to see them" — and assembles a list of cheques on which payment has been stopped. While automation has sped up proceedings for the customer and taken some of the drudgery away from staff jobs, there is still a choking amount of boring paperwork necessary to track all the transactions through the branch.

9:10 A.M. Each teller removes her cash from her own safety deposit box, keeping a maximum of $2,500 in her drawer to limit hold-up takes. To help keep amounts that low, the once-deep slots for bills have been made shallow by the addition of wooden blocks. A teller low in funds (a couple of sizeable withdrawals can empty the drawer) takes cash from her safety deposit box, where she keeps a daily total of $10,000 to $15,000. Twice a week, Monday and Wednesday, each must do a day-end balance. On Monday the total is taken because this is a "shipping branch," that is, it takes in more money than it needs and ships out money following weekend deposits. Armoured Brinks trucks take the cash to Toronto (for a charge of 73 cents per $1,000) and often cart out up to $180,000. On Wednesday the count is done so that bank-wide cash figures can be passed along to the Bank of Canada, as required by law. This day, the branch holds $309,000 in currency and coin, including about £1,000 and $15,000 in U.S. currency for exchange.

9:25 A.M. The branch is not yet open to customers. Personal loan officer Neil McMillan stands at the counter and calls for attention. This is the weekly pep talk and sales address to all staff. All the phones are put on hold as everyone comes out of offices and moves closer. "I've counted it up," he begins, "and we've got 243 years' banking experience among us. What does that have in common with the Visa campaign? Well, your experience and your input are very important." A printed questionnaire is handed out to gather views on how long the September push for new credit-card customers should run. Ideas are sought for the campaign and for prizes for the person who signs up the most card-holders. "Days off," someone shouts. "Money," calls someone else. "To hell with trophies," laughs Lynn McConnell. Posters are discussed, window paintings, the length of the campaign (one week or two), how to set goals. "Will the majority rule," McMillan is asked, "or will management make up its mind?" "The majority rules," he says. Ledger clerk Julie Cox, herself Dutch-born, suggests a list be drawn up of the languages spoken in the branch. A quick check discovers that Serbo-Croatian, Dutch, and German are spoken, but not Portuguese, the main language of the Kaufman workforce across the street. The meeting is good-humoured, but the lunchroom chatter later is concerned: why push credit cards at people who perhaps can't afford them when times are already bad? It is a question never put to management.

9:40 A.M. A customer phone call is fielded by Ric Knapp at his desk in the middle of the banking floor. The caller is sure she was given too little on a withdrawal yesterday. "Did you count it in front of the teller?" he asks. "Well," comes the reply, "I just thumbed it. But I'm sure I'm short." Knapp orders the teller to do a complete count of her money. (Tellers can be $5 over or under on a day without it being called a difference. Up to $50, the teller must find her error, although the count does not need to be verified by a senior officer. Over $50, the money has to be counted in detail by someone else. If the discrepancy is over $100, and not located within three days, written notification is sent to the division. Over $1,000, after an overnight wait to see if the error is discovered by the computer centre, Toronto head office must be telephoned. Tellers, however, no longer have to make up shortages. Until five years ago, there was a token payment required: 10 per cent of the shortage up to a $25 levy. Any excess is treated like an unclaimed balance, wending its way after ten years to the Bank of Canada, where it sits waiting to be claimed.)

9:46 A.M. Manager Bill Ellis sets up a lunch with a local chartered accountant, now practising on his own, who may have access to funds for small business ventures. For Ellis, in the branch for fourteen months, his new job during a recession is not as exciting as his previous role as a bank deal-maker. As a manager for commercial development in the area, he worked out of his car, putting together loans in the high-flying times. "It's not a lot of fun being a banker these days," he says. "Most businesses not making it have had management problems, haven't cut back on staff or inventory. I saw it coming in the fall of '81, when the retailers on the street were holding clearance sales *before* Christmas. A couple of years ago, a business took six months to go sour. Now they can go on you in three weeks."

9:48 A.M. The first customer stands outside the door waiting for opening.

9:50 A.M. First teller Lynn McConnell is trying to decide how much money the branch will need during the day. It needs enough to function, so it doesn't run out an hour before closing, but only the minimum, for security reasons, should be available outside time-lock conditions. In addition to each teller's amount in the safety deposit boxes, McConnell keeps some money in the cash room behind bullet-proof one-way glass. It is this amount she is estimating by weighing various factors: it's a Friday before a long weekend, but many of the factories are closed on annual vacation; yesterday was quiet, so today (when the branch is open late, until six) may be busier; a lot of end-of-month pension cheques will be coming in to be cashed. The drama of this daily guessing game is further heightened by the fact that opening and closing are the riskiest times of the day, because the amount of cash available in the branch is at its greatest. During banking hours, most of it is under time lock.

It was just at closing earlier in the week that a Canada Trust branch a few blocks down King Street was robbed. A single gunman herded everyone into the safe and made off with an estimated $15,000 to $20,000. Each teller at this TD branch, as at all financial institutions in the area, has a piece of paper stuck near her drawer with the serial numbers of ten recorded $10 bills taken in the hold-up. Every teller keeps ten such bills herself with known serial numbers so that when the drawer is emptied at gunpoint, the known bills go in the pile. Underneath the counter at each teller's window are two special buttons that trigger an alarm at the police station when a teller presses them together. "You know," says McConnell, "I'd almost like to go through a hold-up just to see how I'd react. Almost. I worry about it. If anyone came in and knew our system and got me in that cash room, I don't know . . ." Her voice trails off. A twelve-year veteran of banks in Ontario and Quebec, she was once followed for days by a bank customer who was a loony Vietnam veteran. She was in constant fear. "When a teller was killed in Montreal, it was on my mind. I worry about it yet, but I can't let it bother me or I wouldn't work here." As head teller, McConnell's salary is about $15,000, not much higher than the tellers' starting rate of $12,000. McConnell's salary after twelve years is about the same as that of a university graduate who enters the TD's management training programme, called Banklab. They start in the $15,000 to $17,000 range. Commerce grads entering the commercial credit programme earn $19,000 to $22,000 to start, and MBAs begin at $25,000.

9:54 A.M. Securities officer Jeri-Gay MacDonald, after umpteen tries on the direct line to the money market in Toronto, finally gets through to receive that morning's quote on rates paid on term deposits over $100,000. For thirty-day money, the bank will pay 15 per cent, one and a quarter points above the rate paid on amounts up to $100,000. For terms up to a year, 14.75. A list of other rates arrives in the courier bag, but these large wholesale rates can change in seconds. Even if a customer were to call within minutes of MacDonald's call to Toronto, she'd have to check again.

9:56 A.M. McConnell finalizes her figures and picks an amount for the day's cash on hand — $55,000 on top of what each teller has in her safety deposit box. If the branch does run out, another branch — even of another bank — will bail them out. It happened recently, and two staffers had to jump into a car and borrow $15,000 from a Royal branch nearby.

9:58 A.M. Cigarettes are doused, coffee cups disappear — for there is no smoking, drinking, or eating in sight of customers during banking hours. The only other similar rules: no blue jeans, no alcohol on the premises. Ric Knapp opens the doors. Four customers spill in the back, nine in the front, and form a single line. Each of the six tellers punches her five-digit access code number into the IBM computer terminal at her elbow, the terminals signal back in orangey-brown type on the screen. Open for business.

10:04 A.M. Bill Ellis takes a call from another area TD manager. This is the "buddy system": a check made once a day, usually around opening or closing. If the call is not accepted, or the two agreed-upon key sentences are not exchanged, it is a sign of trouble and the other manager alerts the police. The conversation, to anyone else, is business-like and meaningless, so that a call can even interrupt a meeting and be carried out with others in earshot. "I think the price of gold will be unsteady for a while," might be the opening line. "And silver is likely to have the ups and downs, too," the second might respond. The phrases safely passed, they might chat for a few minutes before returning to their duties. In a cabinet, a file folder called the emergency kit is maintained for each of the senior people at the branch. It contains photos of family members, phone numbers of schools and neighbours, the business phone of a spouse — any information that might help check a claimed abduction or alert a family to danger.

10:10 A.M. A teller approaches Knapp with a deposit of $1,100 from a customer. Any deposit or withdrawal greater than $1,000 has to be checked to watch for kiting — changing money from one account or branch to another, removing the money before it actually arrives, then withdrawing it from the first as well. Knowing this customer, Knapp approves.

10:12 A.M. McConnell brings a $1,000 bill to John Doerrfer. "Weren't the police in the other day worried about thousands?" she asks, waving an old-series carmine-red bill with the Queen's portrait. "They were," he agrees, "but it was to see if we had *issued* any thousands." This one looks OK; McConnell can pick off a tiny planchette — a dot of specially inked paper that can be removed from a genuine bill — with her fingernail.

10:15 A.M. At the side counter, Jeri-Gay MacDonald helps a customer retrieving an insurance policy, used as collateral on a loan that is now paid off.

10:16 A.M. An elderly couple totters through the branch, heading for the vault where they have a safety deposit box, one of 513 for rent. The bank key opens the first lock, their key the second, and they take the box to a cubbyhole to inspect its contents.

10:22 A.M. Eleven customers in line, and although the wait is only about four minutes, Bill Ellis is out of his office, ranging back and forth behind the teller line. "Why isn't that eighth teller open?" he asks. Informed that one teller is looking for a missing $100, he paces for a while longer, then disappears back into his office.

10:30 A.M. A man sits with loan officer Neil McMillan, going over his income for a car loan on a $15,000 Pontiac. He is not a regular customer of the branch, so McMillan takes full details of his employment and income. Then comes the key figuring: against monthly take-home pay are listed all pay-outs, to see what cash he'd have left to pay off the car. Other credit cards and amounts owing are listed, as are mortgages. It appears he can afford the $400 monthly payment over four years. The amount, $15,000, is Neil's limit, so he could approve on the spot, but he wants to run one final check. He walks to the back of the branch to a computer terminal hooked into the Ontario Credit Bureau, dials a telephone number, and keys in his access code. The machine chatters back, typing its code name onto a paper roll: "Medusa available." He enters the customer's name, address, and social insurance number. There is a two-second pause before the machine leaps to life, repeating the information on the individual, then listing loan and credit card information dating back almost twenty years. A $4,000 loan paid off four years ago at another TD branch; $1,800 owing on Visa; a few hundred dollars on four credit cards from department stores and an oil company; all payments up to date. No credit problems, so McMillan approves the loan for the full amount. The man signs a chattel agreement — if his payments lapse, the bank can seize the car. The loan interest rate is 20.5 per cent. "When I first came in five years ago, it was 12.5 per cent — and new car loans were 11.5 per cent. People are learning to adjust," McMillan says. "I'm the one that's having the hard time." With new commercial business down in the branch, he's looking to beef up consumer business — that's why his office was recently moved just inside the front door from the end of the line at the back of the branch. "If a guy wants to buy two snowmobiles," he said, "I'm not going to moralize and ask him why." The tough part comes when someone is turned down. "I try to take the positive approach. The plain fact is: sometimes they can't afford it."

10:37 A.M. The cash of the teller whose customer called earlier is $20 short, not $100 over. Knapp phones the customer and lets her know. "Are you sure you didn't lose it after you left here?" She is. Further checks fail to turn it up; the customer begins to have doubts about where she lost it. The bank does not pay. If the customer had persisted, the bank might have paid, according to Knapp. Each situation is decided by a judgement call, on the individual merits.

10:45 A.M. For the first time, there is no one in line. Two tellers lock up and slip downstairs for a coffee.

10:50 A.M. Debra Lappage, manager Ellis's secretary, receives a call from another branch about a possible forgery using a business firm's cheques. For speed, she writes the names on an eight-by-eleven-inch piece of paper in block letters, heading the sheet RAPIDALERT. Downstairs at the photocopy machine, she runs off twenty copies, then distributes one to each teller and several desks around the branch.

11:12 A.M. Manager Ellis is on the phone to a lawyer (a favourite profession, along with chartered accountants, for business referrals), trying to organize a squash game for later in the week to drum up business. His lending limits to a new customer are $100,000. A renewal loan can go as high as $200,000 before he needs approval from higher-ups. He earns $55,000 a year and has a home with a swimming pool. "I have to live the same lifestyle as my major customers." To help out, his $50,000 mortgage is held by the bank at 3 per cent, his Visa is 3 per cent below the going rate, and he participates in a stock purchase savings plan where the bank puts in 50 cents for every dollar he contributes, to a maximum of $600 a year.

11:15 A.M. John Doerffer juggles work schedules. Several senior people are away on holidays and he is trying to plan peak-hour part-time needs for the next few weeks. With an annual payroll to branch staff of $500,000 (plus benefits), personnel work consumes time. With the recession, however, turnover — which had been as high as 60 per cent on the teller line two years earlier — is now down near zero. Squeezed bank profits have also meant that staff do double duty for holidaying colleagues.

11:23 A.M. A teller realizes she has too much money in her drawer, so counts out $4,000 and "crosses" it to McConnell. In return she gets a 293, a receipt form, for the amount. McConnell, who has just taken in an $8,000 cash deposit from a nearby business, calls down the line: "Anyone else?" Another $1,800 is handed over, stacked, and taken into the cash room. There, in the eight-by-eight-foot cubicle, she puts the cash in a drawer and closes it, thus sending the money tumbling through a trapdoor into a small vault on time lock known as a "bandit barrier." To get at the money during the day, a key is needed, then a five-minute wait before the box can be opened. If it is not opened within thirty seconds, another five-minute wait is required.

11:31 A.M. A phone call comes from the businessman who Ellis expected would produce funds before the day ended. An investor had been found in Toronto, and the customer is sure the money will be forthcoming. "I'll wait," says Ellis.

11:50 A.M. Ellis reviews a file prior to his lunch appointment, hoping that the meeting might bring new sources of funds for a client — up to $500,000 is available through this man, he understands — but meanwhile, government-backed programmes remain the best bet. Under the Small Business Loans Act, he can lend up to $100,000 guaranteed by government at a rate not exceeding prime plus 1 per cent. If the business goes bust, the bank gets its money back — although it collects no interest after bankruptcy. "Not all bankers are aggressive with these programmes. I am. I just love them."

12 NOON. Other staff think about lunch, too. A few head downstairs with lunch in paper bags, someone else orders in a pizza, three go across the street for some soup and the salad bar. Ellis heads to the Charcoal, five miles away, for chopped sirloin and a fishing trip with his lunch partner. They talk about dreary business conditions, local scoundrels they know, and how to identify an entrepreneur with an idea that might make it. "The entrepreneur is a strange cat," says Ellis. "He thinks he's right and the rest of the world is wrong. He's either good in production or in marketing — rarely in both." While the men are kindred souls, and discuss balance sheets and borrowing power, the session goes nowhere. Concludes Ellis later: "He doesn't have a source of equity. I don't think we'll be doing much business."

2:05 P.M. Three people in line and one woman at the counter, closing out an account with $24.05 in it. The atmosphere, although correct, is decidedly frosty. "She's had some trouble with NSF [not sufficient funds] cheques," says ledger clerk Julie Cox. "I guess she decided to go elsewhere."

2:20 P.M. A brown envelope arrives for Ellis. In it, a card and a note from one of the men he'd asked to put a mortgage on his house to back up business loans. The card was bought by the man's wife (who'd signed the mortgage agreement) for her husband. He has sent it on to Ellis to make a point. The drawing shows two hockey players hacking away at each other. The printed message: "Don't get mad, get even." The handwritten note sounds more hurt than belligerent. The last line reads: "I thought all bankers arn't [*sic*] the same." He shows both the card and the letter to senior assistant manager Ron Cotnam. The professional action may have been appropriate, but there was a personal cost. "I thought I'd made some headway with him, but I guess I've got a way to go yet," Ellis says with a rueful smile. The card rides out the day on his credenza, beside the picture of his two children, a reminder that bearing bad news or keeping the bank's money safe rarely means making friends.

2:38 P.M. A factory worker in his fifties sidles slowly up to a teller and hesitantly presents two cheques to be cashed. After working thirty years, he is unemployed. It was either him or a younger man with a family, so the firm laid him off because he had only a year to go before retirement. One of the cheques is his last salary, the other his first unemployment insurance payment ever. He explains all of this to the teller, embarrassed to be taking, as he puts it, "welfare." He stands looking at the two stacks of bills after they had been counted out, almost as if he were going to walk away without the cash from the UI pile. "You've paid into it all these years," the teller finally says, "you deserve to collect." He picks up both and walks wordlessly away, with shoulders rounded by the weight of worry.

2:47 P.M. Assistant credit manager Lorne Greene, his blond hair tightly curled around a full face, is talking about his career and his hopes. A 1975 university graduate, he's been through the TD's Banklab in downtown Toronto, where training staff tries to present real-life counter situations for six weeks of force-fed learning. Following that, a week in a branch, and another six weeks of Banklab. He's done consumer lending but prefers his current area, commercial business. "You're going to see a new breed of bankers," he says. "It's a lot harder to be a banker these days. Technical knowledge will not be enough, you need to know how to work with people, too." The next step, he hoped, would be senior accounts officer, but with the economic slowdown, promotions have lost their momentum. "In banking you can go as far as you want," he says proudly, then leans forward and adds slowly, "but timing *is* important." The fast track of the past has turned muddy and he is a long way from the big boys at head office.

2:58 P.M. A teller tries to summon up an account on the terminal, but she is cut short with a two-word epithet: "System busy." A wail goes down the teller line. The words mean each balance has to be checked against print-out sheets and no passbooks can be updated. Still, it is better than being off entirely, or "down," as computer jargon has it. There have been few problems since all the Visa information was added in June 1982. Then the overloaded system could quit for up to an hour. Two years ago, it would die for a day at a time. Still, the tellers agree computers make life easier. Passbooks no longer need to be hand-written, interest is credited automatically, they help with balancing at day's end, and people see their deposits going in immediately and receive their balance more quickly.

3:08 P.M. A vacationing couple saunter in, produce their chequebook and Visa card, and ask for a balance in their Alberta account. The computer, functioning again, complies.

3:20 P.M. The day is slower than most Fridays, when the line-up often stretches to the door, even with a teller open just for cheque-cashing. Today, two close early, complete their "blotters" (a green card properly known as a teller's cash-book reconciliation), and stow away their funds for the following day. They pitch in with the "intersorting," the process of organizing all account transactions in account number order in wooden slots near the cash room.

3:40 P.M. Ellis receives another call from the businessman who said he'd be putting money in. "It's still coming," he says. "I'm still waiting," Ellis replies. (It took four months, but a financial reorganization through the federal government's Small Business Loans Act, along with money in return for ownership from employees, allowed the business to keep going.)

3:58 P.M. A man presents himself noisily at the counter near the back door and complains about charges levied on his chequing account. Pointing to his printed statement, he says: "I've got service charges, overdraft charges, and a maintenance charge. What are all these?" he demands. "Canada Trust sure doesn't charge me all of these for what it does." It takes two people, but after five minutes he's remembered that the system on his account was changed that month at his request, causing the variety of charges that appear, totalling less than they would have been under the previous system.

4:10 P.M. Eileen Hendry, a dicta-typist filling in for a vacationing colleague, finalizes loan applications and assembles them for the courier bag to

Toronto, where they will be programmed into the computer. Julie Cox is filling out similar programming forms — accounts opened and closed and any other major changes in the system. Teller Bridget McBrien opens her safety deposit box to get additional cash for the final push towards closing at six.

4:17 P.M. Teller Joan Ibele knocks on the cash-room door. Inside, McConnell glances up through the one-way glass and lets her in. Ibele runs a stack of cheques drawn on the branch through the Countess, a currency and document counter in the corner. Across the cheque, in purple streaks, is stamped the date and the branch.

4:22 P.M. Ron Cotnam reviews the day and the past six months like a hospital administrator watching the joy of the maternity ward ending and the worry of intensive care beginning. "Most loan interviews are pretty tense these days. We're looking at things more closely to see if it's just Band-aid financing or for growth. But banks have been at fault, too, giving loans on a cash-flow basis. As the economy turns, people look back and say, 'You shouldn't have given them the money.'" In the previous six months, the branch has seen six loans go sour, all under $100,000. The three worrisome borrowers this day are all larger, with total assets among them of $5 million to $8 million as the hard times spread.

4:30 P.M. The task of intersorting is fully under way. Kim Ruge is nabbing help wherever she can, to spread the tedium around.

4:40 P.M. More tellers close, so balances can be struck before the courier bag heads for Toronto at five. Monday through Wednesday, when the branch closes at four-thirty, all work makes it into the Toronto run. Thursday and Friday a day gets lost on any transaction after five. If a deposit is made, credit is given, however, even though the branch doesn't get the money (in this case with a holiday Monday coming) until Tuesday. The bags are being filled, a green one with TD items and mail for head office, a red one containing cheques drawn on other banks and work for programming.

4:45 P.M. McConnell, who is going away on a camping vacation that weekend, starts to balance her money. She counts all coin and currency, runs her numbers through the terminal and an adding machine. "Every teller gets the feeling in the pit of her stomach when she starts: is it going to come out OK?" Bill payments are all totalled, as are cheques deposited or cashed. She is short $143. Back through all the numbers. Nothing found. Is it the utility bills paid by customers, perhaps they were posted twice? More checking.

4:50 P.M. No word from the European investor who was to bolster the sagging local manufacturer. Ellis orders that a "letter of demand" be prepared and sent. He has called the loan. There will, however, be no receiver and lock-changing; legal advice from head office has told him to give the manufacturer ten days' notice. If the European money—or any money—comes within that time, the letter signed by Ellis and Cotnam will be withdrawn. If no money is found, sixty people will be out of work, and the firm will face creditors, including the TD, hovering like seagulls at the last piece of garbage. (Within two weeks, the federal and provincial sales tax departments—both owed money by the firm—try to move in on some of the assets held by the bank as collateral on its loans. Ellis thought there was agreement among the creditors, but this move alters things. Not wanting to fall further back in the creditor line, and risk losing his money, he calls his loan. The company goes into receivership.)

5:12 P.M. McConnell gives up looking for the $143. "The data centre will find it. An error ticket will come Tuesday. I'm going to phone in next week. It'll bug me the whole time I'm on my holidays." (It turned out to be a deposit posted twice, discovered when all the items were "ticked back" the following week.)

5:20 P.M. The men, most of whom have been in since seven-thirty, start to drift away: McMillan to pick up his car at the garage; Greene home with his wife, who stops in with a tow-headed boy; some others across the street for a beer. Left behind are John Doerffer and ten women. This, someone says, is what separates the men from the women in a branch: the men get to go home earlier. Beyond the joke, however, is the reality that the men also have all the top jobs. There are no male tellers.

5:35 P.M. Customer traffic is light; only three tellers are open. As each closes, coins are slid into brown envelopes, cash is counted, bundles are dropped into a bin at their feet, along with the teller's stamp and money order forms, everything swept away into the respective safety deposit boxes.

5:42 P.M. A pasty-faced man with a silly grin dripping from his chin walks in with a mousy woman who appears to be his secretary. He waves a fistful of cheques: "Here's a dirty job for someone." A dozen cheques to be certified. Ruge rolls her eyes, but smiles, takes them, sits down at her desk, and begins stamping each: "Certified cheque, do not destroy." While each is recorded separately, and marked with the Protectograph figures, Pasty-face carries on a vapid conversation with a nearby teller all about his secretary and how she wants the weekend off. The secretary pays no attention as she hands over a current-account deposit book filled out for the firm's day. She gives the man some cash. "How do you like that," he leers, "a secretary that doesn't know enough to put her boss's pay in an envelope." He collects one from the counter and stuffs his money in. The tellers all listen, unsympathetically, as Pasty-face carries on about the difficulty of getting good help. Finally, his secretary grabs his tie and leads him out the door, still nattering.

5:55 P.M. The last few customers scuttle in, glaring at the clock.

6 P.M. The doors are locked and the tellers close in earnest.

6:16 P.M. A critical time as money, perhaps $75,000, comes from the cash room to the vault where it is stowed away in a wall safe by McConnell and Doerffer. The time mechanism is set for eighty-five hours, meaning that it cannot be opened until after the holiday weekend.

6:22 P.M. All the money under time lock, the tellers who have been waiting near the door can now leave. Until then, the outside door is opened for no one.

6:30 P.M. Doerffer wheels the last of the carts into the vault, filling it entirely. He heaves the huge door closed and he and Knapp fumble for their combination numbers to lock it. A final check around the branch to make sure nothing is left behind.

6:36 P.M. As last man out, Doerffer shuts the inside signalling door, checks the lock and closes the front door behind him. He gives it a shake and never looks back. Above, the sign circles and winks on the roof.

In all, while there may have been no tears shed for people in trouble, there was little joy in the day's events, either. And while there are procedures in the manual for every eventuality, there is a place for simple patience, too. Bound by a siege mentality, and the common bond that comes from institutional service, the staff react amazingly well to the stupidities of customer demands. Through it all, the focus that gives the function meaning — the money — has no meaning of its own. It is at once the very reason for the existence of the building and the jobs, the magnet for fraud artists and bounders, even the driving force for the staff since it buys their groceries, too. But money in the branch, all bundled and belonging to someone else, becomes mere bits of coloured paper, worthless because it has no value in the vacuum behind the counter. Among the customers who must suffer through some mistakes amid the maze of services and hear of the bankruptcies without understanding the reasons, the bankers know that their public image ranges from tepid in good times to terrible when the world turns sour. Sighs Ron Cotnam: "We don't have many friends out there any more." For the bad news bears, perhaps little else is possible.

SIX

THE MAN WITH THE MIDAS TOUCH

William Mulholland

CHAIRMAN, THE BANK OF MONTREAL

WHITE WITH BLUE STRIPES and discreetly lettered CF-BNK, the Hawker-Siddeley 125 sits on the airport tarmac like an ocelot straining at an unaccustomed leash. This is the ultimate status symbol, the corporate magic carpet awaiting the bidding of its passenger, its new made-in-California Garrett engines whining expectantly.

Word flashes from the executive offices in downtown Toronto that Bank of Montreal chairman Bill Mulholland has left for the airport thirty minutes behind schedule. Mulholland considers tardiness to be his privilege, like some potentate out among the peasants. Once, late for an Air France flight to Germany, he told an associate, "Why don't you phone someone and tell them to hold the plane for me?" Another time he was to sail on the *Queen Elizabeth 2* to Europe from New York. He told his secretary to phone Cunard with the news that he'd be late and that they should hold the sailing. Came the response: "We wouldn't wait for the Forty-second Highlanders, the Olympic riding team, or Queen Elizabeth herself, and we certainly wouldn't wait for your Mr. Mulholland." Nor did they, pulling away from the dock, as usual, on time. Mulholland rented a helicopter and landed on the ship's deck at sea.

This morning, twenty-five minutes after word of his progress is received, the black Cadillac eases towards the airplane's door and silently stops. Out Mulholland clambers and strides towards the craft with the measured gait of a man who knows that whoever he's about to meet, whether here or at the other end of the country, will wait. He settles himself down in his accustomed seat, facing the rear on the plane's right side, next to his colleague B of M vice-chairman Hart MacDougall. He sets up his briefcase in the aisle and plunks the rest of his load in his lap: an economic study from the C. D. Howe Institute, the day's *Wall Street Journal*, and Anthony Sampson's *The Money Lenders*.

The green leather seat squeaks as he leans forward and looks out the porthole window beside him to see the other corporate jets nearby. "Let's count the house. There's Noranda . . . and Inco." MacDougall joins the game. "There's Northern Telecom. I guess they're waiting for [chairman] Walter [Light]. There's an Amax Falcon. I wonder where they're going?" A discussion ensues between the two about the various Amax holdings in Newfoundland, molybdenum mines in British Columbia, and the deals they've done over the years, as they all the while try to make sense of the other plane's hulking presence in a nearby hangar. Concludes Mulholland, eyes twinkling, "You go through all that, and probably it's been chartered to someone else. But it's interesting to know who's where. It's like a crossword puzzle."

Just one more set of mental gymnastics for the master gamester, William David Mulholland, chairman of the Bank of Montreal, Canada's oldest chartered bank. At $65 billion in assets and growing, it's the third-largest, moving to pass the sluggish Canadian Imperial Bank of Commerce for second place. Under him stretch 1,200 branches coast-to-coast, twenty-seven thousand people in his employ, offices open twenty-two hours of every working day somewhere in the world. Mulholland splits his week — three days at head office in Montreal, two in Toronto — travelling constantly to take the pulse, touch the people. He is the turnaround king, the man who took over a moribund B of M in 1975 and kick-started it into action, making it a high flyer. His annual salary — tops among bankers in the country — is $550,000.

His bank spent its first 150 years slowly building its assets to some $7 billion in 1967; in 1978 alone it punched another $7 billion onto the books. These days the money machine has slowed a bit from the heady days of 1980–81; growth is a mere $2 billion annually. When he took over, the Bank of Montreal's international loans were mostly to other banks — so-called interbank loans — where the profit margin is tiny. He propelled them into syndicated Eurodollar loans (U.S. dollars held outside the U.S.), where the profit margins are larger and there are management fees for putting deals together.

By 1979, the Bank of Montreal was the number one lead manager in the world, putting together more syndicated loans than any other bank, competing with U.S. giants such as Bank of America and Chase Manhattan. At the peak of this pyramid, where Mulholland sits, the deals have become mind-boggling. He put together a $1.25-billion refinancing package for Hydro-Québec in January 1980, lining up the major participants himself. When it was all over, forty-nine banks and financial institutions from eleven countries had participated. His bank was lead manager in a $3-billion loan to Joseph E. Seagram and Sons Inc. There was also the 1980 Woodside deal, admired throughout the world for its creativity, when the bank was lead manager for the $1.4-billion financing of natural gas development on the Western Australian continental shelf. The bank's growth has been so phenomenal that Mulholland was able to tell a December 1981 news conference: "It's no longer a Canadian bank with international appendages; it's an international bank that happens to be based in Canada."

Mulholland stands slightly stooped in the airplane's aisle, with his elbows resting against the chair backs, facing the front of the cabin. At five-foot-nine and pushing 190 pounds, he looks like a Notre Dame full-back gone a bit bulbous. A cap of close-cropped grey hair tops a head perched directly on his body, for he seems to have no neck, his shoulders appear frozen in an eternal shrug. His cheeks are shiny, almost lustrous beneath brown eyes that can transfix, searing through skin and bone to the very soul. As he speaks, there is often a sound that seems to begin somewhere in the back of his mouth, a noise that might be an incipient chuckle, but it moves down into the throat to become a closed-mouth gulp, continuing for up to eight staccato bursts. Audible across a room, these swallowed chortles serve as punctuation for a just-uttered sentence or a warning that there are sterner words to come. They can be self-congratulatory ("Good point, don't you agree?") or carry an impatient challenge ("Beat me on that one"). Sometimes he will wait for some brave soul to begin a sentence, then override the first half-dozen faltering words with words of his own, washing out the other's like waves erasing letters scratched in sand. He will pick up from where he left off, or launch a new probe as if no one else had spoken, or for that matter, even existed, except as a wall against which his own ideas might be tried in order to test their firmness and vigour. Not to mention the strength and mettle of the wall.

As the plane skims along at 420 knots thirty-five thousand feet up, somewhere east of Winnipeg, banking is the farthest thing from Mulholland's mind as he recounts Second World War stories from his days in the Philippines. He tells of one particular crossroads guarded by a lone soldier who often came under sniper fire from a guerrilla in the hills. The sign for safe passage through the crossroads was an erect sentry. If he was not visible, or could be seen belly-down in the ditch, you waited until it was all clear. The sniper, it seems, was a notoriously bad shot, but could always succeed at pinning the sentry down as he pumped random bullets into the ground. Mulholland is laughing so hard at this silly side of battle that tears are forming in the corners of his eyes, his entire body is shaking, his coffee sloshes around in the mug that's tipped precariously in his left hand as the other hand circles the air, describing the scene.

To become perhaps the single most admired financier in the country,

Bill Mulholland has had to drive himself and exercise occasional ruthlessness. He has chewed through underlings: a couple of chief general managers, a posse of vice-presidents, and other faceless folks further down in his organization, while bringing up through the ranks, or in from outside, those who have met his favour. Less than a decade ago, the banks were the last of the paternalistic enclaves, organizations that would take a man from the cradle of high school graduation and coddle him until the grave of pension payments. Success was always possible, if not guaranteed; but if success was tardy or did not arrive, there was always some sinecure, a small womb of an office somewhere in which to hide. Not under Mulholland.

When he took over the Bank of Montreal in January 1975, he usually worked from nine-thirty in the morning to ten-thirty at night, often taking a couple of satchels of papers home. Hard-working but not always efficient, he would spend an hour on the phone when two minutes would have done. At meetings, he would hold forth for ninety minutes on unrelated topics and then demand that the other attendees state the case they came to plead in the five minutes remaining. Come five o'clock, he would become a whirling dervish of activity, firing off orders, filling up the evenings of associates who'd been waiting outside his office all day, like aircraft stacked above an airport by a controller eternally on work-to-rule. Maintains Ronald Kovas, president and chief executive officer of J. Walter Thompson, one of the bank's advertising agencies: "What Mulholland cares about is the intensity of your interest."

Viewed from within, Mulholland's disregard for people can hurt, as Stan Davison, now a vice-chairman resident in Calgary, can attest. "Mulholland has been able to wring more out of the machinery than anybody else. He operates on the theory that if you can't stand the heat, you get out of the kitchen. And he pours on the heat. He doesn't seem to have any regard for his effect on people. He doesn't seem aware that they will get upset." In 1978, when then chairman Fred McNeil wanted to give Mulholland the title of chief executive officer along with that of president to keep him challenged, the resources committee of the board of directors stalled the move for a year. "There was a lot of doubt," admits McNeil, "about Bill's people-handling."

But the hard-headed methods worked. Those who could not make it have left. Those who could, have succeeded with him. All the while, his family — Nancy and the nine kids (five sons and four daughters, the inevitable by-product, as she puts it, "of an Irish Catholic and a Free Methodist") — didn't see much of him when he was at the bank, just as they hadn't when he was at Morgan Stanley or Brinco. Their main time together is spent climbing into the two family vehicles, a late 1960s car and a GMC wagon, and tooling from their home in Montreal's snooty Westmount to their six-bedroom country house on 110 acres near Foster in the Eastern Townships. When he's not off with the boys, fishing for Quebec salmon or hunting chamois, the elusive goat-like antelope in the mountains of Germany, he's here in this house, first built in 1837 with higgledy-piggledy additions since. There's a barn that he's had rebuilt right down to the fifty-seven-foot-long main beam, but he is more likely to keep his five horses (including one that's eighteen years old) and two ponies a few miles away near Lake of Two Mountains, where he belongs to the Hunt Club and rides to the hounds several times a year. On Thanksgiving weekends, he'll sometimes do two hunts in three days, working the horse so hard you can hear its sweat hit the ground in great droplets when he stops to tighten the saddle. Fred McNeil, a rider himself at sixty-seven who will climb onto his western saddle and go off with the cowboys, still warns Mulholland about falls. Mulholland, who's cracked a few ribs in his day, never listens. His other rural pursuit is to tend a few fruit trees on the land around the Foster house. He fashions himself as a sharecropper, puts in vegetables and flowers — violets, peonies, iris, and other spring bloomers including a hundred-foot-long row of lilac bushes along the drive.

The house is a place to restore the soul and repair the family fabric after the success of three high-velocity careers in his first fifty years. The costs are great to achieve these heights. "You cheat on your family," he admits. "That's the honest answer." Would he do it differently? "If I was starting at the beginning knowing what I know now, yes. If I was starting over again knowing what I knew then, probably not."

Born in Albany, New York, on June 16, 1926, William David Mulholland was raised in a strict Catholic home with an added whammy of Presbyterianism. Both grandmothers were Catholic, both grandfathers Presbyterian. He grew up with one sister and was sent for schooling to Christian Brothers, not just a strict Catholic school, but a Catholic *military* school, where the accent was on performance in class and in sports.

After graduation in 1944, he volunteered for the army, telling his family only after the fact, when his mother's protests would be in vain. He was posted to Fort Benning, Georgia, where basic training was an eye-opening combination of live ammo, rough horseplay, and practical jokes. One of the more benign exercises was to booby-trap the barracks of another company. Smoke bombs in the ventilation systems were a favourite trick; one was placed the night before he and his comrades were to be commissioned, so that everybody's uniform on the parade square reeked of smoke.

During his six months at what he calls the "Benning School for Boys," live ammunition meant many tense moments. One occurred when Mulholland was training in a small town built on the base to simulate a site for rush-and-capture operation. He and a partner were to run across an open area, flatten themselves against a house wall, toss in a grenade, jump in the window, and then clear the house of "enemy" troops from the top down. Amid the smoke and confusion, Mulholland, thinking his partner had already tossed in the grenade, hurled himself through the first-floor window. As he stood up to get his bearings, he heard the ominous clunk of a live grenade hitting the floor five feet away. "My heart was right at my teeth. I hit the floor as soon as I saw it." Miraculously, Mulholland came through the explosion without a scratch. His partner was kicked out of the army. It wouldn't be the last time Mulholland would survive an event that spelled the end for others.

The war was almost over when Mulholland was sent to the Philippines. As a weapons instructor, he became a cannon company commander, overseeing six self-propelled howitzers in the hills of the islands as his 342nd Company chased leftover Japanese soldiers who didn't know the war was lost and guerrillas who were more bandits than anything else. These were the early days of the Communist-led Hukbalahap Rebellion, an uprising that began in the Luzon area, where Mulholland was stationed, in response to the leadership imposed by General Douglas MacArthur, who had landed in the Philippines in October 1944.

The Huk Rebellion was a chaotic struggle, with few rules and even fewer classic battles. In fact, Mulholland's beloved howitzers were never fired at the enemy. "We tried to persuade them to come peacefully, even bribed them to give up." Equally difficult was the job of training the headstrong Filipinos who were to take over the policing role from the Americans. "You cannot line the men up and charge the hill," he'd tell them in exasperation. "I tried to explain to them it wasn't like the movies. You had to take them by the scruff of the neck and say whoa." He learned to be scornful of incompetence, to endure duty watches and the chaos of night firing—and not to take himself too seriously. Even his appointment as company commander didn't go to his young head. "In the land of the blind," he says simply, "the one-eyed man is king." The army also taught him how a bureaucracy can become weighed down with paper. "Don't ever believe that armies run on ammunition, food, and gasoline. They don't. They run on paper. They make the bank look streamlined, svelte, efficient, lean," he says, pausing ironically after each adjective.

As the Pacific war ended, commissions in the nationalist army of Chiang Kai-shek were available, and for a while he even considered life as a mercenary. "I was only nineteen. I considered all sorts of stupid things." The U.S. government position towards Chiang Kai-shek, however, changed from benignly favourable to opposed, so he headed back to the U.S. and started at Harvard in February 1947. He wanted to become a doctor, but just barely passed biology. A professor finally came upon the reason when he put Mulholland through a series of microscope tests: he is red–green colour-blind. To this day when he's describing a scene, including the colours, his wife gives him a baleful stare and says: "You've got to be kidding." Next on the list was law. "It was right down to the wire, I was going to go into law. [Not going was] obviously a big mistake when I see the lawyer's bills these days." He offers a typically self-deprecating explanation about how he chose economics and the Master of Business Administration programme. "The way I make all tough decisions — flip a coin. You're only wrong 50 per cent of the time. You just blunder along." In the summers, he worked as a policeman and guide in the parks of New York State, where his father was lands and forests director.

America's top corporations used the Harvard business school as a hunting ground for young talent. It was one of his professors who set Mulholland's career in motion by blithely suggesting: "You ought to see Harry Morgan." Responded Mulholland: "Who the hell is Harry Morgan?"

Henry Sturgis Morgan, born in London, England, in 1900, was a grandson of J. Pierpont Morgan and the younger son of international financier J. P. Morgan. A Harvard graduate himself, in 1923 he entered J. P. Morgan & Company, the centre of the empire built by his grandfather and his father. That same year he married as only a Morgan would: well. His wife was a daughter of the secretary of the navy, a descendant of two U.S. presidents. In 1935, "young Harry" Morgan, as he had become known on Wall Street, joined with Harold Stanley and William Ewing to form Morgan Stanley, to carry on the business of underwriting and wholesaling securities as an investment bank.

Morgan met Mulholland on campus and was sufficiently impressed to invite him to a further meeting at Morgan Stanley's Wall Street offices. After a long talk with Mulholland, Morgan finally said: "Why don't we go in and meet the fellows?" The final inquisition came in the next room where, in a circle of chairs, were assembled ten of the firm's fifteen partners. Mulholland was hired, one of three Harvard grads in the firm. The other two were named Morgan. It was 1952.

In the early years, he did all the things an apprentice executive should, including marrying a girl who was introduced to him by his mother. Nancy, from nearby New Scotland, New York, came over one night with her mother, who was a friend of Mulholland's mother. "She has a daughter I think you'll like," his mother had mentioned. Within three years they were married. Before the wedding Mulholland, by then five years with the firm, and five years away from being made a partner, asked for his vacation time and a couple of half-days as well. "I suppose," said the senior partner, before Mulholland had even spoken, "you're going to tell me you're going to get married." He squinted at Mulholland from behind his glasses and sent up clouds of smoke from his pipe. "I suppose you won't be any god-damned good now." More smoke from the pipe; sheepish smiles from Mulholland. "Just get the hell out of here and come back when it's all over. You'll be no good to us until then."

The marriage weathered much through the early years. While at Morgan Stanley, Mulholland would usually work until about eleven at night. The next day he'd have breakfast with his children, do a little work at home, then arrive at the office about nine-thirty. It was during this period, squeezed in with all the other deals, that Mulholland made his name across the continent by masterminding a $500-million bond deal — the largest such sale ever carried out by a corporation and the largest ever handled privately in U.S. history. The project involved was equally immense: the billion-dollar Churchill Falls (then called Hamilton Falls) hydroelectric power project in Labrador. He was to spend twenty years with this project and the company involved, Brinco Ltd. For all his success since, those years may well have been his happiest time. "Banking isn't really a *fun* business," he says. "It's not like mining — you can *see* mining. You don't very often *see* money. And when you do, one bill just looks like another."

Shortly after the intricate financing negotiations were successfully concluded, Mulholland was made a partner by Harry Morgan and his fame spread. Also planted were the seeds of the debate that rages to this day between Newfoundland and Quebec about the costs of hydro power. Quebec's long-term contract allows that province to buy cheap power from Newfoundland and sell it at much higher prices to New York State. There's also the question of where the border is. Twenty years later, in 1981, Mulholland would say: "We spent six figures on lawyers, trying to find a way of talking about the border without mentioning the word. Then we went back and spent several more months trying to include wording about a border we hadn't mentiond so it could be movable. If you think that issue can be settled, you're a real optimist. Twenty years ago I thought it could, too." Finally, after hearings, numerous trips to Ottawa, endless ego-soothing meetings with premiers, mandarins, and other powers, the deal was in place, including a government tax exemption on the bonds that Mulholland bullied through Ottawa in a week. Hydro-Québec, finally agreeing that all conditions were satisfied, passed the contract along to Premier Daniel Johnson, who authorized signing on July 10, 1968.

On November 11, 1969, the Brinco jet was feeling its way down over Labrador, a landing made more difficult than usual by the rain lashing the craft and a dense fog that reduced visibility. Suddenly, the side of a mountain filled the cockpit window as the craft crashed into the Smallwood mine, strewing wreckage over several of the thirty-foot open-pit terraces from which iron ore was being stripped. Among the dead were Brinco boss Don McParland and seven other key executives, including Eric Lambert, vice-president for finance, with whom Mulholland had worked closely. As word of the crash spread in the company, in the corporate community, and in New York, the name that kept coming up was Bill Mulholland's. No one knew more about the operations of Churchill Falls and its financing; no one, it was agreed, could guide Brinco through this time and into the future as Mulholland could.

Mulholland agreed to become president and CEO, sold his Morgan Stanley partnership, and purchased a hundred thousand shares of Brinco. At forty-three, he moved his wife and then eight children to Montreal in January 1970 to take over a company with empty executive shelves. Even as he made the change, the next career step was already coming into place. Appointed chairman of Brinco at the May annual meeting was Robert D. (Pete) Mulholland (no relation), who was also vice-chairman of the Bank of Montreal. In July 1970, Bill Mulholland was named to the board of the Bank of Montreal. As he sat there at the foot of the boardroom table (there was a pecking order based on seniority), watching the genteel Arnold Hart preside as chairman, he could not have imagined that before the decade was half over he would be the bank's president, and within another half-dozen years, its chairman.

Just as working at Morgan Stanley among the giants of finance was a learning process — as if Mulholland had been a sapling planted in a redwood forest under perfect conditions — being transplanted to Brinco gave him that next growth spurt. He quickly seized control of a company paralyzed by the loss of its top executives, beat off the contractors who circled like vultures looking for payoffs on the million-dollar-a-day project, and rid Brinco of those who tried to use the upheaval for self-promotion.

It was an immense and mind-boggling project. The Churchill Falls development was the world's sixth-largest hydro development, a bigger construction project than the St. Lawrence Seaway. Construction had created a body of water half the size of Lake Ontario in order to produce seven million horsepower. Throughout, his credo from St. Luke hung in Mulholland's office: "For which of you, intending to build a tower, sitteth not down first and counteth the cost, whether he have sufficient to finish it? Lest haply, after he hath laid the foundation, and is not able to finish it, all that behold it begin to mock him, saying, This man began to build, and was not able to finish." Mulholland brought the project in under budget and five months ahead of schedule.

Mulholland would watch the Canadian bankers, both from his seat on the Bank of Montreal board and from his position in the financial community. Brinco colleague David Willock once commented to him on the success of Fred McNeil, an outsider, running the Bank of Montreal. "It's not hard," agreed Mulholland, "when you're not a conventional Canadian banker." Mulholland took a high profile at Brinco, enjoying the limelight in ways that pointed ahead to grander roles. If he were giving a luncheon speech to financial analysts at Montreal's Ritz-Carlton Hotel, he'd work on it all morning, writing and rewriting. Secretaries would furiously type his final version, and it would be handed to him as surreptitiously as possible at the head table minutes before he had to rise in his place and begin speaking. When he was called upon, he'd stand, look down at his just-arrived text, peer out at the audience, and quip: "Well, I wonder what the boys want me to say today?"

When the Newfoundland government bought out the hydroelectric project in 1974, Brinco became an empty vessel. Mulholland was ready for another challenge. It wasn't long in coming.

The Bank of Montreal, founded in 1817, had long been one of the country's premier banks. As late as the 1920s and 1930s, under Montreal tycoon Sir Herbert Holt, the Bank of Montreal was the biggest in Canada. Over the next several decades, however, it slipped, and by the time the 1960s were half over, the place was stagnant. Under the chairmanship of the polished, if undynamic, Arnold Hart, some changes were initiated, not the least of which was the addition of Fred McNeil in 1966 as vice-president for organization and personnel. A former journalist, West Coast consultant, and Ford executive, McNeil brought with him the winds of change. Even so, by 1974, in the words of Don McCallum, then the bank's agent in New York: "There were a lot of worms in there."

Early in the 1970s, computer installation was behind schedule and costs were running 50 per cent higher than planned. The bank also chose a solo route on its charge card. Rather than join the other Big Five banks in Chargex (later called Visa), it would gain the Mastercharge (later Mastercard) licence for Canada, but at the time, the B of M just seemed to be stumbling.

Finally, the bank got stung on interest rates, believing they were going to fall. The bank loaned money for long terms to lock in borrowers and took in short-term money from depositors. They were speculating that as time went by, the long-term loans would stay high, the short-term deposit rates would fall, and the bank's spread would improve. They guessed wrong. And so it was that in January 1975, Norman Heimlich, the respected bank analyst then with the Montreal-based firm F. H. Deacon Hodgson, would write of the Bank of Montreal that it was "undoubtedly Canada's worst performing bank since the 1967 Bank Act [revision]." The B of M, Canada's oldest bank, was calling itself "The First Canadian Bank," or "The First." In the street, it was jokingly called "The Worst." Recalls Fred McNeil: "We didn't have enough horsepower to run that bank. I was swimming in a maelstrom." McNeil had had his eye on Mulholland, both on the bank board and at Brinco.

One day in 1974, Newfoundland finance minister John Crosbie visited McNeil in Montreal to say the Newfoundland government was going to buy Churchill Falls from Brinco. The purpose of the visit was to explain that the B of M, traditionally the province's bank, wouldn't be financing the deal. It led, however, to something else, because shortly after, the two Mulhollands, Bill and Pete, came to McNeil's office to bring him up to date on the goings-on. With Churchill Falls gone, Bill Mulholland's job was shrinking, so McNeil asked him: "What are you going to do?" Replied Mulholland, offhandedly: "Oh, I don't know, Rio Tinto wants me to go to London, but I'm not inclined to do that." McNeil asked him if he liked Montreal, and Mulholland told him he did. McNeil had already discussed Mulholland with Hart, so he pressed on. The two Mulhollands and McNeil were going to a cocktail party, so McNeil asked Pete to go ahead in his own car so he could continue the discussion with Bill on the way. Later, McNeil reported to Hart: "I think we've got a chance of getting him. Let's do it." Mulholland had made it clear he would only come if he were made president; Hart was so convinced it was the right move that he offered to resign as chairman so McNeil could move up, opening up a slot for Mulholland.

No one, however, was prepared for the fight to come from the board's executive committee, in opposition to the appointment of an American citizen. "There was quite a lot of trouble with the board on this," understates McNeil, looking back. "It seems to have been a traditional concept, among both the politicians in Ottawa and other Canadians, that a Canadian should head up a Canadian bank." Mulholland's tenuous Canadian connection — his fur-trading great-grandfather had married a Trois-Rivières woman — did not satisfy Mulholland's main opposition on the board of directors, former Shell chairman Vasey Ash. Nor was Ash impressed when reminded that the presidents during the first ninety-six years of the bank's existence numbered among them men born in England and Scotland — and two Americans. Mulholland was asked if he would become a Canadian citizen if he were given the job. His response, taken back to the board's executive committee, was: "Obviously, if I'm going to spend my life in Canada, I will — but I'm not going to make an undertaking." (He has yet to become a Canadian citizen.)

Finally, after a ninety-minute debate at one executive committee meeting, Stelco chairman Peter Gordon, chairman of the board's manpower resources committee, said in exasperation: "I don't care if he's a Zulu carrying a spear, he's the best man we can get. We'd better go and get him." Immediate support came from Budd Rieger, of Canadian Corporate Management, who jumped in and said: "For God's sake, yes, let's do it." The debate was over. Mulholland was hired as president, the fifth in ten years, at an annual salary of $175,000, about the same pay as he'd been receiving at Brinco. The turnaround king had arrived.

In the early days, there was no small amount of animosity towards the new boy who moved onto the executive floor in head office on St. James Street in Old Montreal in January 1975. McNeil had been the only other outsider, and until Mulholland arrived, men who'd come up through the banking ranks dominated the executive. The previous president, Len Walker, who died shortly after gaining office, had been a lifelong banker. Unlike Fred McNeil, who was both tough and "just folks," Mulholland made few friends, choosing instead to stalk the halls, suddenly plunking himself down at the desk of an unsuspecting employee — at any level of management — fixing him with a cold eye, and asking: "And what do *you* do?" Within a year of taking over, he could talk knowledgeably for up to ten minutes about every one of the 350 individuals in the bank, from the rank of general manager up. Trouble was, some of them didn't do very much. Mulholland moved quickly to change that.

He called in key people from the various departments and read the Riot Act. His message to each was similar and began with him waving a two-page memo at the gathered group, saying: "I'm going to read this, and it's going to be painful." Recalls one attendee: "It was all laid out. I went back knowing how many people I had to cut and how much money I had to get off the balance sheet."

Staff numbers, and thereby costs, were slashed dramatically. One analyst had said that the bank was overloaded by as many as five thousand people, many of whom had been hired by department heads trying to respond to a McKinsey & Co. management study in the 1960s, which urged department managers to *look* like department managers by having lots of underlings. While Mulholland didn't agree with the five-thousand estimate, he did say: "You always take the position you're overstaffed." The bank had ballooned from 19,305 employees in 1971 to 26,114 in 1975, an increase of more than one-third. During Mulholland's first five years, the net increase was a mere 790 employees. Of no small help was Mulholland's luck in arriving just as the computer system was finally up and running. That meant two fewer jobs in each of the bank's 1,200 branches over the next few years. One billion dollars was taken off the balance sheets within a few months by taking money out of short-term, low-profit investments and moving it to higher-profit commercial loans. The commercial loan portion of the international portfolio, for example, was raised from 40 per cent of the total to 70 per cent. "We pulled the bank up very sharply," Mulholland recalls.

The restraint lasted two years — 1975 and 1976 — "and that's as long as you can do that." The technique was simple, since a balance sheet naturally runs down unless it's added to. "It isn't what you do to it, it's what you *stop* doing." Knowing when to start again comes from both "tangible evidence and a sixth sense," he admits. "It's not an exact science."

Mulholland's methods were an extension of his frugal personal ways. An avid salmon fisherman (he often fishes with finance minister Marc Lalonde), he spent four days while with Morgan Stanley at the Price Brothers fishing camp on Quebec's Petit Saint Jean River, which flows into the Saguenay some twenty miles upstream from Tadoussac. There, as the guest of broker and friend Miles Price, Mulholland relaxed amid the rustic private-lodge-and-cabins setting. Mulholland had brought several rods with him, but became taken with a bamboo cane rod brought by someone else. Handmade by Andy Barr, a small red-headed Scotsman in Montreal, the rod was a 3¾-ounce model, about halfway along the range that runs from one to seven ounces. Towards the end of the stay, Mulholland allowed as how he wanted one like it. Miles Price said he'd order one when he returned to Montreal, did, paid for it, and sent it on to Mulholland in New York a few weeks later, along with the invoice for $150. After a couple of months had passed and Mulholland hadn't reimbursed Price, Price brought the oversight to Mulholland's attention.

"I thought it was a gift," said Mulholland.

"Well," replied Price, "I did give you the invoice."

Snapped Mulholland: "Why don't you just expense it."

The Bank of Montreal's computer system, now recognized to be a leader among the Canadian banks, gave the bank an edge among the Big Five in the kinds of services it could offer, including the first multi-branch banking plan in 1977, daily interest savings accounts in 1979, and experimental home banking in 1983. Other areas that received Mulholland's immediate attention during his fourteen-hour days were departmental budgeting, cost control in the branches, an improved equity-to-asset ratio, more outsiders inserted into upper management, and an aggressive advertising campaign.

Not everything he tried succeeded. In fact, there were a few disasters along the way. Firstbank Acceptances, a new instrument, were introduced in 1978 with much fanfare and support from Mulholland. An acceptance is a promissory note or draft that binds both the bank and the borrower and can be used as day-loan collateral or rediscounted at the Bank of Canada. Aimed at new corporate customers, it superficially resembled traditional banker's acceptances, but was, in fact, commercial paper with a bank guarantee. Firstbank Acceptances were aimed mainly at companies — especially utilities and finance companies — who didn't qualify for existing acceptances. The bank thus offered eligible customers the option of borrowing on a direct credit line at a rate linked to the bank's day-to-day cost of money.

Mulholland pushed the new vehicle hard, although not everyone running the operation in Toronto agreed it was a good idea. He wanted the already competitive rates dropped further in phase two, but even such profit-cutting didn't stimulate demand. Finally, Mulholland, in an imperial disowning of paternity, ordered Firstbank Acceptances off the face of the earth, asking: "Who the hell thought of this idea in the first place?"

The successes outnumbered the failures, however, and the bank began moving into the position of being the "hot shop." "I just knew when the engine had caught, some time early in 1977," Mulholland told Terence Corcoran of the *Financial Times* in 1978.

Not everyone at the bank had the strength to stand the constant barrage. Fresh troops were required; by 1978, of the thirty vice-presidents working out of head office, fewer than one-third had been there in 1975. In one six-month period in 1979, seven senior bankers fled, beaten, for one reason or another, by Mulholland. They were Peter Oosthuizen, executive vice-president and general manager of international, recruited by Mulholland from Citibank in 1975; Bruce Campbell, a corporate banking group senior vice-president in charge of all credit policies, after thirty-one years with the bank; Derek Whittle, for the previous year senior vice-president, Alberta division, after twenty-five years with the bank; senior vice-president Barry Hull, the IBM whiz-kid who got the computer system up and running after what had been seen as five years of floundering; Robert Sillcox, senior vice-president for investments; J. R. Crysdale, who joined in 1971 from the investment community and ran funds management before the arrival of Sillcox (he was put into corporate cold storage in 1975, and finally left in frustration in 1976 after writing Mulholland an impassioned five-page letter of resignation); and John McNeil, vice-president for investments, who had just joined in 1975, under Mulholland.

The place looked and felt like a combat zone, and the sight of executives pulling the ripcords on their parachutes and bailing out became common. Little wonder. Mulholland had liked the smaller group working on Churchill Falls, where he could rely on a few select colleagues, particularly under pressure. At the bank, he'd explode over perceived incompetence, using blunt language and demeaning descriptives such as "you stupid son-of-a-bitch" in the midst of meetings. Or he'd blurt: "I told you to fix that three months ago. Why isn't it fixed? Now tell me about it." Commenting on the technique, Fred McNeil says: "That doesn't wash. If you have capable guys around you, they don't tolerate that kind of crap."

Another of Mulholland's less hurtful, but more mysterious methods was to try to lead his colleagues indirectly to the decisions he wanted. As a result, meetings would conclude and senior officers would disperse to do just the opposite to Mulholland's wishes — because they simply did not understand his cryptic messages. Typical was Peter Oosthuizen in international. Hart MacDougall, who managed to survive the Mulholland change-over and become a vice-chairman, had the office beside the beleaguered Oosthuizen, whom he'd often discover heading off in the wrong direction.

"What the hell are you doing that for?" MacDougall would ask.

"That's what the president wants."

"Are you talking about last Monday's meeting?"

"Yeah," Oosthuizen would reply, "it was pretty clear."

"That isn't the way I interpret it."

Oosthuizen would then ask Mulholland for clarification, and time after time, Oosthuizen would have got it wrong, causing him to lament: "I don't understand his riddles."

For Mulholland it just was his way of developing people, of shaking up an institution that had been a safe haven. Rather than give direct orders or specific choices, he wanted his underlings to find solutions themselves. When they arrived proudly at the right place, as likely as not Mulholland would dismiss their success by saying: "What took you so long?" as if he had always known the answer.

Fred McNeil explains: "The investment banker never puts all his cards on the table. He always likes to keep a few options open, so people go out a bit uncertain at times as to what the hell he means, and if they had any sense they'd say: 'Is this what you mean?' But they don't. He tends to intimidate. He's also a lot brighter than many of his associates."

Joining the Bank of Montreal under Mulholland, recalls one vice-president, "was like getting on a moving sidewalk going along at a hundred miles per hour. You didn't have three months to get oriented. You might have four weeks. Not very many people would climb on, stumble a bit, get up and dust themselves off, and move along."

Competence and intelligence weren't always enough. The right chemistry was essential. Mulholland might respect someone's skills, but not like him as a person. If that was the case, all was lost. It was left to executive vice-president Don Payne, who himself departed after twenty-three years with the bank, to take one vice-president aside and say: "You've got bad chemistry with the president." It was typical of Mulholland to delegate the job of putting someone in corporate limbo. He does not like such confrontation. The VP's duties dried up, no information flowed his way, and repeated requests to Mulholland for explanation went unanswered. He was gone within a year. Mulholland will not be drawn into a discussion on any of the departed. "The last thing we'll do is rake over old coals," he says. "A wrong word from me would not be helpful to them. They always leave in good auspices, well looked after."

Comments Stelco chairman Peter Gordon: "He has difficulty delegating.... He recognizes that most people aren't as capable as he is and as a result, he really wants to have the final say. I'd have some trouble working for him."

So did others. One of the flock to leave in 1979 was John McNeil, who now works for Sun Life in Boston. He readily admits: "In a personal sense, I detest him. I didn't care for his management style. He didn't need to be so inhuman to people." Mulholland can show another side in certain situations, however. When vice-chairman Hart MacDougall's son was in a coma, he ordered MacDougall off the job and home with his family. He was the first person in to see vice-president Ted Pratt in a Montreal hospital after a cancer operation. When his own youngest child, Bruce, came down with peritonitis in October 1981, Mulholland cancelled a business trip to Japan, so that he could stay close to home. However, he pulled president Bill Bradford away from a Florida vacation to do the honours abroad.

In public, one of Mulholland's favourite sports is taking pot-shots at his colleagues and watching them writhe. Annually the bank executives criss-cross the country, usually in January and February, forecasting the economy to customers and the media in eleven cities via the Annual Economic Outlook Conference. In the bank, it's called the "road show."

A panel of four bankers, led in a couple of cities by Mulholland, elsewhere by deputy chairman Grant Reuber or other stand-ins, talk about prospects and project numbers on a screen for groups as large as two thousand.

One year, when Mulholland and vice-president John McNeil were part of the panel, Mulholland introduced McNeil's presentation by saying: "I see the podium is equipped with a clock and alarm system. Mr. McNeil is next. I think I'll set it." McNeil took his place at the podium, made an elaborate show of turning off the clock, and said to the audience and to the notoriously late Mulholland: "I admire the chairman's new-found devotion to punctuality." It was a cutting dialogue that was repeated at two more presentations and for McNeil it was the beginning of the end. Mulholland dismisses McNeil's departure from investments as being caused by the bank's decision to get out of bonds. McNeil disagrees, and as he says goodbye to a visitor, he speaks wistfully of the days he stood up to Mulholland. "I believe a cat can look at the king, and that..." his voice trails away, and the visitor fills in the missing words: "says it all." McNeil nods and whispers, "Maybe," and turns away.

Mulholland stands on the raised dais, three colleagues ranged out to his right, his chin propped in the heel of his left hand, fingers curled on his cheek. His lips move, mouth working away on a lozenge, and his eyes glitter with amusement as he looks out at the oil-patch bigwigs assembled at the Westin Hotel in Calgary in February 1982 for that year's Outlook Conference. "I get a sense of pending tragedy," he begins, "when I see the smiling hopeful faces, and I know what's in store for you. You'll go out trembling wrecks, dabbing at your eyes." The audience of about forty shifts and smiles, bracing for the bad economic news. The messenger can gather a crew with clout: Bill Richards, president of Dome; Ron Southern, president and CEO of Atco; Bob Brawn, president and CEO of Turbo Resources; Fred Mannix Jr. of Loram; Ed Czaja, president of Alsands; John Beddome, chairman of TransCanada PipeLines; Gerry Henderson, president of Chevron; Dick Haskayne, president and CEO of Home Oil. There is a smattering of developers, too: Harold Milavsky, president and CEO of Trizec; Gerald Knowlton, chairman of Knowlton Realty; and the inimitable N. R. (Buck) Crump, former chairman of Canadian Pacific Railway. Mulholland parks himself so the panellists can make their presentations and proceeds to act throughout like a bored child seeing a movie for the second time. He chortles to himself for no apparent reason, writes notes and passes them to his colleagues, then waits expectantly for their reaction. He smirks out at the audience as if to see when the eye-dabbing begins.

These are his people, assembled to hear his words and the wisdom of his institution, and he enjoys being the font from which all knowledge flows. At the reception before dinner, he swims around the room like a happy blowfish swollen with pride, moving about in the warm and friendly waters, basking in the sheer joy of hospitable surroundings, any predator safely sent to the far reaches of the ocean. Dinner is served on Wedgwood china in the Bonavista Room and comes complete with two kinds of wine, freely poured at all eight tables. There's Graves Cruse at $17.50 the bottle and Beaujolais Villages at $21.75. Smoked salmon, consommé au sherry, filet of beef aux fines herbes, bouquetière of fresh vegetables are followed by a palate-clearing butter lettuce salad and, finally, raspberry sherbet. Liqueurs are served; tobacco is passed. The bank's tab, per person, is $38.50 with, as the hotel insists, a guarantee of sixty-five. Perhaps forty-five show up, and the food costs $2,300 — the wine is extra.

Guest speaker, headliner, and comic relief is economic guru Arthur Laffer, the laid-back Californian who invented the Laffer curve, which argues a free-enterprise point of view that government revenues don't increase indefinitely with tax rate increases. Normally his fee for such a night runs $8,000 (U.S.), but the bank has bought the A. D. Laffer and Associates package. For about $15,000 (U.S.), it joins his other 150 corporate clients in North America and Europe, who receive up to a dozen basic research reports a year, a monthly update, access to Washington seminars, and visits from staffers and others writing reports — including a visit like this by Laffer.

Praise, even if purchased, flows later from Laffer, who says: "I do two or three of these things a week. They're stuffy. Mulholland's different. I meet all the CEOs of the banks [and] he comes across as one of the few who really knows what's going on. Unlike the rest, he has an awareness of politics and economics. He's not a right-wing tycoon type — just the opposite. He understands the concepts, the trade-offs, the politics. To use the Yiddish word, he's a *maven*. He really knows where things are at."

Mulholland rises to introduce Laffer, as proud of his captive presence as Ponce de León was when he brought Florida natives back to the Spanish court. He ploughs through some prepared biographical notes, then settles into a stand-up comic routine. "Mr. Laffer has told me," he begins, barely able to swallow his laughter before delivering the punch line, "that his favourite curve happened when a bikini dropped off one shoulder." Mulholland waits and delivers the next line with perfect timing: "That's *my* kind of economist." Then he takes on Laffer's critics and his well-known Republican leanings. "Whatever charges have been made against Laffer, being a Democrat is not one of them.... I've long admired men who have risen from humble beginnings," Mulholland says, and then dead-pans: "Dr. Laffer was educated at Yale." And, finally introducing the speech topic: "He will recommend Canada be unilingually French and a few other stimulating concepts."

Laffer, a cheerful elf, delivers a fifty-minute machine-gun barrage of jokes ("California is the cereal state. Take out the fruit and nuts and you're still left with the flakes"); economic homilies ("Inflation reduces the values of real liabilities"); and a call for less government involvement and lower taxes ("What country in Europe has the lowest tax rate? Switzerland") The roomful of free-enterprisers nods regularly in agreement. There is a smatter of questions and the group is dismissed finally by the banker whose grace and favour allowed them into the presence of a real live celebrity.

It is ten-thirty by the mental time clock that began ticking inside Bill Mulholland's head thirteen hours ago when he left Toronto for Calgary in his corporate plane. A five-and-a-half-hour flight, afternoon meetings with local staff, a two-hour presentation on the economy, a reception, then dinner, and through it all not a hair out of place, not one stumbled word at the end of a long day of non-stop talk. Even his beard doesn't seem to grow at the wrong time, as if the bristles can be halted by royal fiat.

Outside the hotel, and across the street from the sidewalk where the hookers sell their wares, the Calgary Place Cinema marquee bills the film *Rollover*. As the doyens depart into the night, the movie's advertising poster telegraphs its message towards hooker and banker alike: "The most erotic thing in their life was money."

As the jet works its way down from the sky towards the prairies and pump-jacks around Calgary, the banker wrestles with the meaning of money in *his* life. "It's a funny business, a business of intangibles. After all these years, I've never personally made a loan." Some deals are pointed out to him, including the $1.25-billion bond issue he put together for Hydro-Québec in an afternoon. He dismisses it with a wave of the hand: "I don't regard that as a loan." He roams off into a discussion about the best ways of working with and through people. "You don't tell people which loan to make; you don't tell your geologist where to drill."

He stares out the window, looking for answers amid the clouds. "I've never been prepared for any job I've done." He talks of measuring the performance of those beneath him, those who do things he's never done himself. At Brinco, he brought in outside geologists to sit with the Brinco geologists and argue what they knew. Mulholland would just listen to the debate's ebb and flow, to see how his boys made out against the experts. He did the same at the bank, calling in computer aces to go against his computer department. He'd be the withdrawn observer, the king upon the dais, watching the clash and clang of combat as his troops jousted with the best that the other side could send. If his knights were still standing at the end of the day, they must be good. If not — well, they were expendable.

The jet is on its final approach for Calgary airport as Mulholland scrambles to explain, even to himself, why he is a banker. "Banking is intellectually challenging — if you enjoy doing puzzles." He takes a run from another vantage point. "You're doing it from duty. N*ot* doing it is *not* acceptable. It's not the sort of thing you take off like a coat. You just can't go to the directors and say, 'Chaps, I've had enough.'

"I don't really *do* much banking. For those who do banking, it probably is fun. I don't get to do the banking equivalent of kicking the tires or scratching the dirt. I used to like going out with the geologists when I was at Brinco, out into the field. T*hat* was fun. I'd feel guilty — the Presbyterian genes in me coming out, I guess. There's nothing in banking like that."

In the end, perhaps it is an ego need, the same joy that a father feels towards a son and heir, some posterity assured, the capacity to create something that will continue even beyond the grave. "The question is," Mulholland says, "can you mass-produce? Do you want to achieve a self-perpetuating process, one that goes on after you walk out? The ultimate accolade is when they say: 'Mulholland, we don't need you any more.' Like man's earliest effort, you have created a tool that can be used over and over again. In fact, there's no way of knowing how you did until after you've left." With that as final pronouncement, as the craft touches down, he puts on his banker's coat, sets a black Persian lamb wedge hat carefully on his head and climbs into another Cadillac come to do his bidding in another town. Driver, he says, to immortality, please.

SEVEN

THE LAST OF THE JUMBOS

The Aquitaine Take-over

During the take-over fever that infected Canadian business in 1981, the bankers were quietly fuelling the process with money. The largest single deal was done by the Canada Development Corporation, as it tapped three Canadian banks for $2.1 billion in a loan that almost fell through.

PROLOGUE

In the beginning, it looked as if the last of the jumbos would never come off. In the end, it nearly didn't. The tumultuous deal was worth $2.1 billion, and it brought together a bubbling brew of typically Canadian ingredients: a nationalist government policy, the National Energy Program; the Canada Development Corporation (CDC), 49 per cent government-owned; a foreign oil subsidiary, Aquitaine of Canada; its French parents, Société Nationale Elf Aquitaine; and an American multinational, Texasgulf Inc. Throughout the negotiations, CDC officers — with lawyers at both elbows — conducted secret negotiations, knowing that any breach of confidentiality would cause the stock market to soar, adding untold millions to the eventual share purchase price. Before the strange brew could come to a boil, the essential catalyst was added: a bevy of bankers. Without these men, the deal, the largest single corporate take-over financing ever done in Canada, would not have been possible.

For the nationalists, the deal was something to shout about. For CDC, the purchase of Aquitaine of Canada and the Canadian assets of Texasgulf meant they joined their voracious corporate brothers in buying out high-priced companies. For the bankers, they were on the inside of a gigantic corporate take-over, moving money around faster than a tax lawyer could blink. Those were heady days, and everyone's ego was well fed at the groaning take-over table. But then the world changed. Oil prices, projected to rise out of sight, didn't. Cash flows meant to finance such expenditures fell short. With the benefit of hindsight, bankers saw they should have been balking at deals such as this one and the Dome grab for Hudson's Bay Oil and Gas — but they didn't. Their egos needed feeding, too, and their fear was of being left out, thought less of, if they didn't finance whatever came their way.

This is the story of how one take-over was financed just as the economic bubble burst, sending the country into a depression not seen since the 1930s. The bankers, who have tried to play doctor these past two years, were also involved in spreading the disease.

One target should have been enough to satisfy the CDC's lust for growth. Aquitaine stood fifteenth among Canada's oil and gas liquids producers and thirteenth among natural gas producers. The second target, Texasgulf's Canadian arm, had zinc, copper, silver, lead, tin, and cadmium as well as sulphur, potash, oil, and gas. The Texasgulf empire embraced the giant Kidd Creek Mines at Timmins, Ontario, the largest open-pit mines in the world and the corporate crown jewel. By acquiring both targets, CDC created a new company — Canterra Energy Ltd. — which was the eleventh-largest oil company in Canada and the fourth-largest owned by Canadians. It holds the number eleven position in production, stands seventh in Western Canadian land holdings, fourth in frontier lands, and third in the Beaufort after Dome and Gulf, and is the world's largest producer of sulphur. All of this was snared with borrowed money.

The CDC was first dreamed about by finance minister Walter Gordon in the 1960s, but it was his pragmatic successor Edgar Benson who finally gave birth to it in 1971. Pro-Canada and profit-oriented, the CDC has always been chided by both sides of the political spectrum. Says chief executive officer H. Anthony Hampson: "The left doesn't think it's socialist enough, the right doesn't see any need for it. Because the government's still involved, people say we're wasting money or not propping things up."

It began with $250 million in government money and ownership of Polysar, the former Sarnia, Ontario, crown corporation. Since 1974, all financing has been by Canadian individuals and institutions, with government ownership diminishing as time passed. By 1979, it owned 65 per cent of CDC's $2.5 billion in assets. In 1981, the government owned 49 per cent, as more and more shares were released to the buying public. Under Hampson, CDC had been an aggressive investor in Texasgulf Inc., working ownership up to 36 per cent, as well as becoming owner of 60 per cent of Petrosar's $760-million refinery and petrochemical plant. In addition, the CDC bought the Canadian holdings of Tenneco Inc., which it renamed CDC Oil & Gas; Connaught Medical Research Laboratories; and a handful of venture capital companies.

CDC is a holding company with a mandate to invest in Canadian industry, although not necessarily to repatriate foreign-held assets. When Hampson decided to swallow an oil giant, however, the field was filled only with subsidiaries of foreign firms. In 1977 a lengthy list of possible targets was drawn up. Unsuccessful bids were made on various companies: Hamilton Brothers, Kaiser, and Mesa among them. Other possibilities included Unitex, Union, and Amaratta, but nothing jelled. One name kept cropping up: Aquitaine of Canada, suggested by Ron Freeman of Salomon Brothers, a New York financial house that acted for both CDC and Aquitaine's French parent company, popularly known as Elf.

In November 1980, the federal government announced the National Energy Program (NEP), the nationalistic policy meant to increase Canadian ownership in oil and gas to at least 50 per cent by 1990. While it would be the final stimulus to successful negotiations, NEP also meant uncertainty for a time, until the rules were understood. Hampson temporarily halted the hunt for take-overs.

Born in Montreal in 1930, and educated at McGill and Cambridge, H. Anthony Hampson is a quiet, even courtly, man. His early jobs were scattered along the Montreal–Toronto–Ottawa triangle in both the public and the private sectors. As a finance department employee, he was on loan to Walter Gordon's Royal Commission on Canada's Economic Prospects from 1955 to 1957; from 1961 to 1964, he served as secretary of the Royal Commission on Banking and Finance (the Porter Commission). He was research director for a Toronto investment firm, then vice-president of Paul Desmarais's Power Corporation from 1964 to 1968 and president of Capital Management Ltd., a Power subsidiary, from 1968 until 1972, when he joined CDC.

That the CDC has succeeded at all is due to Hampson's tenacity, a trait he applies to his personal life as well as to his business. About five years ago his weight rose to 200 pounds, but he beat it back to a more slender 180 pounds on a six-foot-three frame. He has a way of standing with a willow-like backward lean that makes him look pompous as he peers down his nose at his interlocutor. His mouth is like a letter-box opening, all squared off and capable of only two shapes: open and closed. He knows when each is required, for he is a man of few words. He owns a Dufour 33 sailboat, on which he and his sometime companion, lawyer Connie Brown, plied the waters of Lake Ontario during that hectic take-over time.

The overall strategy to acquire Aquitaine was set by Hampson from a maze of rooms in the renovated former Eaton's College Street store in Toronto. The day-to-day negotiations, however, were carried out by CDC executive vice-president John Hague, with the banking business masterminded by treasurer Jim O'Reilly and chief financial officer Gerry McGoey.

After the initial brouhaha about NEP subsided, the burly and bushy-bearded Hague met in New York with Michel Rapaccioli, president of Aquitaine Inc., the holding company for Elf's U.S. investments. Also at the February 26, 1981, meeting were Gilbert Rutman, Elf's vice-chairman from Paris, and Jean-Yves Chereau, vice-president for North America and Australia. Elf, known world-wide for its exploration success, particularly on frontier acreage, was both puzzled and perturbed. "They were clearly groping," said Hague, "with what the hell to do with the National Energy Program. They were quite down on Canada." The two-hour session ended with an agreement to look at various proposals before meeting again in a month.

On March 23, Rapaccioli met with Hague at the CDC offices in Toronto. Hague mentioned CDC's 36 per cent ownership in the U.S. firm, Texasgulf, and pointed out that CDC had often thought it would prefer owning all of Texasgulf's Canadian assets, rather than a chunk of the whole multinational. Knowing that Elf was interested in a U.S. firm (it had recently lost out in a take-over bid for U.S. resource conglomerate Kerr-McGee), Hague held out the possibility of a multi-tiered deal: Elf could buy all of Texasgulf, including CDC's share; then Elf would transfer the Canadian portion to CDC, while selling Aquitaine of Canada to CDC.

Trying to figure out what the Canadian assets of Texasgulf were worth as part of the whole would be difficult, they agreed. Further, the tax implications in moving ownership of parts of Texasgulf from the U.S. to Canada were complex. However, the plan did fit with Elf's interest in gaining assets in the U.S., while getting out of Canada. Further, part of CDC's payment to Elf for Aquitaine would come in the form of swapped Texasgulf ownership, rather than cash. With currency exchange controls in place in France, the swap was a plus for Elf, because it meant less cash would be repatriated to France.

An April 2 lunch date in Paris was set so their bosses could meet to agree in principle to a deal. At the three-hour lunch in the Elf offices on the Left Bank with chairman Albin Chalandon, Hampson quickly discovered there was an interest in selling Aquitaine. It was further agreed that if both that deal and the complex Texasgulf deal were done, they must be kept separate. CDC, for example, didn't want to become involved in an unsuccessful take-over of Texasgulf and thereby lose out on the Aquitaine purchase. A working group of lawyers was established, to see if both deals were possible under the laws of the three countries, and an end-of-April deadline was set for a verdict. Neither side wanted protracted negotiations.

The lawyers found some solutions and some sticking points. The group included Art Scace and Jack Blair of the Toronto law firm of McCarthy & McCarthy; Herb Gallant and Bob Prescoe from Fried, Frank in New York; and other counsel from Sullivan & Cromwell in New York and Fraser & Beatty in Toronto. Their brief, showing how Texasgulf's Canadian assets might be hived off, was delivered to Hague's condominium in midtown Toronto Easter Sunday. It showed a chasm on valuations. CDC thought Aquitaine was worth $1.2 billion; Elf had pegged it at $1.9 billion.

CDC treasurer Jim O'Reilly is thin-faced and a little grey around the gills. When he sits, his gangly arms and legs fold up around him like various pieces of a collapsing chaise longue. It was up to him to see what money was available, for without funds there could be no deal. On May 7, he put out the first feeler to the bankers at King and Bay, about a mile due south of CDC headquarters. O'Reilly called John Graham, one of three vice-presidents in the Bank of Montreal's commercial and industrial division.

"Does the bank," asked O'Reilly, "have a level of exposure [debt] with the CDC beyond which you would be uncomfortable?"

Assuming a deal was in the wind and wanting to measure its size, Graham countered with a question. "How large would it be?"

"We would need financing of seven or eight hundred million," replied O'Reilly.

Graham made the further assumption that the figure represented half the deal and that another bank (or perhaps a share issue) would cover the rest. In those circumstances, Graham told him, the bank would not feel uncomfortable.

With the promise of easy money in their jeans, John Hague and Jack O'Brien, president of CDC Oil & Gas, flew to Paris for the final push with Elf. They held two days of meetings, May 16 and 17, in a hotel suite on the top floor of the Paris Hilton, overlooking the Seine. During the first morning, they argued about the amount of Aquitaine's gas reserves, but before lunch, Hague told Elf that CDC was prepared to move its bid price up from $60 a share to $68. It was a massive jump, worth about $180 million to Elf, and was meant to get the stalled talks moving, because both Hague and O'Brien were, in Hague's words, "a little pissed off." They left and went down the street for a leisurely lunch with a bottle of white wine, followed by a long walk in the springtime sun, to let Elf consider its position. At four, when talks resumed, Elf vice-president of finance Michel Moreau radiated a change of tone. After a management meeting, Elf had decided it wanted a deal, too. For the first time, Elf named a price per share for Aquitaine. At $78, it was almost within the range of $67.50 to $77.50 that Hampson had previously set for Hague. Negotiations now proceeded quickly and within thirty minutes, the midpoint, $74, was agreed upon.

Next came the thorny issue of what percentage of Texasgulf was in Canadian assets. Elf would bid on the open market to buy all the Texasgulf stock. CDC would sell its 36 per cent to Elf. But Elf wanted to fix a price that day. CDC said that was impossible, that the price would have to wait until the day of the bid; at that time, a price set above the going market price would give all shareholders a reason to sell to Elf. Elf was talking about $45, while that week the stock was trading at $31.50. Nor was there agreement on what the Canadian assets of Texasgulf — the portion CDC wanted — formed as a percentage of the whole company.

Elf's opening position was that half of the company's assets were in Canada. The effect of that view was to increase the price of the portion CDC wanted, because it was Hague's view that Canadian assets were a much smaller proportion of the whole company, somewhere in the 35 to 45 per cent range. Elf finally agreed that the Canadian assets were, perhaps, only 45 per cent, but Elf wouldn't budge from its view that $45 was a fair price per share of Texasgulf, regardless of how the market might swing before the Elf bid was announced. No more progress was made Saturday except that the two agreed that they needed to make some contingency plans in case the Texasgulf bid failed; neither wanted to end up a minority shareholder. The Canadians flew home on Victoria Day, May 18.

The next day, Richard Mollison, president of Texasgulf Inc., was in Toronto to meet with Hampson, who was also a Texasgulf director because of CDC's holdings in Texasgulf. Even though CDC's negotiations with Elf about Texasgulf were nearing completion, the conversation between the two was limited to management and compensation matters due to be on the agenda of the June Texasgulf board meeting. Secrecy was holding, but interlocking board directorships would be problematic again. In the tight world of Canadian corporations and North American finance, there was a banker on the Texasgulf board, too: TD's Dick Thomson.

The monthly CDC board meeting held in Winnipeg May 21 was a stormy session. The first agenda item was Prime Minister Pierre Trudeau's coup attempt. He had wanted Maurice Strong, an old ally, to be named CDC chairman, but backed off prior to the meeting, submitting instead a new plan to have two additional government appointees added to an expanded board, in order to have a larger say in what the CDC did, perhaps to use it for nationalistic ownership purposes.

The first speaker was Trudeau emissary Ian Stewart, an *ex officio* member of the board and deputy minister of finance. At the end of his twenty-minute speech, the directors were polled; every one said he would resign if Trudeau's two nominees were added. Defeated, Stewart left the room, and the board proceeded to the second confidential agenda item: the Aquitaine/Texasgulf deal. Because there had been a number of Canadian firms buying U.S. companies in recent months, there might be "quite considerable flak" from American political and corporate circles over the plan, Hampson told the board. He also pointed out that there "was a fair amount of financial exposure." Pointing to the possible $2 billion in debt that CDC would have, he said: "We'll be pretty fully levered, but this is the last thing we're going to do for a while." Director Pierre Côté, chairman of Celanese Canada Inc., spoke out against it, but he found little support and in the end, the board gave approval in principle to proceed with further negotiations.

The Game Begins

The courting of the banks now began in earnest. The following week, on Wednesday, May 27, the Bank of Montreal, already aware that the CDC was up to something after O'Reilly's call to John Graham, invited the CDC brass around for lunch, ostensibly to introduce Bill Bradford, incoming bank president.

Among the bankers present at lunch were vice-chairman Hart MacDougall, deputy chairman Grant Reuber, senior vice-president Doug Gibson, and Graham. Representing the CDC were Hampson, Hague, McGoey, and O'Reilly. After pre-meal drinks, they all sat around a long table in a dining room on the sixty-eighth floor of First Canadian Place. It was a relaxed atmosphere, with some kidding between Hampson and Reuber about the 1975 CDC share issue. The banks, Hampson reminded them, hadn't been all that helpful. The issue, Reuber laughed, wasn't all that profitable. The general atmosphere was clubby. Each knew the other's strengths and needed those relationships. And each knew the other's foibles and was prepared to turn a blind, if business-like, eye. This was no half-baked application for a car loan.

Over dessert and coffee, Hampson addressed the group from his chair. He described CDC's various corporate operations and brought the bankers up to date on some of its operations and plans. Finally, in an almost off-handed manner, Hampson said: "What would the bank's response be to a line of credit of a billion or a billion and a half for a major acquisition?"

Replied MacDougall smoothly: "Assuming the evaluations are correct and the bank agrees with the financial aspects of the operation and the acquisition, we can do a credit that large."

"We may try you on for size in the next couple of weeks," said Hampson.

"Try us on," said MacDougall.

It was a more public confirmation of the private trial balloon floated three weeks earlier by O'Reilly, intended to make sure that Hampson was not embarrassed by the wrong answer nor MacDougall surprised by the question.

The game was on. That afternoon, McGoey and Hampson discussed banking strategy. First, they removed the public relations fluff from the bank's statement. "I don't interpret their remark," McGoey told Hampson, "as meaning, 'We will finance a billion-and-a-half take-over by ourselves.' I interpret it as, 'Yes, we would like to be a very substantial player.'" Hampson decided that the CDC should be speaking to a number of banks about the deal, since the CDC, like much of corporate Canada, was watching all the banks more closely than it once did. Explained McGoey: "You watch how CIBC deals with a Turbo or a Massey. You watch how the Bank of Nova Scotia deals with the fishing industry. You watch how the Royal deals with oil and gas. Those are the early warning signals for a change in philosophy, for a change in lending practice."

CDC preferred to involve all the Big Five Canadian banks. That way, exposure would be shared and, if there was a competing bid for the quarry, all the banks would already be on CDC's side. However, there were problems with some of the Big Five. The Toronto-Dominion was CDC's main bank, the "house" bank, but TD chairman Dick Thomson was on the Texasgulf board (along with Hampson). Because of the anti-Canadian backlash noted by Hampson, every possible delaying tactic could be used against the take-over, including lawsuits against directors. CDC did not want to embarrass Thomson by assuming he'd be interested in financing part of the take-over when he wasn't, so decided to give him an early warning to discover if the TD wanted to participate or allow him to withdraw with honour.

As for the Commerce, it had just suffered through a public feud when Brascan Ltd. had made a grab for the U.S.-based F. W. Woolworth Co. Both Brascan and Woolworth were Commerce customers. First, the Commerce had hesitated to finance the take-over, arousing Brascan's ire; then it put up the money and made Woolworth mad. Lawsuits flew and, in the end, the Royal nabbed the Woolworth account. For its part, the CDC feared its move could cause similar problems in the U.S., and the Commerce was a banker to Texasgulf. McGoey and Hampson concluded that the Commerce "would more than likely over-react" if approached for financing. No requests would be made.

The Bank of Nova Scotia, they decided, was "too low-profile." Said

McGoey: "We just did not think they would be able to come up with the size of loan and the commitments that would be required." Also, there was the matter of the Petrosar term-preferred issue a few years earlier. The Bank of Nova Scotia had stayed out of the deal because of a "philosophic belief" against that form of after-tax financing. In the mind of CDC, Scotiabank had excluded itself from the fraternity. Scotiabank would not be approached.

Finally, there was the Royal. It should be approached because of its oil and gas expertise — and because CDC wanted three banks involved.

The next Monday, June 1, Hampson hopped on the subway to call on Robin Korthals, TD president (chairman Thomson was away), in his TD Centre office. He explained the deal, noting that Thomson was on the Texasgulf board and that TD was a banker to Texasgulf, but leaving the decision up to the TD. Hampson left with the feeling that the TD wasn't certain which way to go.

Korthals summarized the meeting and his views in a memo. "We have a real conflict," it said, "in the Texasgulf case, and I told Tony it would not be politic for us to offer to finance the cash portion of the Canadian asset purchase." The memo was circulated to vice-chairmen F.G. (Ted) McDowell and Bob Dickson as well as to senior vice-president Ernest Mercier, who added a handwritten comment: "Rumors of action between CDC and TG upset both stocks on Friday, but Aquitaine wasn't involved in the rumors." (Texasgulf jumped $5 per share that day to $40.50; CDC was up 75 cents to $13.50.)

Meanwhile, Hampson continued his rounds and called on the Royal June 3. He already had an appointment with Royal president Jock Finlayson for two-thirty, at which he and Noranda Manufacturing Ltd. chairman Len Lumbers pitched Finlayson for a corporate donation to a five-year $15-million fund-raising campaign for Toronto's York University. About four o'clock, Lumbers left, and Finlayson was joined by executive vice-president Joe Regan and senior vice-president Paul Taylor.

Hampson began the forty-five-minute meeting by stressing the need for confidentiality, then said that CDC was negotiating to buy Aquitaine, with the final price likely to be in the $1.5-billion range. Because the Royal had no business with Texasgulf, that part of the deal didn't need to be mentioned. He told them that CDC would likely go beyond its traditional two-bank relationship with the Bank of Montreal and TD by adding a third. Flattered by the offer of new business, Finlayson expressed interest. Concluded Hampson: "If something develops, our financial people will get in touch with you."

On Monday, June 8, Dick Thomson was back in his office and read Korthals's memo. As a Texasgulf director, Thomson was a member of the audit committee and personally owned a thousand shares. Though taken aback at the bid idea, his first loyalty was to the TD and the CDC's request for secrecy, not to Texasgulf.

Thomson telephoned Hampson to express his concern, saying he was "worried about the political backlash to Canada," and pointing out that one company was dominated by the Canadian government, the other by the French, and that they were both "dividing up a public American corporation." Fearing an international debate that might turn into a slanging match, Thomson added: "The politics of that bothers me." The TD, however, did not back out of the financing. Not yet.

Nor was the CDC to be stopped by Thomson's warning. The CDC's O'Reilly had already telephoned Doug Gibson at the Bank of Montreal the previous week, asking for a meeting. Gibson had pulled John Graham off holidays, and the two bankers met with O'Reilly on June 9. O'Reilly asked the bank to develop a proposal for a $1.4-billion financing. "We understood it to be competitive," said Graham later, although no other bank was approached to draw up a specific proposal.

While Graham worked on his proposal that week, John Hague finalized a deal with Elf on June 11 that would tie the two companies together on the Texasgulf offer. Elf feared that even with CDC's 36 per cent interest pledged, insufficient shares might be tendered by other shareholders for Elf to gain control. Each agreed to buy the other out, so that there was no surprise partner, and they agreed they would need to have two-thirds of the Texasgulf shares between them after the bid in order to proceed. It wasn't a lack of trust so much as possible surprises that they were trying to eliminate.

Hampson, by now in Europe for Polysar meetings, interrupted his schedule on Friday, June 12, to fly from London to Paris for another lunch with Aquitaine chairman Chalandon. It appeared that socialist candidate François Mitterrand would win the French elections, and Hampson wanted to be sure where any Aquitaine deal would stand with the new government. Reassured by Elf that any new government would not block something in progress, Hampson pressed on with Polysar meetings in Wiesbaden, Freiburg, and Brussels.

That weekend, John Graham finalized his financing proposal and delivered it to B of M senior credit manager Don McLean at home. In it, Graham recommended that the Bank of Montreal swallow $600 million itself and syndicate, or share, the rest out to other banks, both Canadian and foreign. McLean took it to Montreal for study at the regular Monday credit review committee, but before B of M could respond, the CDC strategy switched.

With a CDC board meeting now a mere eight days away, O'Reilly phoned the three banks — TD, Royal, and Montreal — on Wednesday, June 17, requesting that each attend a meeting in the CDC south boardroom the following day. If CDC was going to move, it was now or never. The price might go higher or lower, but as Hampson put it: "There's a time when you buy things and that's when people want to sell 'em."

All three banks responded positively to the call, although the TD's position puzzled the CDC. Said McGoey: "They indicated support for the acquisition. The fact that they would attend the meeting indicated to us a support for the transaction." Also, O'Reilly had met a week or so earlier with Mercier and one of his assistant general managers, Blair Slade, to make sure that the TD was not worried about such a potentially hostile take-over. It was, said McGoey, "bizarre. We couldn't understand. Dick Thomson was trying to get Tony Hampson to stop, [yet] his people were bullish on the acquisition."

The first mention of the code names under which the transactions would be known came during the telephone calls to the bankers. Every take-over has such cover phrases to help maintain secrecy when documents are typed or a conversation is overheard. In the days to come, no one talked of Aquitaine, it was "Chinook." Texasgulf became "Waters."

The Club Gathers

It was an uneasy alliance in CDC's south boardroom. Once the three banks gathered like this at the behest of a client, they were no longer full-tilt competitors, but they weren't quite colleagues either, since there was nothing yet to bind them into one negotiating team. As with all such loans where the risk was spread around, they soon would be, thus reinforcing the club atmosphere in which they work. Poker-faced Joe Regan led the Royal group, accompanied by Paul Taylor and Mike Waiser, who worked on the CDC account. The Bank of Montreal sent Doug Gibson and John Graham. For the TD were Blair Slade and an associate. For the CDC, McGoey and O'Reilly.

CDC handed out its Aquitaine acquisition document, an inch-thick stack of paper in a black three-ring binder. Each bank studied its copy separately, exchanging few comments. McGoey walked them through the evaluations that morning, aided by slides on an overhead projector, and by noon the banks had already decided — without having seen the Texasgulf half of the deal — that it was too large for the three of them to take on by themselves. It would have to be put out for syndication and shared with a number of other banks. McGoey further proved the need for other institutions by saying: "There is a second part. One bank knows more than the others." The Montreal and the Royal looked at each other and quickly realized it was neither of them, although the TD did not state the obvious. Joe Regan, who had let TD's Slade carry much of the bank questioning in the morning, chastised the CDC: "How can we make any credit decision when we don't know the other piece of the puzzle?"

Still trying to keep the two deals separate, McGoey responded: "We really want the credits to stand on their own. You'll find out at some point in time."

The bankers were getting testy. The Royal and the Montreal felt that something was being withheld, and their suspicions were aroused. For John Graham, who had prepared the B of M proposal at CDC's request a week earlier, what he was now hearing didn't seem entirely consistent with what he had known earlier. Finally, the CDC relented. McGoey turned to O'Reilly and said: "We'll have to give them a full briefing on the other half."

The afternoon was taken up with explanations about the Texasgulf deal, with the total financing required now reaching $1.7 billion. The situation was further confused by TD's position. It wanted to stay away from supplying funds to do the Texasgulf portion, but take a larger share, proportionately, of the Aquitaine "tranche" (slice), so that it would carry one-third of the total value of the two deals. The banks pressed for more information and it was agreed they would meet again the following day to hear a presentation from CDC Oil & Gas president Jack O'Brien.

They also agreed that because of the total deal's size, it would have to be syndicated. The deal could not be done in Canadian dollars; they were too expensive at the time. Investors were demanding high interest rates for funds on deposit with the banks. As a result, said Taylor: "We're funding ourselves, in Canadian dollars, above prime." In addition, CDC's original hope for a multi-currency loan, allowing the corporation to switch around during the term of the loan and play the exchange rates, was also rejected as having too many wrinkles that would be costly for the banks to administer, thus reducing their profit. "The bells and whistles are becoming expensive for us," said Taylor.

In return, if it was to give up flexibility, and such money-saving arrangements, CDC wanted iron-clad assurances that the three banks, having heard the deal, would finance it. McGoey and O'Reilly repeatedly asked about the banks' policies on hostile take-overs. They didn't want to get launched and find a bank had to back out for policy reasons. That would mean that the CDC would have to scuttle around, find someone else, and possibly pay more for the money because word would spread that there were extra risks involved. "The last thing we want to be worried about," said McGoey, "is our banking group." The day ended with all three banks pledging loyalty and continued participation — but without the final policy clearance that CDC continued to demand. That reluctance would almost prove to be the undoing of the deal.

Jack O'Brien, president of CDC Oil & Gas, began the briefing on Friday explaining how much debt CDC felt Aquitaine's cash-flow could carry. With less than a week before the CDC board meeting, it was essential that pricing and other terms be settled quickly. CDC wanted this deal done in half the usual two months, a demand that compounded the problems already inherent in its size.

In order to reduce the number of possible legal targets and court entanglements that could be invoked to stall the deal, any participation by U.S. banks was ruled out. As O'Reilly put it: "There's no reason to toss another pea in the soup." The banks demanded security in the form of Aquitaine stock. As part of the negotiating dance, CDC expressed surprise at this request. No borrower wants to pledge security, it reduces flexibility. On the other hand, no bank would do a deal this size without some financial back-stopping. Once the banks took that position, O'Reilly agreed: "We more or less had to go along with it. If they had any sense, they knew that." The banks also wanted CDC to pick the agent, or lead, bank from the three participating banks.

The CDC wanted to keep all banks equal and not pick an agent bank, thereby hoping to play one off against the other and cut the rates. The banks persisted, arguing that the agent bank could be responsible for answering the legal questions about a hostile take-over, thus letting the other two off the hook. CDC finally relented, choosing the TD because it had already been investigating the question. The choice satisfied the banks, but left the CDC scratching its head about the TD's reluctance to talk about the policy question. At one point, McGoey turned to his colleague, O'Reilly, and whispered: "There's something wrong here. The TD has had over a week to look at it."

The meeting broke up about four-thirty, and a pricing meeting was set for the next day. That Saturday session, however, would include different participants.

That evening, Joe Regan and Paul Taylor had returned to their offices at the Royal, called in financial analyst Mike Randall, and were just nicely under way when Regan's phone rang. It was a Bell operator: "Stand by for a conference call." Within seconds, he was connected with TD's Blair Slade as well as Gibson and Graham from the Bank of Montreal.

Slade dropped a bombshell: "We have decided, for various reasons, that we have a conflict of interest. We're getting out." For long, agonizing seconds, no one spoke. Finally, Regan made some sympathetic comment and said: "Tell the CDC to call us as soon as you've told them. We're on a short time fuse." Goodbyes were said all around, Regan hung up and swore. "It seems late," said Taylor, "given how long they knew."

The CDC was blissfully unaware that its worst fears had just been realized. With five days left before the board meeting and twelve hours before a pricing meeting for a loan approaching $2 billion, the agent bank had just dropped out. "There was a business decision and a banking decision," TD president Robin Korthals said later. "In retrospect, we should have made our final decision sooner, but you want to get the business, so you avoid that decision as long as possible."

In all likelihood, the TD hoped that the CDC would have backed out on its own — perhaps after listening to Thomson's arguments. In that event the TD, CDC's long-time banker, would not have been forced to withdraw. When it appeared that CDC was committed, U.S. counsel's advice of a potential conflict was heeded and the aggressive Slade had to be called off. And he had the embarrassing job of telling the CDC. CDC's McGoey had barely arrived at a dinner party when O'Reilly called to say that he'd just heard from Slade, who said he had something to tell the CDC.

It was about eight-thirty when McGoey reached his office. There he found Slade sitting on a couch, O'Reilly standing, leaning against his desk. Slade, obviously ill at ease, said: "The bank has reviewed this and made a policy decision not to participate." O'Reilly and McGoey exchanged looks of utter disbelief.

"Would you mind saying that again?" asked McGoey.

Slade repeated what was apparently a well-rehearsed sentence.

"Blair," said McGoey, "let me make sure I understand this. What you know today is no different from what you knew two weeks ago."

"No."

"There are no facts, no credit considerations, nothing that is different."

"No. It's a policy decision."

McGoey asked him if he was aware what the TD's last-minute pull-out could do to pricing of the loan—perhaps the whole deal. Slade told him he'd informed the other two banks and they were waiting for CDC's call.

McGoey bit his tongue and said: "There's no point in discussing this any further. Thank you for your input. Would you please have all acquisition documents back on our desk by tomorrow."

Hiding their rage, O'Reilly and McGoey walked Slade to the elevator. On the way back, the two CDC colleagues tried to make sense out of the decision and wondered what to do about the meeting in the morning. With U.S. banks ruled out, and now two Canadian banks with conflicts, they phoned Doug Gibson at his Bank of Montreal office. "We assume you're aware of the TD response?" The voice at the other end could have belonged to an undertaker, it sounded so gloomy. "Yes," replied Gibson, "we're aware. What would you like to do?" The CDC pair said they'd be down in half an hour. The call completed, McGoey said to O'Reilly: "Where the hell are we going to get $600 million in twelve hours?"

It was O'Reilly who suggested an unlikely saviour, the Bank of Nova Scotia, ruled out previously because CDC believed it could not or would not take on such a large loan. O'Reilly was a back-fence neighbour of Peter Godsoe, a bright, young, well-connected executive vice-president at Scotiabank, and had often swum in Godsoe's swimming pool.

He phoned Godsoe at home about nine. "Are you going away this weekend?"

"Yes," came Godsoe's reply, "would you like to use my pool?"

"No, this is a business call," said O'Reilly. McGoey addressed the speakerphone. "We'd like to know the answer to three questions. Assuming that the credit will stand up, would the Bank of Nova Scotia be willing to participate with $600 million as a third member of an acquisition? Two, is there concern about hostile take-overs? Three, how fast can we get a response?"

"What's your number? I'll be back to you." The Godsoe family weekend at his mother's farm north of Toronto was cancelled. He phoned Ced Ritchie, Scotiabank chairman, at his Don Mills home. "CDC is up to something and it's very, very major," he told Ritchie. "It's bound to be oil and gas. I don't know who, but I can make a few educated guesses." Among the guesses was Aquitaine. Ritchie's response was positive, but he suggested Godsoe run it by president Gordon Bell and another executive vice-president, Scott McDonald. Neither was available, so Godsoe phoned McGoey and O'Reilly. "We're in. We don't see any major problem. We can't make a credit decision yet but we don't see any policy problem." With a potential third bank in their pocket, McGoey and O'Reilly climbed on the subway and rode down to meet the other two.

After hours, First Canadian Place is locked up as tight as a maximum-security prison. McGoey and O'Reilly presented themselves to the guard in the lobby. He'd been told to expect them and led them up to the twenty-fourth floor after telephoning ahead. There they walked through another reception area with television monitors and approached the locked glass doors leading to offices. Both McGoey and O'Reilly were identified through the glass by the bankers within, before the security guard opened the door with his key.

They all trooped quietly by the Inuit art and wall hangings to the conference room in the northwest corner of the floor. McGoey and O'Reilly sat on one side of the doughnut-shaped table, with three from the Royal (including Taylor and Regan) across to the left and three from the Montreal (including Gibson and Graham) across to the right. The mahogany table is fifteen feet across, forty feet in circumference, ringed by chairs covered in black and grey pin-stripe velveteen. In the corner, a five-foot-high podium stands, packed with buttons that run the Technics sound system and projection equipment. On one wall, a blackboard, against another wall, a credenza; on the windows hang drapes, sheers, and venetian blinds. In a far corner, a small fabric wall hanging depicting a large pack of wolves. McGoey and O'Reilly felt as if the wolves were circling towards them, for the unspoken question bristling in the room from the bankers was: What did the TD know that caused it to drop out?

McGoey and O'Reilly spent the first thirty minutes explaining that the TD move was a policy decision and did not reflect at all on the credit-worthiness of the deal. Finally convinced, Gibson spoke for all of the bankers: "Where do we go from here?" The bankers wanted at least two more banks brought in. The CDC didn't. Even with a third bank at the ready, the CDC wanted to keep the group to two if possible, fearing that a third would delay proceedings by taking time to catch up. Said McGoey: "We want you to take a billion each."

It was one of the few times anyone remembered seeing the impassive Regan register any emotion. McGoey had managed to cause a slight wrinkling of the crow's-feet around Regan's eyes. "You'll have to give us some time," Regan said. "You've got an hour," replied McGoey.

The two banks headed for separate offices to telephone more senior officials. Returning with Regan as spokesman, they said: "With two banks, it's too large. Additional banks should be brought to the table." The banks also wanted the next day's meeting postponed and the presentation to the CDC board delayed beyond next Thursday, so that the other banks could catch up.

The banks were informed that a preliminary call had already been made to the Bank of Nova Scotia. "If it is doable," asked McGoey, "and we can get a third bank, are you changing your policy to take $600 million each?" The Royal and the Montreal agreed they would stay with a three-way split but expressed doubts that Scotiabank would come in. By now a little wary of bank promises, McGoey and O'Reilly phoned Godsoe again.

"The size is no problem," Godsoe told them. "Six hundred million is not out of the question. We can absorb it ourselves. There's no problem with a hostile take-over," he reiterated, "all other things being equal." They described the deal in more detail, naming names and telling him that the TD had dropped out, thus precipitating the last-minute phone call to him. He agreed to meet them the next morning at eight at CDC offices to go over the acquisition documents, to discuss the deal with chairman Ritchie, and to be ready to meet with the other two banks by ten o'clock.

The new third banking colleague was announced to some surprised comments.

COOKIE WEEKEND

Saturday, June 20, did not begin auspiciously for Peter Godsoe. Tooling down Avenue Road, on his way to meet the CDC and begin a weekend of work, he was nabbed in a radar trap and waved down by a policeman. "Jesus," he thought, "greater love hath no man." In the parking lot behind the CDC offices, he met colleague Bruce Birmingham, in charge of the bank's U.S. operations, whom he'd phoned the night before. After trying unsuccessfully at several locked doors, they finally found their way in. Over coffee and doughnuts, Godsoe, Birmingham, O'Reilly, and McGoey studied the acquisition documents that the other banks had seen two days before. After an hour, Godsoe and Birmingham headed to their offices on King Street, across Bay from the Bank of Montreal's First Canadian Place. Ritchie pored over the binder brought by Godsoe, agreed the numbers looked sound, and waved aside concern about a potentially hostile take-over. As Ritchie put it, banks are like railways, "they carry all kinds of freight."

Back at the CDC, McGoey thought he'd get a quick haircut across the street. His mind on the deal, he paid no attention to the barber until he was finished. Looking in the mirror, he cried in alarm, "My God, man, what have you done?" He looked like a Buddhist monk.

When he and O'Reilly arrived about eleven-thirty Doug Gibson made some mild remark about his appearance. McGoey, whose hair is usually modishly long, raised his voice for all to hear and quipped: "I figured you fellows would clip me, so I might as well get it down as close as I could before we started." Still concerned about the late arrival of Scotiabank, O'Reilly asked Godsoe if he had caught up to the others. Godsoe and Birmingham, it turned out, both knew some of the players in the room — Godsoe had been in New York when Regan was — and they already had a fair amount of knowledge about CDC, Aquitaine, and Texasgulf between them. Godsoe was pleased and replied: "We thought we were going to come into a deal we knew nothing about, but we found out we knew a lot more about it than we thought."

With the roller-coaster ride of the day before, when the previous banking group looked secure, still fresh in everyone's memory, Joe Regan turned to O'Reilly and dead-panned: "Jim, maybe you want to change the banking group again."

The initial tension broken, they settled around the table: McGoey and

O'Reilly for the CDC; Godsoe and Birmingham for Scotiabank; Regan, Taylor, and their junior associate Mike Waiser for the Royal; Gibson, Graham, and account manager Gary Sills for the Bank of Montreal. They were now bound together by the same tightening rope and they'd all have to live for the next ten years with prices and terms set this weekend. It was the kind of deal that could make — or break — an individual's reputation.

The chubby-cheeked and cheery-faced Paul Taylor later put it this way: "It's a high. It's positive stress. It's what we do banking for. It's exciting to be a part, a little piece of a major event. Getting a crack at it is a positive thing, both for yourself and for your bank. If you get it right, you'll make quite a bit of money for your bank. If it's a good deal, it's a positive thing personally for you in your career.

"Knowing things that others don't isn't all that important. That goes with the territory — just like being a priest. I've been through a half a dozen of these deals and there's an adrenalin level that has to be reached — especially when there's a time element. It brings out the best and worst of you. You get testy, you have fun, you fight, you do it eighteen hours a day. We worked three weekends in a row. That's part of corporate culture. It becomes so interesting that nobody notices it's Saturday morning."

Among the bankers' initial concerns that Saturday morning was the number of "back doors" available to the borrower. The CDC wanted a few escape hatches, ways to sell off assets at some future date, methods to retain flexibility to acquire something else or maintain cash flow for other plans. The bankers wanted to nail all those back doors shut, to make sure the corporation didn't do something next month or next year that changed its capacity to repay the loan. The main job that weekend was to put into place a short-term loan that would supply the money for the Aquitaine purchase and be replaced by the larger syndicated loan that would take a month to set up. Pricing and terms for that long-term loan, however, would be established by this group. But first, O'Reilly had to be convinced that the loan should be syndicated out to a score or more banks. The telling argument was the reminder that with this deal CDC was becoming an international player and would want to come back, at some point, to the big European banks. This loan, led by three Canadian banks and shared by the European banks, would be an excellent introduction.

Next they discussed pricing. As with most syndicated loans, the rate was to be based on what's known as the London Inter-Bank Offered Rate (LIBOR). Essentially a floating rate, it changes every three months. Loan interest rates are set in relation to the LIBOR rate and move automatically

— up or down — with LIBOR. The CDC, of course, thought it should have the best rate possible — LIBOR with nothing added. The banks, just as predictably, wanted to set a rate over LIBOR — that extra margin or spread was where they would make their profit.

The banks proposed that the rates for the first two years be half a percentage point over LIBOR, then five years at five-eighths and three years at three-quarters. "What about one-third?" asked O'Reilly. "This is a great credit, our reputation in Europe is excellent." The haggling had begun. More sophisticated than buying a new car, perhaps, but the techniques are little different. The three-quarters disappeared, replaced by one-half for five years, five-eighths for five years. The CDC moved to three-eighths, O'Reilly pointing to deals he'd seen done at that level. Rates are moving up, he was told. Behind all pricing considerations was the view, too, that with CDC's 49 per cent government ownership, it would be viewed in Europe as more of a government agency than it really was. "Our usual greed," said Taylor, "was tempered by concern for the credit of the country. It's in the best interests of Canadians and Canadian bankers to be perceived in the best light. We would have been shirking our responsibilities as Canadians if we didn't go for the best price. We wanted success, but not to be overly successful. You don't want banks clamouring for the deal or turning their backs on it."

For all the combined professional competence and personal camaraderie, no one could organize lunch. Doug Gibson did manage to rustle up some pots of coffee from the executive pantry across the hall, but while it was well equipped with a fridge, stove, and coffee-maker, there was nothing to eat but boxes of Peek Frean cookies. The ten men straggled through the day fuelled only on cookies and coffee, dubbing Gibson the "cookie monster."

The price and term haggling finally ended at about five-thirty, amid groaning stomachs, when it was agreed that the loan would be priced at one-half over LIBOR for the first five years, five-eighths over LIBOR for the second five. Then the banks called colleagues in their respective London offices, where the loan would be syndicated, to hear their views. Godsoe phoned Chris Barnes, Graham phoned Alex Yankovich, Taylor phoned Nick Johnston. All were told to gather in London the next afternoon and to think about a deal in which, at the moment, they knew only code names, numbers, and credit-worthiness.

On Sunday, June 21, the bankers gathered without the borrower in the twenty-fourth-floor B of M conference room at nine-thirty to talk about an important consideration, one in which they needed to have a united front: fees. When Jim O'Reilly arrived at ten-thirty — better prepared that day, with a sandwich and a banana in a paper bag—the banks were ready. He needn't have bothered with a lunch; loyal secretaries had been summoned to run food errands as well as type the one-page document that was ready for O'Reilly and McGoey when they arrived.

It outlined the margin, terms, and conditions already agreed to, and set the syndication fee for doing the deal at $10 million. Each of the three lead banks would take a piece and pass along the rest to the other thirty banks who would eventually become involved. The first call to London was placed about ten-thirty. CDC withdrew from the room while Ed Mercaldo, Regan, and Godsoe talked with Barnes, Yankovich, and Johnston. Mercaldo, a senior vice-president for international, was Yankovich's boss and had joined the B of M's team that day particularly to pitch for the agent's job now that the TD had dropped out.

London's initial view was quite different from Toronto's. First they discussed which banks might be involved in the syndicated loan, looking particularly at Middle Eastern bankers who were becoming more active at that time. London wanted a free hand in the selection. Toronto pointed out that CDC wanted European bankers. London said the deal would take six weeks; Toronto said it had to be done in three. The room was filled with transatlantic voices saying: "No way." "You guys are crazy."

The conversation turned to pricing. London seemed to be looking at things too mechanistically, looking only at numbers, and not taking any long-term relationship into account. Term was also debated: London thought it should run seven to eight, Toronto wanted ten. Finally, Toronto pointed out that what they were putting forward was closer to what the client wanted and would agree to. London should think about it; they'd all talk again in two hours.

In Toronto, those two hours were spent pitching CDC as to which bank would be agent, and who would "run the book." The agent bank works essentially as a trustee, carries on communications with the other banks involved, distributes the annual reports, receives payments, parcels them out, and handles any ensuing negotiations. In addition to a fee, there is prestige involved in being agent: that bank is listed at the top of the page-sized magazine advertisement that enumerates all the eventual bank participants in descending order of the size of their share in the loan. These "tombstones," as the ads are called, are carefully scrutinized by analysts and corporations looking to see who's doing the big deals. The bank that "runs the book" invites the other banks to participate in the syndication, sends out the telexes, and ensures that information is shared with all the banks involved. The job is short-lived and is over within a matter of weeks when the loan is signed.

Because it was last in, Scotiabank said it did not want to pitch for either job, so O'Reilly and McGoey retired down the hall to Doug Gibson's office, where the Bank of Montreal and the Royal made presentations each lasting about fifteen minutes. Mercaldo spoke for the B of M, stressing the bank's track record of having done more agency work than any other Canadian bank. "We've consistently been voted by other banks," he pointed out, "as best lead manager." The fee suggested: $25,000 per year or, depending on the number of banks that would eventually participate, $500 per bank each year of the loan.

Paul Taylor made Royal's case, concentrating mainly on the expertise of Royal's merchant bank in London — Orion — in loan syndication and Eurobond capacity. He pointed out, for example, that the Royal was the only Canadian bank to own a merchant bank, with sixty computerized telexes that would disperse information quickly.

At one-thirty McGoey and O'Reilly announced that the Montreal would be the agent, Royal would run the book. For its part, the Bank of Nova Scotia would perform the honorific role of hosting the closing banquet, where all the participating banks sign the loan agreement.

They placed their next call to London at two; during that conversation the important pricing details had to be worked out. There was no chance to widen the circle much further, call in other experts, because every time information was passed on to someone else, the chance of a leak grew. As Peter Godsoe put it later: "You had to crack this whole thing over a weekend in secrecy, so you weren't trying to go out and test markets. They had to be in a position Friday to make an announcement. It was just a ticking time bomb. As it was, the news leaked badly." He worried particularly about those dealers who might try to buy and sell blocks quickly. "If the price starts to get arbitraged up, that can kill the whole deal."

The two o'clock London call was more successful. The London bankers agreed to let Toronto pick the banks, since CDC had some old friends it wanted to keep happy and also wished to take the opportunity to introduce itself to some key Swiss and German banks. Said Bruce Birmingham: "These are long-run relationships. You can't screw anybody. As in most things in life, you don't hold the upper hand for long." Most important, the pricing was finally settled. A ten-year term with five years at a half and five at five-eighths over LIBOR — what the Toronto bankers had proposed Saturday. One of the early restrictions was changed, from two years without prepayment to one year. The grace period (when no principal is repaid, only interest) was set at five years.

Because the pecking order on the tombstone was all-important, the syndication levels were also established: a $75-million participation made a bank a co-manager; $50 million, a manager; $25 million, a participant.

And because the deal, like most syndicated loans, would be based on British rates and written under British law, British counsel would be needed. Allen & Overy was a London firm known to all; lawyer Philip Wood was acceptable to all as an expert in drafting the necessary legal wording to bind all the parties together. (While Wood did much of the drafting, he was replaced late in July by an associate with the marvellous name of Jonathan Horsefall Turner.) Canadian counsel was also picked — Ted Weir of McMillan and Binch — to act for the banks in drawing up the loan agreement. Finally, about four-thirty, the Toronto bankers began a draft of the letter of agreement that would bind the banks to provide $675 million in bridge financing, the first "tranche" in the deal for the Aquitaine bid Friday. The banks would be ready but there were a few unknown twists and turns in the short road that lay ahead.

By the next day, Monday, June 22, the circle of people aware of the deal was widening. Meanwhile, a time noose was tightening around the main players. At the banks, officers at lower echelons were brought in to draw up the documents, even as senior officers gave final approval to the numbers put together over the weekend. The Bank of Nova Scotia was the first to signal CDC with formal approval for the deal, about two-thirty. After that, the Royal; by evening, the Bank of Montreal was in.

For Tony Hampson, it was a day of telephone calls. One from Texasgulf's Richard Mollison relayed news of continuing rumours. Hampson maintained a stony silence about the deal that would involve his fellow director and his company. Another came from Dick Thomson, who wanted to explain TD's Friday pull-out directly to Hampson and continued to urge that CDC drop the deal. Again, each man was carefully wearing the appropriate hat for the conversation, but both were aware that they each had other roles in the deal. While Thomson has never revealed his full reason for opposing the deal, he must have been concerned about the size of the debt-loads being taken on by Canadian firms as they bid up oil assets. As a participant in Dome's $2-billion loan, he refused Dome chairman Jack Gallagher when he came looking for more a few weeks later. Thomson has since admitted the bank was wrong to loan these kinds of sums. His concern, seen then only as impractical conservatism, turned out to be accurate as other loans turned sour in 1982.

Meanwhile, a slip-up at the CDC had sent the market buzzing. Tam Deachman, a Vancouver-based PR man for CDC, was in Toronto to be briefed about the deal by manager of public relations Jim Smith. When a call came from the Dow Jones news agency, Smith, assuming it was about a matter previously announced, asked Deachman to handle it.

The next thing Smith heard was Deachman saying to Dow Jones: "We've heard this rumour. We've been running all over Vancouver trying to find out what's going on." Then, he added: "We have no intention of selling our shares." Within minutes the Dow wire was chattering with an item that said: "A spokesman said CDC has no intention of selling its shares in Texasgulf." With a sinking heart, Smith phoned Toronto Dow bureau chief Pat Wallace to say that Deachman was not an official spokesman. "Are you denying it?" asked Wallace. "No," replied Smith, hedging his words, "we have no comment." Wallace said he wouldn't change the item unless CDC denied it. Smith was stuck. He could lie and deny it; he could be truthful and blow the deal. He stuck with his "no comment" and hoped for the best, knowing that the news-wire would continue its earlier, inaccurate version. Official word was being passed by CDC, meanwhile, to the Ontario Securities Commission in regard to the bid for Aquitaine. Whenever one firm plans to buy more than 10 per cent of another firm, the OSC ensures that all other shareholders receive the same offer. CDC counsel Nigel Gray spoke that day with director Charles Salter and legal adviser Keith Boast, telling them that CDC had not settled on price and "had not come to a landing yet on the follow-up offer" for the rest of the shares. The OSC said it would watch the market.

For their part, the bankers and the lawyers had joined forces in a Royal Bank meeting room to begin drafting the bridging loan that would be in place until the full loan was syndicated. Scotiabank's Bruce Birmingham brought along Dennis Belcher, a general manager, special loan services, to take over from Godsoe and himself. Also at the meeting were Montreal's John Graham and Ed Mercaldo, Royal's Paul Taylor and in-house counsel Mike Setesky, the two from Scotiabank, and bank counsel Ted Weir. They drew up, over the next two days, a three-page letter of offer to CDC that would form the basis of the loan agreement. Documentation was necessary for the bridge financing that would acquire Aquitaine and finance the cash payment to Texasgulf. In all, $1.75 billion was divided three ways — with the initial drawdown of $675 million to purchase the Aquitaine shares Friday to be made up of (U.S.) $225 million from each of the three banks. While one team did the loan documentation (the agreement, amending letters, promissory notes, indentures) for a black binder and presentation to the CDC board, another group began work on the syndicated loan agreement that would supersede the bridging agreement. Only the two-team approach could cut the usual fifty-to-sixty-day time in half, as CDC wanted.

Lawyer Ted Weir was joined by Philip Wood of Allen & Overy. Behind Wood's ebullience and upper-crust British public school accent was a practical man with a talent for drafting the phrases and paragraphs in what was to be a 135-page loan agreement signed by five dozen people.

Wood and Weir also acted as referees between the borrower and the bankers. As Belcher put it: "The borrower starts wanting a simple order to pay over a number of years with no conditions. The banks want hefty conditions. Counsel helps by negotiating the two together." Bankers also began arriving from London, with B of M's Alex Yankovich the first in at one o'clock to help draft the offering circular that would go to other banks to encourage their participation.

It wasn't just banker and borrower who argued, however. There were some disputes among the three banks, too. One, for example, concerned the first principal payment. There would be a five-year grace period, but when would payment start? In the sixtieth month? In the sixty-sixth month? They finally settled on the sixty-sixth and specified that eleven equal semi-annual payments would retire the loan.

These meetings, going ten hours a day, filled the first three days of the week amid continuing concerns about leaks, as the Aquitaine stock, which had been sitting quietly at $62 a share the previous week, suddenly jumped more than $7 a share on Monday. Wednesday, June 24, brought concerns about secrecy to a head. What happened then, coupled with CDC's last-minute change in the offer, just about blew the deal out of the water.

Even as the bankers were feverishly working in secret, McGoey received a call from his Vancouver friend David Thompson, chief financial officer of Teck Corp., a mining and resource company. The two old friends regularly fell together when each visited the other's city. McGoey was aware that Teck was working with Aquitaine of Canada on a frontier partnership (Aquitaine of Canada was kept in the dark by its French parent about the CDC deal) and didn't want Thompson to be suspicious. Hoping to put Thompson off the track, McGoey accepted his invitation to get together for a drink. They met at five in the National Club on Bay Street, a venerable institution in the shadow of the bank towers. There was a function on upstairs, so for privacy they met in the empty women's lounge near the men's washroom downstairs. Thompson pulled something from his briefcase — a document with Aquitaine and Teck printed on it. "Let me see that," said McGoey.

"Oh, no," replied Thompson, "it's nothing you want to see," and thrust it back into his briefcase. "I hear you're after an elephant," Thompson fished.

"What are you talking about?"

"Rumours on the street," repeated Thompson, "say that you're after an elephant."

"What's an elephant?" asked McGoey, feigning stupidity.

"I hear it's a very large oil company."

"Which one is it this time?" replied McGoey lamely. "Usually we're going to acquire Gulf or Esso or Petro-Can. What's the outrageous rumour this time?"

When Thompson's answer came, it wasn't so outrageous. "I hear you're after Aquitaine." McGoey continued to pretend nothing was happening, but Thompson began to describe a take-over scenario, not just of Aquitaine, but involving Texasgulf as well, where the Canadian assets were stripped out and held by CDC. Except for the complex tax arrangements that had been worked out, he described 80 per cent of the deal in place and offered Teck as a financial partner. McGoey denied the scenario, convincing Thompson that with a hostile management and the tax problems such a deal would be too difficult. McGoey could barely contain himself and flew back to the office to phone the banks.

"There's a leak somewhere, where the hell is it?" Each stoutly denied being the source.

About six-thirty, around the corner from the National Club, John Graham was preparing to walk to Union Station and grab an eastbound GO train for his home in Scarborough when the Royal's Paul Taylor called. "Why don't you stop by for a few minutes?" He wouldn't get home for another ten hours. In a deal involving countless long nights, the longest was just getting under way.

While McGoey was being amazed and the meeting was heating up at Paul Taylor's office, a think session was about to begin at John Hague's condominium, where he had invited some of his CDC colleagues that evening for supper and final consideration of the deal. In addition to co-workers Hampson, McGoey, O'Reilly, and O'Brien, others attending were New York lawyer Herb Gallant from Fried, Frank as well as Washington consultant Dick Whelan. Whelan, a former journalist, had been a campaign manager for George Bush in his run for the U.S. presidency. Bush had also been a Texasgulf director, so Whelan's Republican connections were helpful in assessing the political response in the U.S. to the bid they were about to make on Texasgulf with Elf. In Whelan's view, it was simply a question of price. If Elf set a satisfactory bid price on Friday, there would be no political flak, he said. The others were dubious. There was a series of noisy battles on at the time — NuWest/Cities Service; Dome/Conoco — this could be another, they feared. In the end, Whelan was right, but the rest — bearing in mind that the price for Texasgulf had not yet been set and Aquitaine had last talked of a $45 offer (and it had closed that day at $45) — decided to be a bit more conservative than they'd originally planned. Rather than go for 74 per cent of Aquitaine on Friday, they dropped the chunk they would seek to 49 per cent, deciding to go after the rest later. After dinner, McGoey and O'Reilly went to tell the bankers of the major change in the deal.

The bankers, Taylor, Graham, and Birmingham, were meanwhile wrestling with security. CDC was pledging Aquitaine shares as collateral, the very shares that they were acquiring with the borrowed money. But would the CDC have legal ownership? Among the Aquitaine assets in Alberta, for example, was a pipeline. To transfer ownership from Elf to CDC, permission would have to be granted by the Alberta Public Utilities Commission. What if that body refused and CDC in turn could not pledge it against the loan? "Well now," said the Royal's Taylor when the point was discovered, "that *is* a bombshell." They had been consulting Alberta counsel, phoning CDC people, but could not resolve the problem. Recalled Bruce Birmingham: "We went round and round. It started looming as a big issue. We reworked it about five times."

About midnight, McGoey and O'Reilly joined the bankers in the Royal Bank Tower, wending their way past photocopy and coffee machines to the grotty room where the bankers had been meeting. They dropped another bombshell on the already blitzed banks, saying they were changing CDC's offer from 75 per cent of Aquitaine shares to 49 per cent. The bankers were flabbergasted. This was a major alteration in the transaction. It meant that CDC would own less of Aquitaine in the beginning, receive less money from that investment, and therefore be less likely to service the substantial debt CDC wanted to take on. Joe Regan was brought in from his home in Don Mills, hurried calls were made to Montreal head office, and a tense hour was spent while the CDC twosome convinced the bankers the credit-worthiness wasn't altered.

There was further difficulty involved in getting the ownership of the Canadian assets of Texasgulf, a Delaware company, transferred to Canada and into one of several corporate vehicles between the date Elf and CDC would acquire Texasgulf and the actual date when the assets would be divided between the two. Meanwhile, CDC would be borrowing about $536 million (the exact amount wasn't known that night), loaning it to Elf, and Elf in turn would loan it down to a transitory company that would do the acquisition. The goal, once all that was understood, was to assure that the interest on that loan would eventually be put against the assets of one of the vehicles, for tax purposes. "We needed a CDC guy to tell us how the whole thing would blend," said Birmingham. The steps were so complex that they were still going on a year later as the assets moved through corporate vehicles before coming to their final resting place. To this day, most of the people in that meeting get glazed eyes when they try to explain the intricacies of the deal.

The pipeline was also debated, and after O'Reilly and McGoey finally left at one-thirty, the bankers discussed things for another hour, trying to finalize the wording in a seven-page document, called "Agreement pledging the Aquitaine shares" with CDC Petroleum Inc., another vehicle in the deal. It had to be in place before the money was advanced.

Finally, about three o'clock, their minds gone to mush with too much talk, they agreed to reassemble in the morning. John Graham took a taxi home to Scarborough, showered, changed, and was back at work by six-thirty. Ted Weir headed to his office on the thirty-eighth floor of the Royal Bank Plaza, did some more drafting on the commitment letter, and grabbed a few hours' sleep on a three-seater couch in an anteroom off the firm's boardroom.

Regan returned home, while Taylor, Birmingham, Belcher, and Waiser, who all lived outside Toronto, fled to the nearest beds — the Royal York Hotel, where they discovered that checking in at that late hour meant a cut-rate of $40 for a room. In the morning, after hurried purchase of toiletries in the Royal York (and new shirts later in the morning), the bankers and lawyers assembled again. Weir had come up with the saving words on the pipeline problem: "If any approval was necessary the pledge would become effective upon that authorization being obtained." By the cold grey light of dawn, it all looked so simple. As Graham put it: "It was a pledge but not a pledge." Said Taylor: "When you work sixteen hours a day, you waste four because you're tired. You get on tangents. The next morning you see it could have been done in twenty minutes, not the three hours it took."

All this material for the board was available from two o'clock for the five o'clock meeting. In addition to the pledging agreement and acquisition documents, there was the twelve-page bridging agreement done by the banks that detailed a (U.S.) $1.75-billion credit facility. Signed by Taylor, Birmingham, and Graham, it committed each of the three banks to putting up $583,333,333. Typed on June 23, signed on June 25, it was, in effect, a self-destructing document that would be replaced by the loan agreement.

Thinking that the CDC would decide quickly, the bankers met at the Bank of Montreal at five to wait for the board's signal, like observers in St. Peter's Square looking for the plume of white smoke when a pope is chosen. As time dragged and they heard that the board was still debating the two deals, Birmingham invited everyone to the Ontario Club for drinks in the leather chairs at the back of the lounge. Another hour passed, still no word from CDC, so the dozen of them walked up to Hy's Restaurant for dinner.

The board decision took almost five hours. In addition to the deal itself, the board was worried about the price Elf would offer for Texasgulf. Since CDC would be selling its 36 per cent to Elf, CDC wanted to sell at the right price. Also, it had to be high enough for other shareholders to tender and the deal to fly. Although John Hague spent an hour on the phone talking to Elf, then several more telephone hours from the bar of a nearby restaurant, Barberian's, he was not able to persuade Elf to raise its price to where the CDC board felt it should be: $50. (The stock had closed that day at $45, up from $31 barely six weeks earlier. Aquitaine had reached $68, up from $59 in mid-May.) Finally, the CDC board approved the deal about nine-thirty, subject to the bid price being $50.

Word was now leaking so badly that at one point during the meeting, Tony Hampson's secretary, Diana White, brought him a note that he read out at the end of the meeting. It was from Teck president Norm Keevil, saying he had to get through to Hampson because he knew that the board was discussing Aquitaine and Texasgulf. Teck wanted to participate and offer financing assistance.

Of the fifteen directors attending, five (including Dome Petroleum chairman Jack Gallagher and Pierre Côté) voted against the deals. Ten were in favour.

After the meeting, Hampson, CDC senior vice-president Claude Marchand, Jim O'Reilly, Ted Weir, and John Graham headed for the airport and a commercial flight to New York. There they would finalize the offer with Elf the next morning and make the appropriate announcements before the market opened at ten o'clock. Difficulties with U.S. air traffic controllers meant that no planes were flying to New York. Various options, including renting a car for the drive, were considered and rejected. No bank plane was available on such short notice, although John Graham checked on both the Royal's and the B of M's planes. Hampson, cool throughout the delay and hopeful that they would be able to fly out in the morning, finally said: "Let's all go home."

At six the next morning, John Hague received a call from one of his New York lawyers, saying that he'd just come from the printers where the Elf offer was being finalized. His sense was that Elf would raise its bid on Texasgulf to $50. After Hague had come into the office and joined colleague Nigel Gray and McCarthy lawyer Jack Blein, another call from New York said Elf wasn't going to bid $50.

At seven, Hampson, Weir, Graham, and Jim O'Reilly flew out of Toronto; they arrived in the New York law offices of Sullivan & Cromwell just half an hour before the market opened. Elf, which had been locked into the $45 price since the Paris meeting, was also represented, but Hampson and the Elf people sat in separate rooms and did not speak directly. Instead, both telephoned John Hague in Toronto. As ten o'clock approached, Hague had Hampson on one line and Elf on the other — and no deal. Hampson wasn't going to close on Aquitaine, Elf wouldn't budge on the Texasgulf price. Then, suddenly, at 9:58 A.M., with the market set to open in two minutes, Elf signed for $50, Hampson signed, the announcement was on the stock wires, and trading was halted in both Aquitaine and Texasgulf. The wraps were off Chinook and Waters.

Hampson phoned Texasgulf's Mollison. "I would rather have been there in person to say what I'm going to say," he began. "We have received," Hampson told him, "an offer from Elf Aquitaine that we thought was particularly attractive to all the shareholders. We intend to accept it." Mollison was momentarily nonplussed, but recovered sufficiently later in the day to begin making arrangements to hire New York lawyer Joe Flom, a deft manoeuvrer who had fought in the Brascan–Woolworth take-over.

Representing the banks that morning at Sullivan & Cromwell were John Graham and Ted Weir, watching over the transfer of the cash payment from CDC to Elf, ensuring that Aquitaine shares received in return were properly pledged. The money, some (U.S.) $675 million, was transferred from the Bank of Montreal in New York to Citibank, then on to the U.S. Federal Reserve, where it was given a wire-transfer number before being sent back to Elf's banker. One of Elf's lawyers kept hovering in the doorway, looking in at the three of them waiting for the phone call to signify the process was finished. "Have the wire transfers been made yet?" he'd ask. They'd shake their heads and two minutes later he'd be back with the same question. Champagne was planned for the boardroom once the deal was done, so finally the hovering lawyer threatened them with the ultimate: "You're not going to get any champagne until you get those numbers."

Finally, close to noon, Elf was advised that funds had been received, the numbers were passed along, and a Citibank representative arrived with a share certificate for Weir and Graham. They stood and stared at it. Registered to CDC Petroleum, it was for 10,567,000 shares, 49 per cent of Aquitaine Canada. The artwork showed a young woman draped in a classic white gown, holding up the object of the whole hunt: a vial of oil. On the skyline behind her, the hope of the future: rows of lofty oil derricks.

The toast took place in the boardroom with good French vintage champagne bubbling onto the carpet and people spilling out into the hallways to share in the moment of triumph. Then O'Reilly, Weir, and Graham left, nodding to the receptionist, who said brightly: "Have you said goodbye to everybody?" "We only met one person," said O'Reilly, thinking of the nervous Elf lawyer, "and he didn't like us."

By five-thirty, John Graham was back in his Toronto Bank of Montreal offices and had reported the successful day to Doug Gibson. Then he said: "I'm going to go home, have a couple of stiff ones, and tell my wife what I've been doing these last ten days."

The next day, Saturday, Texasgulf director Tony Hampson put on his CDC hat and explained his move to the Texasgulf directors at an emergency board meeting in Stamford, Connecticut. Special guest at the meeting was lawyer Joe Flom. Hampson explained at length the reasons for CDC's interest in Aquitaine and how Texasgulf became involved in the deal. He also stoutly defended his silence on the issue until then. "I felt that I had no obligation to disclose this possibility to the directors or to the management of Texasgulf." He then withdrew from the meeting, knowing that day that he could no longer wear a Texasgulf director's hat. Whelan, the Washington adviser, had been right. Texasgulf was willing to sell, it was just a matter of price. The directors did not want a long lawsuit. There was no need for Joe Flom and his arsenal of defensive tactics.

While the meeting was going on in Stamford, the bankers gathered again, this time around Paul Taylor's backyard pool in Oakville, west of Toronto. The six bankers — Taylor and Nick Johnston from Orion; B of M's Graham and his man from London, Alex Yankovich; Scotiabank's Dennis Belcher and Chris Barnes — sat in the sun, with papers blowing about, drank the odd gin, and redrafted the offering circular so that Yankovich and Barnes could catch the early-evening British Airways flight back to London and begin sending out the telexes. Sixty bankers would be officially informed of the details in an offering circular that ran thirty typed pages.

But before the offering circular was sent, a preliminary phone call was made to test the water. Since it created an IOU to be invited to participate, there was some jockeying among the three banks during the meetings that began the week as to who would place the calls and what banks would be on the list. CDC's O'Reilly wanted two Japanese banks approached — Fuji Bank and the Industrial Bank of Japan — simply because they had regularly called on him. He also added other favourites, Bank Leu of Switzerland and Deutsche Gironzentrale of Germany, because they had done work on a financing that hadn't proceeded and he felt he owed them one.

To achieve fairness in the selection, there was a coin toss, won by the Bank of Montreal, meaning it got to pick first from the list of sixty. The Royal won a second toss, so Scotiabank chose third until each bank had twenty banks to phone with the initial pitch.

On July 5, negotiations over the Texasgulf price continued, with Morgan Stanley representing Texasgulf and Salomon Brothers representing Elf. The Texasgulf offer price would be increased from $50 to $56, with CDC and Elf splitting the added amount. By July 6, a first draft of the syndicated loan agreement was ready and on Wednesday, July 8, CDC met with all the bankers and lawyers. At times the debate became rancorous. One clause was stuffed in to cover any unforeseen increased cost, such as a withholding tax imposed by the central bank. "Objectionable," complained CDC counsel Nigel Gray. "Non-negotiable," said the banks. In the end, the banks won. "There's not a helluva lot you can do about it," admitted Gray. "To a large extent, you are relying on the banks and their expertise."

During the next two days, the banks bound CDC hand and foot. For example, the loan agreement made such sweeping statements as: "The borrower will not without the prior written consent of the banks enter into any merger or consolidation." Subsidiaries were given debt-load ceilings. Working capital could not be less than $400 million. Various financial ratios were dictated by the banks. The CDC won only on the odd point such as future disposals by Petrosar, which did not need bank approval because CDC had only 60 per cent ownership, not full control.

By July 12, a draft loan agreement was sent out to the thirty banks that had agreed to come in on the syndicated loan, now at $1.9 billion, reflecting the increased payment to Texasgulf. On July 15, Belcher left for London to make arrangements for the CDC closing in London at the Guildhall, July 22. He arranged for pens in London (everyone signing the agreement keeps one with the amount printed on it) and four engraved silver trays for the managers' dinner the night before the closing. On July 16, however, the CDC board met in St. John's and fouled up his plans. First, it decided to raise a little more money for general purposes, so bumped the loan a further $200 million to $2.1 billion. Second, while protocol said the closing should be in London, Hampson wanted it in Toronto, for nationalistic reasons.

John Graham had gone pickerel fishing when he received a message to call colleague Garry Sills. When he returned the call, Sills said: "They want $200 million more." "Oh, my God," said Graham. He was at a pay phone and had used his last quarter, so he phoned Regan collect. Once they'd talked, Graham phoned Godsoe and could hear Godsoe (whose mother's name was also Graham) making noises as if he wasn't going to accept the charges: "Which one of my cousins is that?" In the end, the additional $200 million was picked up by banks that had already subscribed.

Toronto's Royal York Hotel was hurriedly booked for the closing, now set for July 23, and on July 21 Dennis Belcher came scrambling back from London. He had the seventy-nine Cross pens stuffed in his suitcase, each printed with the now out-of-date $1.9-billion loan figure. The four silver trays—engraved with the wrong date—were in a plastic bag. He had no Customs declarations, so the trays and pens were impounded at the airport. Belcher was aghast. The managers' dinner was the following evening; he could never arrange replacements in time. The next day, Customs agreed to release the goods, upon payment of $1,000 in duty. Belcher dispatched a colleague in a taxi to the airport to pick them up, mere hours away from the time when the trays would be presented by Scotiabank chairman Ced Ritchie that evening.

At first, the Royal York had refused to rent the Royal Suite for the managers' dinner. Traditionally reserved for Princess Margaret, the suite had just been refurbished. Upon receiving the request, a hotel official said: "I'm not having a bunch of bankers in there burning holes in the carpet." Eventually convinced, the management made the suite, with its separate sitting and dining rooms, available. Scars on the room were unlikely; the dinner traditionally is held the night before a signing so that any wounds caused among the banks or with the borrower during negotiations could be healed.

Belcher was uptight; the bigwigs were coming: his boss, Scotiabank chairman Ced Ritchie, along with Godsoe and Birmingham; from the CDC, Hampson, Gray, O'Reilly, and McGoey; from the Royal, vice-chairman Robert Utting, Regan, Taylor, and Orion executive director R. A. Chamberlain; Bank of Montreal chairman Bill Mulholland, vice-chairman Hart MacDougall, Yankovich, and Graham. Late in the day, Belcher checked the arrangements with Scotiabank general manager Bob Peel, who knows Ritchie's personal taste. Peel pointed out that Ritchie preferred German wines over the French on the menu. A German white was hastily added. Then, when Belcher checked the liquor cabinet in the suite prior to dinner, he saw a bottle of Scotch, Glenlivet, that he hadn't ordered. When he queried the headwaiter, the reply was swift and scathing: "That," said the headwaiter, sounding his most imperious, "is what Mr. Mulholland drinks."

After drinks, they settled around a long table to a dinner of smoked salmon, filet mignon Rossini, and strawberries Romanoff. And a little needling from Joe Regan, who took the opportunity to tease Bill Mulholland. Regan, who has a cottage on Rice Lake, east of Toronto, had seen an item in a local paper about a vacant lot in nearby Cobourg, owned by the Bank of Montreal. The lot, filled with sewage, was creating a local stink in all senses of the word. Waving the clipping at Mulholland, Regan said: "I've got a lot of relatives down that way, what are you going to do about it?" Mulholland, hearing about it for the first time, hooted along with the rest.

Ritchie presented the trays with the wrong dates to the CDC foursome, then promptly took them back, promising they would be re-engraved and returned. (It took months, and whenever McGoey saw Birmingham, he would kid him that the bank must be waiting for the price of silver to go down.)

Tony Hampson made a graceful speech, much of which he repeated at the closing the following day. "It's one of Canada's strengths," he said, "that we can get a group of banks to participate, commit themselves, and understand a credit so quickly. That's just not available in any other banking system in the world today." At the managers' dinner, he also noted that not all of the Canadian assets or liabilities in Texasgulf were known when the deal was struck and the loan granted. "A lot was based on faith."

While they were digesting the $3,000 repast and buying $108 worth of cigars through room service, work was still proceeding on the loan agreement. CDC wanted a few last-minute changes, and John Graham and Ted Weir were trying to work them out without the time-consuming effort of going back to all the participating banks. They worked in Weir's boardroom until about eleven to check final details as Regan, Ritchie, and Godsoe stayed after dinner to swap stories. They were the last to leave except for a fatigued Belcher, who stayed to count the bottles. One ceremony done; one to go.

At a quarter to ten the next morning, about six dozen bankers, lawyers, and trustees gathered with their single borrower, CDC, in the Quebec Room on the mezzanine floor of the Royal York Hotel. Over Danishes and coffee, they exchanged business tidbits and gossip until ten-thirty, when they moved to the Alberta Room for the signing. There, in a pecking order worthy of feudal times, they were arranged around the room by the monetary level of their participation. Each of the sixty-one people signing the 135-page loan agreement that day kept an original, so the stack beside Tony Hampson was three feet high. He signed each first, then sent them snaking around the room.

Two hours later, the signing not finished, they broke for lunch in the flag-festooned Manitoba Room. Ten-inch-high standards everywhere contained the flags from the eight participating countries — Canada in the middle, surrounded by Britain, Germany, France, Switzerland, Japan, Belgium, and the Netherlands. Lunch began with shrimp cocktail, followed by roast prime rib natural with château potatoes, green beans, sliced mushrooms, and a dessert of bombe Suchard.

And, of course, speeches. As chairman of the lunch, Peter Godsoe spoke first, calling everyone's attention to the pen they'd been using, which said $1.9 billion, not $2.1 billion: "We only had one job in this deal and we screwed that up." Then he repeated a comment that Gerry McGoey had made to him during lunch that, in future, pens for syndicated loan deals should have a bulb thermometer that could be squeezed to read the correct amount.

Signing began again about a quarter to two and was completed in thirty minutes. By two-thirty most of the bankers had fled, and five days later the money began to flow.

An Ontario Securities Commission hearing in September found the take-over and the follow-up provisions in order. On September 26, CDC paid $537 million to Elf and exchanged its shares in Texasgulf. The remaining 25.2 per cent of Aquitaine was acquired in October 1981, for $407 million, for a total cost of $1.6 billion. Except for the months-long tax arrangements, all that was left was division day, when the Canadian assets of Texasgulf were split off and deeded over to CDC.

Division day was to be January 4, 1982, and ceremonies were to take place over a pleasant dinner at La Vendue on New York's Sixty-second Street. Nigel Gray and John Hague flew down to collect the documents, only to discover that some of the share certificates hadn't been seen for twenty years. When they were finally found, two lawyers were dispatched in separate taxis to exchange envelopes in New Jersey, a ludicrous trip that avoided a New York transfer tax that would have been $200,000 on a $2-billion deal. Dinner over, the two lawyers hadn't shown, so the diners left messages and moved on to a bar, the Right Bank, at Madison and Sixty-ninth. When it closed with no lawyers yet in sight, the party moved on to another bar that stayed open even later. Finally, the exchanging lawyers were tracked down by phone. They had lost track of the party and had simply gone home. Roused from bed, they delivered the envelopes at 2:15 A.M. Gray checked the contents quickly, saw that they contained the necessary shares to Kidd Creek Mines, Allan Potash, TG Hydrocarbons, as well as assorted title documents, sealed it, and wrote on the front, "Mattel's 83rd St. and 3rd Ave. 2:15 A.M. Jan. 5/82."

The deal was done. And except for a few niggling points, happily so. CDC, for example, didn't much like paying $60 for the flags ordered by the bankers for the closing banquet or being billed $2,000 for all the pens with the wrong date. They kept quiet about that, but they did protest the $900 bill for six-inch-high lucite blocks containing copies of the tombstone — when a year later they still hadn't received any blocks for distribution to CDC staff. In April 1982, when the CDC finally complained, a dozen were dug up and sent over from the Bank of Montreal.

CDC Oil & Gas and CDC Petroleum disappeared, to be renamed Canterra Energy Ltd. Former Aquitaine of Canada president Bernard Isautier was made president, former CDC Oil & Gas president Jack O'Brien named chairman. The Canadian assets of Texasgulf became Kidd Creek Mines.

The CDC had won its diversity — and gained heavy debt. In 1981, cash flow was $543 million, with about half dedicated to pay interest on all debt. In 1982, cash flow increased to $643 million, but interest payments, because of higher rates, accelerated to $632 million — almost all of cash flow. Interest paid on the jumbo deal alone was $370 million and contributed to CDC's $125-million loss that year. While the company pays, the bankers prosper. Perhaps John Graham's statement is typical: "It was a high point in my career, one that got me a lot of visibility." Like most of the men involved, he has since been promoted. For the three lead banks, each can expect to make about $9 million to $10 million on the deal, peanuts in a $2.1-billion jumbo.

But for the take-over game, the end was at hand. About the time of the closing banquet, finance minister Allan MacEachen called all the senior bankers to Ottawa and ordered that they finance no more takeovers. The pressure caused on the Canadian dollar by all that money leaving the country was too great. The ruling has not yet been revoked. It was the last of the jumbos.

EIGHT

A COUNTRY BOY ON THE RUN

Ced Ritchie

CHAIRMAN, THE BANK OF NOVA SCOTIA

IT WAS LESS than a month after the ill-fated budget of November 1981, and the federal government was once more the hated target of the business community. Robert Johnstone, the newly appointed deputy minister of international trade, had been invited to the stuffy York Club in Toronto for dinner and discussion with about two dozen Toronto businessmen. The group, fed up with Ottawa and fortified by drink, seized the opportunity presented by the private dinner to participate in their favourite blood sport — Ottawa-bashing. Johnstone was an old Ottawa hand, having begun his career two decades earlier in the Bank of Canada. In his previous post as deputy minister of industry, trade, and commerce, he had been involved in the Massey bail-out. Though accustomed to adversarial situations, he was woefully unprepared for the pasting handed out that night.

Toronto's establishment was looking for blood. They wanted Ottawa to understand, after the interventionist — nay, socialist — National Energy Program, announced a year earlier, just how far in the wrong direction finance minister Allan MacEachen's budget was taking the country. Free enterprise, they argued, was dead in the water. There was no room left in the country for risk. It was an old, familiar song.

As the evening wore on, Johnstone became more and more beleaguered and defensive, for he was being castigated about a budget that he'd not been involved with, one that he freely admitted he didn't understand and shouldn't be expected to explain. Finally, he pointed out that specific government views on the economy had been advanced in documents released with the budget. The implication was that if they were printed, they could be believed. Noranda Mines president Adam Zimmerman exploded. "Why should we believe you? Who gives a shit that it's in black and white?"

The atmosphere turned ugly. Suddenly, Johnstone received support from a businessman speaking in a voice edged with sufficient anger to catch everyone's attention. It belonged to Bank of Nova Scotia chairman Ced Ritchie. He took on Zimmerman in three swift interventions, making points about the budget that Johnstone should have cited, the heel of his outstretched hand thumping the table for emphasis. It was enough to defang the venomous attacks; the ugliness in the room dissipated, and everyone was relieved that Ritchie had stepped in. The intervention demonstrated both Ritchie's solid connections with Ottawa and his command over the corporate world.

In the galaxy of business, where there are few shooting stars, Cedric Elmer Ritchie is a distant sun. Although he has power over those who depend on his light and warmth for their very life and growth, he is publicly all but invisible. As the least extroverted of the Big Five bank bosses, he is happy with his self-imposed secretiveness. In 1982 he gave precisely two public speeches: one at the obligatory annual shareholders' meeting in Halifax, the other a ten-minute effort to a shipping conference in Saint John. Early in 1983, he edged farther out of the cocoon with a speech to the Canadian Club of Toronto. Ritchie runs the bank's annual meetings like a small-town station agent eyeing his pocket watch. A binder supplies his every word, right from "Good morning" through to adjournment. He has suggested answers to dozens of potential questions any impertinent shareholder might ask. Even with such fastidious preparation and throttled control, he still sweats out this public appearance; he has been known to feel physically ill on the morning of the meeting.

He soundly dislikes meeting journalists and steadfastly refuses most requests for interviews. In the early 1970s, when he was a member of the executive council of the Canadian Bankers' Association, the members would all make themselves available at breakfast meetings with journalists. Not Ritchie. He would wait outside for the sessions to be over even though they were normally pleasant, non-confrontational occasions. At a branch opening in Moncton, he once consented to an interview with a local reporter. The tone of the article was to be "New Brunswick boy makes good." The toughest question: "Would you counsel a young man to go into banking today?" Even so, Ritchie awaited the interview with fear and survived it with ill-concealed unease.

To assume that Ced Ritchie is simply shy is to miss the point. He is basically insecure. Only among his own kind does he appear all bonhomie and bravado, and much of that is just cover-up bluster. At Conrad Black's must-attend annual black-tie dinner at the Toronto Club following the Hollinger Argus annual meeting, one of *the* Establishment gatherings of the year, Ritchie all but sprints among the knots of high-muck-a-mucks in attendance. He will josh with Inco's Chuck Baird, greet Wood Gundy's Ted Medland like a long-lost friend, and curse amiably at the sight of Power Corporation's Paul Desmarais. "Christ, there's that god-damned Desmarais again," he'll bellow. "And here comes the world's worst banker," Desmarais will retort.

And always the back-slap. Although it seems to be an offensive weapon the way he wields it, the back-slap as practised by Ritchie is really a defence mechanism. Barely five-foot-ten, he is among the shortest of the chief executives at this or most other gatherings. The back-slap is his misguided attempt to even the odds in any encounter. His arm begins the swoop somewhere near belt level, rides upward behind him, gaining speed, until it reaches the zenith of its arc somewhere above his head. Sufficient momentum attained, the hand, closed tightly until then to reduce aerodynamic drag, is unleashed. The fingers splay out, the wrist stiffens, and the arm comes whistling down towards some unsuspecting part of the intended recipient's upper torso. In its full force, properly planted, a Ritchie greeting has made colleagues feel as if they were about to be propelled across the room.

Ritchie scarcely needs such an attention-getting gesture, for he has clout enough without it. At the 1980 Hollinger dinner, for example, among the other conversations he held, he readily pledged his bank to a $100,000 donation after then Iron Ore president Brian Mulroney told Ritchie about his fund-raising campaign for St. Francis Xavier University. He can also commit his bank to a $500-million loan on the strength of his word. But still there is an insecurity that tugs at his insides even when he is in his seat of appointed power, at the regular board meetings. Scotiabank president Gordon Bell explains Ritchie's style this way: "He goes into every board meeting and tables his resignation. If it hasn't been picked up after two hours, he's OK."

His bank, with its twenty-three thousand employees, 1,000 branches in Canada, 100 offices in fifty-two countries, and $50 billion in assets, is strongest in international assets and consumer credit, carries the largest gold inventory of any Canadian bank, but ranks as the weakest in number of corporate accounts. It has an inordinate share of the consumer loan market and has made more than six million consumer loans in the past twenty years. It is a bank for the blue-collar man and the working woman. Thin in the top executive ranks, it is the most conservatively run of the Big Five banks. As a result, during the go-go days of 1980 and 1981, when take-overs were a dime a dozen and financiers fell all over their own feet to fund them, Scotiabank missed out on some of the business. As the recession deepened, however, Scotiabank, along with the TD, was most healthy. With the downturn and business failures, Scotiabank fared better simply because it had fewer loans in the areas that were badly bleeding. Even the *Globe and Mail*, not noted for worshipping corporations, gave this praise in an editorial last year: "The Bank of Nova Scotia has been noted among banks for looking long before it leaps, thus keeping its feet out of many a bog."

Opening-night reception for the 1982 World Bank/International Monetary Fund conference in Toronto. It is the first time in the thirty-eight-year history of the organization that it has come to Canada, and the limousines are lined up four abreast on the street outside the Harbour Castle Hilton convention centre. A knot of the curious cluster at the entrance to watch the passing parade. It is tough to separate hustlers from hangers-on, to know the princes from the paparazzi. Finance ministers and bankers from around the world pour out of limousines the size of tanks, their very anonymity a prize to be guarded. If a terrorist came upon the scene, he would barely know whom to grab, because there are so few recognizable faces.

Amid the flow is Ced Ritchie, his head ducked low, his hand splayed across his cheek to pull a cigarette from his mouth and subtly shield his face from the cameras at the same time. Driving his stocky frame up the escalator, he ploughs into the main hall with the confidence that comes from being among kindred souls—three to four thousand of them. Drink in hand, he fires up another cigarette, then squints against the curling smoke. Finally, he takes a deep breath—as if what he needs is firm resolve more than a firm handshake—as he greets central bank governors, finance ministers, and the upper echelon of the banking community from every non-Communist country in the world. Ced Ritchie doesn't so much enter a room as launch himself through it. Every one of his raw nerve endings seems visible through the regulation blue suit as he moves about the room, gripping dozens of hands with a firm squeeze, his right shoulder ducking towards the floor with a jerk that forces each person in turn to dip downwards in concert. The result is synchronized bobbing and bowing as he hurtles from circle to circle.

He looks older than his fifty-six years. His face is hard-worked, almost haggard, as he rests his chin on the palm of his hand, the fingers pushed up the cheek, deepening the already craggy, vertical furrows that leave ruts so deep they have dark and shadowed bottoms. His eyes are hooded. Twin creases rise from the bridge of his nose, one thrusting higher than the other, giving his face a sideways tilt. In profile, it has a concave shape, the chin and forehead sticking out; the eye seems to turn and offer itself in full view so that he appears like some nursery-rhyme drawing of the man in the moon.

A brief word with some Philippine bankers, some phrases with a passing

Brit, then a longer conversation with Paul Volcker, the man who brought high interest rates to North America. Volcker, chairman of the U.S. Federal Reserve Board, towers over Ritchie by at least a foot. They chat amiably amid the cacophony of the room, trading pleasantries and frequently interrupted by delegates who come to touch Volcker as if to feel for themselves how tough he really is. Ritchie steers away again and continues to thread his way about, ignoring the colour-coded name badges (green for delegates and top advisers; brown for guests, including the senior bankers; blue for ministers of finance and their deputies; orange for journalists), and looking rather for the familiar faces of those he has come to know in his thirty years as an international banker. Here a welcoming handshake, there a heartier back-slap, a final word with Toronto mayor Art Eggleton, and he is gone less than an hour after he arrived.

The following morning, at the official opening, Ritchie, decked out in a grey suit, his blonde wife, Barbara, in tow, moves through the airport-style metal detectors with the rest and takes his seat in a corner section reserved for Canadian special guests. Nearby are TD's Dick Thomson and his wife, Heather; B of M's deputy chairman Grant Reuber; a smattering of former Liberal finance ministers — Mitchell Sharp and Donald Macdonald; a former Clark government minister, Michael Wilson; folks from the investment community, including Latham Burns, chairman of Burns, Fry; Greenshields president Brian Drummond; and Wood Gundy chairman Ted Medland, who takes the seat beside Ritchie. Finance minister Allan MacEachen opens the meeting by calling upon Prime Minister Trudeau, who delivers himself of a bland call for national will, international consensus, and other ethereal ideals. Next up is IMF chairman Abdul-Latif al-Hamad, minister of finance for Kuwait and the first chairman from the Arab world. Throughout, Ritchie sits, his translating device plugged into both ears as al-Hamad rattles along in Arabic. He applauds heartily for Trudeau and for the IMF managing director, Jacques de Larosière. After a morning of pomp and little circumstance, the speeches fall away badly, as Third World countries line up to roll pleas from the podium.

The atmosphere of the conference is generally nervous, as many national economies are ailing, and countries propped up by enormous international loans, like Mexico and Poland, are making noises that they might default. A piece of corridor banter captures the mood. Says one delegate lightly to another, just to start a conversation: "Est-ce la fin du monde?" (Is it the end of the world?) The second replies more thoughtfully: "C'est la fin d'un *certain* monde."

For Ritchie, the week is a blur of parties, receptions, drinks, and canapés. Invited to thirty-four key events that week, he accepted thirteen and shows up for only half of those. The first is one of the most prestigious, the reception given by British consul-general Reginald Holloway at his Toronto home, on the Saturday evening prior to the opening. Invitations are hard to come by. "To get into the British Embassy party," one banker cracks, "you either have to know the Ambassador or the chairman of [British bank] NatWest." Among those Ritchie rubs shoulders with are the chancellor of the exchequer, Sir Geoffrey Howe; Gordon Richardson, governor of the Bank of England; Gerald Bouey, governor of the Bank of Canada; Sir Michael Herries, governor of the Royal Bank of Scotland; Thomas Risk, governor of the Bank of Scotland; A. W. Clausen, president of the World Bank; Lord Moran, British high commissioner; and a flotilla of industrialists and lesser lights.

Ritchie attends no galas of his own. The bank had originally planned a black-tie dinner at the Harbour Castle on Sunday night, which would have attracted two thousand to its glittering spectacle — and cost $150,000. Planning began a year earlier under Robert Peel, the bank's major-domo and chief of protocol. Peel, a debonair man with curly grey hair, knows every banker of note in the world. For him, life is one continuous receiving line. An art buff, he has entrée into Bavarian castles and private collections in New York. Decked out in what for him is almost a uniform — black suit, white shirt, and narrow knit black tie — he has travelled the world with former Scotiabank chairman Bill Nicks and sailed the Mediterranean with the king of Greece. He also tended the ailing Nicks when he was stricken ill in Paris, and was one of the few who ever visited him in his home in Toronto. When the regime changed and Ritchie took over, Peel continued to serve in the new king's court.

A veteran of World Bank/IMF meetings since 1961, Peel took sick early on during the planning for the gala dinner and dance. After some time away from the office, he returned and broached cancellation of the party with Ritchie, saying: "What if I got sick in the final days?" Ritchie was already having second thoughts himself. The economy had turned down, and much of the bank's 150th-anniversary celebrations (except for the publication of a corporate history) had already been cancelled. Ritchie's attitude was: "That's just an ego trip, me sitting up there with prime ministers and presidents. Who needs it?" The dinner was cancelled and lavish entertaining was left to others.

The Bank of Montreal filled the Concert Hall of the Royal York Hotel one night and took a hundred people out on a lake cruise on another; the Toronto-Dominion overran the Art Gallery of Ontario; the province of Ontario spent $200,000 on an evening reception; and the federal government held a concert at Roy Thomson Hall with Jon Vickers and an all-Canadian cast followed by a buffet reception for three thousand guests. By contrast, Scotiabank held three lunches for thirty-eight people in its fourth-floor directors' dining room and two dinners for 160 at the tired but tony Toronto Club.

Of all the events in Ritchie's week, Scotiabank's Toronto Club dinner on Thursday night is the one that catches fire. Canadians attending include Ontario premier William Davis, Crown Life chairman Bob Bandeen, secretary of state for external affairs Mark MacGuigan, and D. G. (Bud) Willmot, chairman of the Molson Companies Ltd. There are commercial bankers from Guatemala, Guyana, Peru, and beyond; central bankers from Bermuda, El Salvador, Kenya, and elsewhere; diplomats from the United Nations, the Philippines, and the People's Republic of China; not to mention a battalion of international organization reps and a bevy of U.S. financiers. Bill Davis speaks, gibing with the assemblage in his best auctioneer style, poking fun at Charles Bronfman and his Montreal Expos, who have just lost out in the pennant race, placing a football bet with Stelco chairman Peter Gordon, and dropping one-liners. For his part, Ritchie delivers a short speech, carefully leaving out a worrisome phrase that described the times as "a week of disturbing news," for this is a night of festivities and merry-making over sole and a German white wine, Alberta beef and a Savigny-les-Serpentières 1974.

Without warning, a woman in a glittering green dress rises to her feet in response to Ritchie's comments. She is Claire Giannini Hoffman, daughter of Amadeo Giannini, the founder of the Bank of America, the world's largest bank. He had started his bank, known first as the Bank of Italy, in San Francisco in 1904. After the earthquake of 1906, Giannini set up shop with a bag of money and a plank amid the rubble and offered to finance reconstruction. His daughter, worried about the present-day Bank of America's changed attitude towards its customers, praises Ritchie and Scotiabank's "great warmth and humanity." She warns: "Don't lose that quality."

When the glamorous week is over, there is time to reflect that the IMF decided little, that its policies would make but a slight difference to an anxious world. What matters to Ced Ritchie and his Canadian peers is that the week has gone without a serious hitch and the tightrope of international finance has stayed secure, if precarious. The world is no wealthier, but then, it isn't their job to create wealth, is it? The bankers merely move the money around, and as long as the haves and the have-nots continue to need each other, the bankers know they will be secure.

Tucked away in the middle of that mad week was a quiet lunch called by Prime Minister Pierre Trudeau that reflected Ritchie's impeccable political connections. Among the other guests was former Canadian Pacific chairman Ian Sinclair, who would take the day's topic to the public — how the government's six-and-five policy could be sold to the private sector. Ritchie is as close to Pierre Trudeau as any businessman in the country. "Of all the bankers," says Bob Johnstone, "Ritchie is probably most *simpatico* with the Liberal Party. He's seen around town more. He is more interested in working with the government than some of the others." Because Ritchie is a former Diefenbaker Conservative who was turned on by Trudeau, Ritchie's connection is both noted and knocked by his peers. Once, at an Ottawa gathering, several businessmen found themselves standing together during a break in proceedings. Among the group were Commerce chairman Russ Harrison, Royal chairman Rowlie Frazee, and Ritchie. Quipped Harrison, pointing at Ritchie: "For the first time they've planted a Liberal mole in the higher echelons of banking."

When corporate and community leaders were invited to Rideau Hall for lunch with Governor General Ed Schreyer and the seven world leaders attending the Montebello economic summit in July 1981, the list of businessmen included was short. Trudeau invited a few people who supported his constitutional position and some Montreal businessmen known in Quebec as "integral Liberals," such as Charles Bronfman, Paul Desmarais, and Mel Dobrin. There were only two businessmen invited from Toronto: Conrad Black and Ced Ritchie.

When Ritchie was given the Order of Canada in 1981, he was told at first he would be allowed only one guest at the reception, since there were sixty recipients and room for a total of 125 people. He would, of course, take his wife, but he wanted to bring their university-aged daughters, Heather and Kim, as well. A phone call to Esmond Butler, secretary to the Governor General, solved the matter. Butler escorted the two girls to the ceremonies and receptions by pretending that they were members of his own family.

In return for access and a hearing in Ottawa, Ritchie gives the government his respect. He would not, for example, ever publicly castigate — or even call into question — Trudeau or his policies. In 1976, when the Royal's Earle McLaughlin launched a particularly virulent attack on Trudeau, Ritchie told people privately that McLaughlin had blundered. Trudeau, said Ritchie, is "too strong an adversary with too many guns at his disposal." He added, "That will be held against McLaughlin for a long time."

Ritchie's loyalties, in certain cases, do include Conservatives. When Darcy McKeough resigned as treasurer of Ontario in 1978, he had lunch with Ritchie the following day. At that point, McKeough had no plans (he is now chairman of Union Gas), and at the end of the lunch, Ritchie said: "I leave you with three thoughts. I'd like to have you join our board. If you'd like to work in a bank, you've got a position here. If you want to go out on your own, you write the cheque and I'll endorse it." Ritchie also knows and has the respect of many civil servants, such as the former and current deputy ministers of finance, Ian Stewart and Marshall (Mickey) Cohen. Ritchie has put his position simply: "You make better headway by talking privately than by criticizing publicly. Too many businessmen just go to Ottawa with a self-serving or a narrow viewpoint. You have to build credibility over time."

And Ritchie has done so, from the days of the Porter Commission, which reviewed the industry prior to the 1967 Bank Act revision, to the 1980s, when he became a key member of the Business Council on National Issues, a high-powered lobby group encompassing only chief executive officers. As a result, when he does lose his temper, he does so carefully, out of sight. In 1978, during the Bank Act hearings, Inspector-General William Kennett was a witness before the Parliamentary committee. In talking about term-preferreds, he used the phrase "a pretty hideous kind of situation" to describe the impact of these financing vehicles on some unsecured creditors. A Canadian Press reporter, misunderstanding Kennett's point, wrote a story that said Kennett was talking about the chartered banks in general. Ritchie read the report in the *Globe and Mail*, became livid, and immediately telephoned Kennett. Without asking for an explanation, Ritchie tore into Kennett as if the man — who had been involved in revising the Bank Act, writing great chunks of it himself — didn't understand banking. Kennett was stunned by the attack and later told someone else: "I don't expect to be treated like some kind of office boy for the banks."

Normally, however, Ritchie offers not criticism but sound proposals, often in conjunction with the competition, particularly Bank of Montreal chairman Bill Mulholland, with whom Ritchie gets along best among all his confrères. "At Bank of Canada meetings," says Mulholland, "more often than not I'll say something and he'll agree." There is a mutual respect as a result of their equally tough competitive instincts. Coming from an investment banking background, Mulholland is a scrapper. So is Ritchie, because he's had to beat his way up from the bottom. Says Mulholland: "He competes more like I'm used to. He's hard, but he's not a hard loser. You can slug it out like hell today and be on good terms and co-operate on something tomorrow. Ced plays hard ball. He's no softie. He's not a bureaucrat, he's a good banker. He knows where the trading room is."

Mulholland and Ritchie combined in a joint proposal to finance minister Allan MacEachen in October 1981. Faced with MacEachen's threat of an excess profits tax on banks in his fall budget unless they did something on their own, staff at Scotiabank and the Bank of Montreal worked up a proposal called the Temporary Housing Interest Stabilization Program (THISP). The scheme, they said, would reduce mortgage rates from the then staggering levels of 20 per cent down to 16.42 per cent. To achieve this they proposed that the government would change tax rules for those individuals who loaned mortgage money to banks and other financial institutions. Such an investor would receive a rate of return lower than the going market rate (the government would make up the difference); thus the mortgage could also be priced below usual rates, because it cost the bank less than the usual rates.

The scheme did not gain acceptance among other bankers. In fact, Mulholland met animosity when he tried it out on the Royal's Frazee (who favoured a deferred-interest plan). In turn, B of M and Scotiabank disagreed with the Royal's plan, arguing that deferring mortgage renewals meant trouble. The staff research presented to Mulholland and Ritchie showed that the number of mortgages to be renewed in 1982 was estimated at an all-time high — some 40 per cent of the $118 billion outstanding. If rates didn't drop in the U.S., the research said, and the Canadian federal government introduced a deferral programme, a log-jam of monstrous proportions would be created. Rolling 1982 renewals ahead to 1983 (along with the 25 per cent of mortgages already scheduled to come due that year) would mean that fully two-thirds of all Canadian mortgages would come up for renewal in 1983. Faced with MacEachen's threat and those calculations, Ritchie and Mulholland opted to unveil THISP. Said Mulholland at the final meeting: "Why don't we let the rabbit out of its cage and see how far it'll run?"

It ran far enough to distract attention from the other ideas in the race, although MacEachen was not mightily impressed. He even went so far as to dump on the idea in the House of Commons with unusually strong language: "Last week I had a suggestion from presidents of two of the banks. They proposed another scheme, which involved the minister of finance and the taxpayers picking up the bill." MacEachen concluded icily: "In these circumstances I would like the banks to strive more diligently to find schemes which would cause them to bleed a bit." In spite of MacEachen's political grandstanding, Ritchie and Mulholland regarded the exercise as a success. As Mulholland said later, speaking for them both: "Some days just stopping things from getting going is an achievement. We brought out an inherent conflict. If you wanted to do something about the problem, we gave them a solution. We played the devil's advocate, put forward the best package we could — but it involved spending some money. If you don't like that, it's a dead end."

It was a dead end. The issue was defused; Ottawa did nothing.

"The minister understood what we were doing," said Mulholland. "He's a very sophisticated man. A lesser man would have gotten angry." Lesser bankers, too.

Ced Ritchie began his stewardship of Scotiabank as a throw-back to previous regimes when all of the banks were one-man bands. His management style is autocratic, his manner demanding. When underlings prepare something for his eyes, they try to second-guess his every whim, fearful that his disapproval of them or their views will mean banishment. More than one employee has been taken aside and told, "You're not welcome in Mr. Ritchie's doorway any more."

Fruitless staff hours are spent preparing presentations for which Ritchie will likely have one of two reactions: immediate embrace or eternal shelving. Once Ritchie makes up his mind, he rarely changes it. Those who argue with him do so at their peril. When Chargex (later Visa) was begun by four banks in 1966, Scotiabank stayed out. In 1973, Scotiabank began to look at getting in — or obtaining the Mastercharge arrangement for Canada. (Mastercharge later entered into an agreement with the Bank of Montreal.) The banks already in Chargex demanded that Scotiabank pay a late-entry fee of $9 million. That fee, coupled with start-up costs and first-year losses, meant an investment of about $20 million. Ritchie wanted Chargex. Gordon Bell, then an assistant general manager for administration, was pushing for Mastercharge. At the final meeting, the others who had favoured Mastercharge fell into line when they heard Ritchie's strong views. Ritchie turned to Bell and asked: "Which is it?" Bell replied, "Mastercharge." Without missing a beat, Ritchie announced: "It'll be Chargex and you're making the board presentation."

Bell presented the pro-Chargex arguments just as if he believed them all along, and received approval from the board of directors. Then Ritchie called him in and said: "Now, you're going to implement it." And he did, for refusal or whining would have meant a career stalled. Says Bell: "He's got the power of life and death. His method is control and involvement. There are a lot of American banks that have been in trouble in the last year or so, banks headed by people without those attributes. They didn't know what was going on within their own banks."

Ritchie does know what's happening at Scotiabank. Of all the senior bankers in the system who have scrabbled their way up from the teller's cage as he did, Ritchie is the one who still has cronies spotted around the place—in the vault, on inspection, in the gold department. Relentlessly loyal, they offer a clean read on the place and allow him to perpetuate the notion that he is really "one of the boys," not the boss at all. His first stop most mornings—as early as before seven—is not his own office but the trading desk on the tenth floor, where he is on a first-name basis with traders Tom Healey and Gus Wong, from whom he finds out the currency exchange rate and the price of gold. At the end of the day, particularly if he's on the road, he'll be the last to bed, staying up to score a few drinks with staff or a customer in hopes that it will bring some business.

"He's a very disarming, unaffected guy," says former Bank of Montreal chairman Fred McNeil. "He will not stay out of putting his fingers in deals. He's a rough-talking guy, and I don't think he's building strength beneath him. He just keeps trying to work harder. That's stupidity. He'll kill himself."

Dying in harness might just be Ced Ritchie's idea of ecstasy—as long as he leaves the bank in good shape. He wants no personal aggrandizement and religiously follows the dictum that his predecessor, Tom Boyles, once gave his PR man: "Your job is to keep the press off our back." For Ritchie, it is the institution, not the individual, that matters. Once when Ferdinand Marcos, president of the Philippines, visited Vancouver, he had meetings with bank officials to talk about current and prospective business. Marcos needed to borrow five limousines; Ritchie's approval was sought. Ritchie refused, saying: "Military dictatorships come and go. I want the bank to go on forever. Let's not get too close to Marcos." Still, in 1978, Ritchie took two dozen directors and their spouses to Manila for a board meeting, one of the few full board meetings held outside the country. There were courtesy calls, tours, glittering dinners at the palace, and a series of gifts exchanged between Ritchie and Marcos and his wife, Imelda. While not wanting to get "too close," Ritchie knew that a show of support for the embattled political regime, a demonstration of the bank's interest in the area, wouldn't hurt business. After all, Ritchie regards himself, as does the Pope, as a direct descendant of those who have gone before. He sees himself in the same courageous mould as the bank's pioneer officers. As he once put it bluntly, when he still headed up the international department: "Our fellows before us weren't afraid to go into these countries and make a buck."

Cedric Elmer Ritchie was born in 1927 in the New Brunswick village of Upper Kent. Nestled on the gently sloping land of the Saint John River valley, Upper Kent was little more than a wide spot in the road, a dozen or so houses. The Great Depression suffocated the two major industries of the region, potatoes and lumber, making times tough for all and prospects grim for the coming generation. Even local magnate Andrew McCain, founder of the McCain Foods empire, had to wait for the 1937 upturn in the potato crop to turn in his ten-year-old flivver for a new Buick.

Ritchie's father died young, leaving his wife to raise their son and daughter herself. A God-fearing United Church member, she was a woman of great strength and character who became postmistress in Upper Kent in order to support her children. After Ritchie finished high school, in 1945, there was no money for university. With the war over, there was little point in joining the army. There was but one way to get the hell out of Bath, where he had attended high school, and that was to join the town's only institution with connections to elsewhere, the bank. The lone bank in town was the Bank of Nova Scotia. While Ritchie's early days were spent far away from the international world he would one day work in, he was influenced by the region's trade connections, forged over a century. Sending seed potatoes to Cuba and other southern islands, lumber to London and beyond, the people in the part of the universe that Ritchie grew up in instinctively understood the interdependence of nations.

Starting as a teller, Ritchie found his initial progress to be slow and based on the wrong criteria. "It wasn't what you did so much as how long you were on the job before you were promoted," he recalls. From the customer's point of view, things were wrong, too: there was reluctance to trust banks as institutions, even fear. People saw bank branches, says Ritchie, as "pieces of paper here, money here, and a cage here." Bankers made customers feel "as if it were a privilege to come into a bank, not as if it were a competitive business."

Eventually Ritchie was promoted to Halifax, then Montreal, and finally to the inspection staff. There he travelled the system, with a fellow inspector, showing up in surprise visits to ensure that each branch was abiding by all the rules and regulations. During the half-dozen years he was on the road, he searched for fraud and picked nits in about 80 per cent of the branches in the system, including the Caribbean. Those years on the road established both his continuing demand for perfection and his high level of plain hard work. They provided wacky moments, too. During the early 1950s, Ritchie was travelling with Bill McMillan (now a vice-president) and J. W. Chisholm (now a general manager in corporate credit). They had just checked into their hotel on a swing through Western Canada when a posse of local police showed up. It seemed that the three bankers fit the description of the notorious bank-robbing Boyd gang from Toronto. The bankers' bags had yet to arrive, and it took some fast explaining to convince the police of their real identities.

On another occasion, Ritchie was sent with fellow inspector Ambrose McGourty to check on a possible kiting operation in Grand Banks, Newfoundland. The matter was cleared up quickly, and the two returned to St. John's for the flight to the mainland. As is often the way on the island, fog closed in and they couldn't fly out. McGourty, not one to miss a chance for a friendly drink or three, stayed away from alcohol the first day, but when the flights remained grounded the second day, he couldn't resist the call of the hotel bar. The following morning, he discovered that his upper dentures were missing. Convinced he'd put them on the toilet tank the night before and they'd been swept away by the chambermaid, McGourty, with Ritchie in tow as counsel, went to the hotel's assistant manager, told him the story, and demanded $300 to replace his upper plate. The assistant manager, with his English accent, director's suit, and white carnation, was not sympathetic. In fact, he suggested that McGourty was probably under the influence and could have lost the plate anywhere.

McGourty protested vigorously and continued to blame the errant chambermaid. Finally, the dispute was taken to the hotel manager for arbitration. With Ritchie, McGourty, and the two hoteliers now gathered, the manager asked his assistant to prove his allegation that McGourty had been drinking. With that, the assistant pulled a wad of bar chits from his pocket and spread them out on the desk. Each had a time-date stamp. The first purchase of the evening was signed by McGourty and charged to his room with a legible, correct signature. As the evening passed, however, each signature became more and more indecipherable until the final drink was paid for by a scratch and several wiggles.

"What have you got to say to that?" demanded the manager.

McGourty looked at Ritchie, faced the manager, and replied: "I'll settle for $150." The hotel paid.

McGourty put Ritchie through his paces in other ways, too. McGourty always carried a baseball cap as well as a ball and glove on the road. When a junior was sent out to travel with him, if he couldn't play a good game of catch, he was given a bad report. Ritchie evidently passed muster, for he was made an assistant inspector in 1954.

It was also on the road that he met his wife. He fell ill in Lethbridge, was admitted to Municipal Hospital, and was tended by a nurse from Saskatoon named Barbara Binnington. Even a lovestruck banker knows his place, however; and it took the passage of two more years and an appointment as accountant in the bank's main branch at 44 King Street West in Toronto before he could stop living out of a suitcase and marry her in 1956.

By then, the bank was in a period of boom. From three hundred branches at the end of the Second World War, it had doubled in size. High overheads had yet to send branch costs skyward, so strength was based on setting up branches in as many locations as possible. For his part, Ritchie was well placed to ride the wave up in the bank through this period of great growth. During the 1960s, chairman Bill Nicks astutely put the bank into both international and consumer loan business, head starts that no other bank has yet been able to overcome. Since 1958, the bank has financed the purchase of more than 2.5 million cars in Canada. The bank now has 54 per cent of its assets in foreign currencies and about 23 per cent of the Canadian consumer loan market; Nicks was building a far different bank from the one Ritchie had joined.

Ritchie progressed through the system as chief accountant in 1960, was made an assistant general manager in 1963, joint general manager in 1966, and chief general manager for international in 1968. The title chief general manager had been reserved until then for the operating head of the whole bank. Giving it to Ritchie indicated both Nicks's high regard for international and his admiration for Ritchie. Momentum was beginning to build behind Ritchie as Nicks's successor. Working twelve-hour days, fuelling himself with chocolate bars to keep his energy level high, Ritchie was conscious of Nicks's grooming hand.

Still, when Nicks picked a president and a potential successor in 1970, he chose not the hard-driving workaholic Ritchie, but the urbane and affable Art Crockett. As a former manager of Toronto main branch, Crockett had played the system well and lived in the right part of town, down the street from Nicks in blue-plate Rosedale. When Crockett was made president, Ritchie became chief general manager — in charge of day-to-day operations — but was very clearly number three. Ten years older than Ritchie, Crockett looked to be tipped for the top. From the outside, at least.

In fact, the race had already been won by Ritchie. Insiders knew that Ritchie was still being groomed and that the appointment of Crockett was just a holding operation, an honorific posting, until Ritchie was ready. Ritchie, however, had little first-hand chance to learn from the master. By 1970, Nicks's marriage dissolved, his wife moved out of the Rosedale house, and Nicks took to travelling more than he had previously. In Paris, he collapsed and was admitted to the American Hospital, where he underwent surgery. Nicks was away from the office for nine months, even missing the shareholders' annual meeting in January 1971. It wasn't really until the fall of 1971, at a board meeting in Vancouver, that colleagues agreed that Nicks was his old self again.

His recovery was brief, however; on January 4, 1972, he was dead of a massive heart attack. Attendees at the funeral saw the ashen face of Ritchie and knew there was more on his mind than sorrow at the passing of a boss. He was also grieving the fact that he hadn't had an opportunity to sit at Nicks's feet for long enough. Some even said that Robert MacIntosh, the outspoken deputy chief general manager and favourite of the Toronto investment community, might get the board's nod. But Ritchie and his close associate Rod Taylor knew better. "Sitting with

Ritchie," recalls Taylor, "the afternoon of Nicks's death, he knew—and he knew I knew—that the mantle would fall to him after certain orderly formalities. You could see him grow—almost from a boy to a man. He became very reflective."

With the annual shareholders' meeting scheduled for Halifax a mere eight days after Nicks's death, no one on the board or in the bank was ready for precipitous moves. President Art Crockett read the speech to the subdued assembly just as it had been written for Nicks. After lengthy deliberation by the board, deputy chairman Tom Boyles was named chairman; no other shifts were announced. By turning to Boyles, with his fifty years in banking, the staid Bank of Nova Scotia signalled business as usual. Yet Boyles, everyone was well aware, was sixty-eight years old; his tenure was sure to be brief. He didn't even bother to move into the chairman's mansion, and it was sold. Boyles didn't like the chauffeur-driven car much either. He and his wife would celebrate Christmas in Peterborough, Ontario, but Boyles was petrified that any car he travelled in might become snowbound. The chauffeur would drop the two of them off at the Bay Street terminal in Toronto and they'd ride to Peterborough by bus.

As the next annual meeting approached (moved to December that year), the executive committee of the board, led by Molson's Donald G. Willmot, stockbroker William C. Harris, and Halifax lawyer Don McInnes, decided that Ritchie should replace Crockett as president and CEO. The executive committee presented its recommendation to the full board and it was accepted with hardly a raised eyebrow. Said director Harrison McCain of the switch: "We thought it was surprising, but not controversial. There was some disappointment for Arthur, because we thought he was a fine fellow, but Ritchie was better for the job." Crockett was made a deputy chairman and passed the next eight years, until he retired, running large real estate developments for the bank, helping out the Canadian Opera Company with fund-raising drives, and a handful of other public-spirited duties.

During the next two years, Ritchie consolidated his position and in 1974 took on the third of the titles, chairman. Boyles was named honorary chairman and, to ease his departure from the executive floor and prevent any possible interference in the running of the bank, Ritchie ordered a suite of offices built for Boyles on the second floor. The renovations cost $85,000. In addition to a book-lined office, a reception area, and a dining room that sat ten, there was a bathroom with marble floors and gold-plated faucets. As Boyles himself described it: "It's the best night-club in the city."

Boyles safely stashed away, Ritchie proceeded to place his own people in key positions. Scott McDonald, a lanky Harvard MBA, was put in charge of international; Peter Godsoe, also a Harvard MBA, was put in charge of the Western hemisphere (both were in their late thirties); Robert MacIntosh, with his doctorate in economics — perhaps the man most surprised that the top job had gone to Ritchie — was made an executive vice-president and put in charge of systems. He left in 1980 to become president of the industry's lobby group, the Canadian Bankers' Association. George Hitchman, the bank's most canny credit man, was named a vice-chairman.

Hitchman, who could be suave and entertaining over dinner with customers, was a tyrant at work. He'd keep the most senior credit officers standing in line outside his office for hours on end, awaiting his time and approval. Hitchman demanded that memos be kept to one page, and at least once a day reamed someone out for slips both real and imagined. One tale has it that Hitchman once took a rare holiday in Florida but collapsed after a week away from his desk. He was returned by ambulance to his office, where he quickly recovered.

Bell was named chief general manager by Ritchie, although very little power was passed to him. Says Harrison McCain of Ritchie's early style as chairman: "The first few years he was determined to run the whole damn bank himself. I hope we've got some good fellows. I hope we've got a fellow good enough to take his place, but I wouldn't swear to it." It wasn't until 1981 that Bell was made president and Ritchie loosened his control on the reins.

Ced Ritchie had taken over a bank that was barely out of the dark ages of paternalism and bigotry. Only a decade earlier, when Walter Bond had been head of the personnel department, he would tell employees, during staff meetings, that two children were enough for any banker. He was not an early exponent of zero population growth, he was just trying to keep down the expenses when staff transfers occurred. He also took a keen interest in an employee's religion and urged regular church attendance. As a Baptist, he favoured those of his persuasion and would arrange for membership at his church, Yorkminster Park. Since he attended services every Sunday himself, he could keep an eye on attendance. In the late 1940s, Catholics were never promoted very high in the ranks and Jews were rarely hired. Under Ritchie, the bank was yanked into the twentieth century when he named Fred Goddard, a Catholic, as general manager of the personnel department. It was a signal that some, at least, of the bad old days were over.

There were other more systematic changes needed. As late as the 1950s, when juniors joined a bank branch, they were required to burn waste paper, change storm windows, shovel sidewalks, mix powder to make ink, and change pen nibs. It was the kind of apprenticeship Ritchie himself had gone through, but he knew it no longer equipped people to become branch managers, let alone head-office hot-shots. In 1976, at his behest, the bank purchased Spencer Hall, a University of Western Ontario women's residence, which it converted to a live-in staff training college with a seventy-three-seat auditorium, a thirty-seat classroom, a twelve-seat conference room, nine seminar rooms, and every modern audio-visual device for the six hundred employees a year who would be trained there. It was Ritchie's view that only through such steps could the level of professionalism among bankers be raised.

Reducing bigotry and paternalism and raising professional standards were perhaps the easiest of Ritchie's problems. He'd inherited a bank that was strong internationally and in consumer loans, but weak in the important areas of corporate clients and marketing. Although Scotiabank ranked fourth in assets of the Big Five, its own surveys said the bank was last in what marketing surveyors call "top of mind." When asked to mention their main bank, consumers inevitably cited BNS least often. Scotiabank was the number one retail bank in only three Canadian cities of any size: St. John's, Halifax, and Ottawa.

Even the bank's signs were confusing. Over the years a plethora of logos (one of which had been designed by Nicks on a napkin), symbols, and typefaces had grown up. Each time someone had a new idea, it was simply piled on top of the rest. When Ritchie was shown examples of the many versions, he shuddered in disbelief and ordered a new logo be devised to replace all the rest. In the mid-1970s a stylized "S" was designed and a bright orange-red colour picked by a Chicago consultant.

The concern about uniformity reaches ridiculous levels; even the use of colour pencils is legislated. When a senior executive at the bank ticks off a memo as read, or gives an initialled OK, he uses an individually designated colour. Ritchie uses scarlet, Bell a sienna brown, McDonald a dark blue, Crockett black, and Hitchman purple. When Boyles was alive, he used green. There was a great hue and cry when Dixon, the company that made Boyles's pencil, announced it would cease producing that colour. Staff was dispatched in every direction to buy up all available stock of the stout, six-sided pencil so that Boyles would be assured a lifetime supply. Prior to directors' meetings, not only does each have several sharpened pencils placed at his chair, but the tips are carefully rubbed on paper several times so that they won't break when first put to use.

Ritchie began to travel extensively, especially to the Far East, where he built loan portfolios in Indonesia, Malaysia, Hong Kong, and Singapore to $2.5 billion, speedy growth by comparison with the $4.5 billion in loans to South America and the Caribbean, where the bank had been active longer. Four trips to Peking since 1974 (including one where he tried to give up smoking but succeeded only in losing his temper) paid off in 1981, when the bank became the first Canadian bank with a branch in China. He travelled regularly to the IMF meetings and the World Bank gatherings and became involved in the lesser-known but in many ways more powerful International Monetary Conference. He learned who mattered and how to differentiate between fakery and finance. Once, before a meeting, he received an invitation from former Chase Manhattan chairman David Rockefeller. Rockefeller, as later became known, had a Cardex system with forty thousand names in it. The invitation would arrive properly addressed, with the banker's name and title correct, and his wife's name as well. Ritchie waved at a colleague this particular invitation for a gathering during the IMF meeting in Manila. "You know," he began, "I get this letter from him saying, 'Dear Ced, I hope you and your wife Barbara will join me for dinner....' And we get there, and he doesn't know us from a hole in the ground. I know Clausen and ... all kinds of people and they know me — but not Rockefeller. I don't think I'll go."

Ritchie can also see the humour in some rather bleak situations. Once, in Trinidad, a local businessman was in the habit of sneaking into the home of a woman who was a teller at a Scotiabank branch in nearby Princes Town. Caught *in flagrante delicto* one night by her father and uncle, the businessman was decapitated. Her branch manager, aghast at the situation, fired her. She complained bitterly, or as Ritchie put it when he'd tell the story, tongue in cheek: "She was mad as hell at being fired just because there was a little trouble at home."

Another event in the bank's recent history roused Ritchie more to embarrassment than to laughter. Although the executive offices have been in Toronto since 1900, the official head office remains in Halifax. As a result, the annual meeting, festivities, and dinner take place there. The shareholders' meeting is always a grim affair, held in the morning, and preparations take days. All the proxies signed by shareholders to be voted by the executive need, for legal purposes, to be on hand and are flown down in boxes on the bank plane. There is nervousness about who stays behind in Toronto "to run the bank," because everyone must be on tap in Halifax, so there is much executive shuttling by plane. Stories abound of drunken employees falling off the train in Halifax in the old days when most travelled by land, but by far the wildest night in modern times occurred in 1975. The scene was the Nova Scotian Hotel. Some five hundred local and Maritime dignitaries and bigwigs had stowed away free booze at the pre-dinner reception as well as countless bottles of wine during the black-tie dinner in the ballroom. The evening had degenerated badly and those there still shake their heads and tell tales of grown men stuffing knives, forks, spoons, and salt and pepper shakers into their pockets for souvenirs.

Guest speaker that evening was a New York lawyer, Harry Harside, who attempted to speak about the international balance of payments. It is a difficult topic at the best of times; even so, the speech ranged on for more than an hour; Harside's grip on the audience was not helped much by his inclination to keep moving away from the microphone. At least once, a note was sent to him to move in closer, but the improved delivery lasted only a few minutes. Throughout, as the din in the room increased, Ritchie and Crockett tried to look cheerful at the head table. Finally, industrialist and Royal Bank director R. B. Cameron stood up and shouted: "I think we've had enough. Let's have a round of applause for our speaker." Most of the people in Cameron's vicinity applauded, hoping it would bring an end to the speech. Harside, however, announced: "I'm not finished." "Well, I am," replied Cameron, and he walked out.

After Harside finally concluded, people fled, only to have the power in the hotel suddenly go out. It wasn't restored until the following morning. The story quickly circulated that Cameron had paid off the hotel engineer to get Harside quietened, but the real cause was more likely the December storm that blew in. Several people, including some directors, were trapped on elevators and needed drinks passed down to them in order to put in the time until they were rescued. Even with candles in all the hospitality suites, surroundings were so dark that, according to one attendee: "You couldn't talk about anyone because you didn't know who was there." It was an evening Ritchie just wanted to forget. He later flew to New York to apologize to Harside. As a result, in future years, courses of the dinner were dropped and the service was speeded up so that there was less pre-meal drinking time.

Ritchie knew that other, more major, changes were needed at Scotiabank, including alterations in the board of directors to make it a more deliberative body. According to one director, "Nicks didn't use the board for anything but necessary legal purposes. I don't think he ever asked the board a serious question for which he expected an answer. Under Ritchie, the board now has a better-articulated voice and a genuine function." He also sought, as his confidence in himself and his underlings grew, to share out power. By the late 1970s, for example, he had established an 8:30 A.M. meeting for himself, Bell, McDonald, Godsoe, and senior credit man Phil Dodd, so that the five came to develop policy together. Ritchie also untied loan limit purse-strings for his three senior men and announced it in a typically offhanded way. Godsoe, who reported to McDonald at the time, phoned Ritchie about a $50-million loan in 1977. Ritchie responded: "Look, Peter, you're paid to make decisions, not phone for help. You don't have limits. Your limit is your judgement."

At the same time as he gave new freedoms in the fiefdom, he also became more hands-on chairman than Nicks had ever been and was happiest when he was dipping into a deal himself. In 1978, for example, he lit out one Sunday in the Bank of Montreal plane with that bank's executive vice-president and general manager, Hart MacDougall; their destination was Calgary, where the two of them met with Nova chief executive officer Bob Blair and loaned him $400 million for his successful purchase of Husky Oil. Ritchie's attitude in the whole affair, as top man out in the trenches, was simple: "Any one of us around this building will get on an airplane and try to do a deal. I don't think you can legislate entirely. I think you also have to demonstrate that it's possible for everyone to get in and mix it up."

As chairman, his personal lifestyle has changed little. He has kept the same home in suburban Don Mills that he had when he became president, although he's added a chalet in the Quebec Laurentians, where he is a strong but clumsy skier. At one time, he owned a farm near Shelburne, Ontario, which he sold, claiming with a smirk that he "couldn't afford the interest payments."

Some are critical of Ritchie as a long-range planner. Says former B of M chairman Fred McNeil: "Ced is one hell of a smart guy, but I don't think he's a philosopher, the type to get to the root of the pattern, know what's causing it, reflect and think about it in a strategic way." Ritchie might find such a charge pretty irrelevant and point to bank performance as the best barometer. There, even with exposure in foreign countries proportionately bigger than the other banks, Scotiabank has an excellent record.

He is perhaps more sanguine than most about the economy, seeing problems as cyclical tests of people, rather than as situations that require new strategies for solutions. He points to the troubled East Coast fishing industry, for example, where his bank has some $400 million in loans to that major industry employing thirty-five thousand people: "We have a responsibility to work out the problems," he says, but cites the royal commission of the 1930s. "Today's problems are the same, the amounts are just higher. Some of the boys who have been loaning in the 1960s and '70s have been doing it in rosy times. George Hitchman was through the 1930s. He's seen it all before." That's why Hitchman, at Ritchie's request, is still working long after retirement. Never mind the strategic needs or the fancy solutions, he'd say to his friend Fred McNeil, give me the right man, a man with some savvy and some experience, and we can work it out.

It is a similar clarion call that attracts him to Sir Harry Oppenheimer, the powerful South African tycoon who finally retired in 1982, at seventy-four, as chairman of the Anglo-American Corporation, staying on as chairman of De Beers Consolidated Mines, which markets 80 per cent of the world's diamonds. In 1982, despite opposition from churches to the bank's doing business in South Africa, Ritchie joined the board of a Bermuda-registered company called Minerals and Resources Corporation (Minorco). With major mining assets around the world of $2 billion, Minorco is Anglo-American's flagship for international expansion. Chairman of Minorco is none other than Sir Harry Oppenheimer, a man Ritchie has described as a "voice of reason" in the apartheid debate.

The Reverend Thomas Anthony, former chairperson of the Taskforce on the Churches and Corporate Responsibility, takes a dim and practical view of Minorco and Ritchie's association with it. Maintains Anthony: "It is money not being reinvested in South Africa for blacks." The Taskforce took after Ritchie in private meetings for his membership on the board and because Scotiabank is the official Canadian seller of the Krugerrand, the South African gold coin prized by gold bugs and other investors. (The bank is the leading gold retailer in this country and purchases 65 per cent of all Canadian gold-mining production.) "This is a touchy situation with the churches," Ritchie admits of his Minorco appointment. "I was surprised at the backlash."

He has long found his position on this issue a difficult one, although he has regular meetings with the Taskforce and has always been candid in private. He once told them in no uncertain terms that they had no monopoly on morals. "I'm just a boy in from the country doing a job. I come downtown to do it, and each night I go home for dinner with my wife and two bright young daughters who ask a lot of questions. You don't need to wear a collar that's turned around to have morals. Everybody who hasn't got a collar turned around isn't a crook—in fact, there are a few I could name who *did* have their collars turned around and *were* crooks."

The relationship he has with the churches is symbolic of Ritchie. In private, he's tough, but in public he'd rather duck. Ritchie may not be a brilliant man, but perhaps a banker does not need to be. As Harrison McCain puts it: "Clever guys aren't running banks, they teach at university. They've got high IQs and read the classics. The guys who run banks have energy and can motivate people, and that's not just by staring out at people from an annual report, it's from moving around, telling people when they're doing a good job, and telling them to get off their ass when they're not."

Ced Ritchie charges about, doing his best at both tasks, like some old-fashioned hall clock that has been wound too tight. It might tell the time, but it makes a helluva racket, and who knows how long it will last. He tests himself every day, and some days he tests himself too hard, pushing his body and mind to the point of snapping, his health to the brink of breaking, and his staff to the edge of collapse. "Ambition," explains his friend Harrison McCain, "is a cruel mistress."

Ced Ritchie left Upper Kent long ago and he doesn't ever want to go back. Some days the insecurity of a fatherless home and the limitations of the small town seem to be just over his shoulder, always in his mind. He will never feel part of the Establishment, no matter how many friends he has in high places in Ottawa, the private clubs of North America, or the palaces of the developing world. For Ced Ritchie, the past is always present, threatening to become his future. Running ever harder is the only revenge.

NINE

The Secret Elite Gather

Inside a Board Meeting

There is no more mystique-laden part of banking than the workings of the high-powered board of directors. Here, for the first time in print, is a detailed, blow-by-blow account of one two-and-a-half-hour board meeting.

"BOARD DAY." Two words that run throughout any bank, commanding attention at every turn, like a messenger announcing the impending arrival of royalty. At the Big Five banks, board members are the secret élite, appointed to gather as often as twice monthly to monitor management, exchange information, approve loans, and pass judgement on the bank's performance. Each board is a veritable Who's Who of Canadian commerce, with corporate interlocks perpetuating the myth that in Canada the levers of power are in too few hands.

For the bank's part, management expects its directors — numbering between thirty-five and fifty — to steer business towards the bank and be available for telephone advice regularly. The boards are large because mergers over the years have added directors, but not large enough to include more than nine women out of the 202 directors on the Big Five boards.

The first female board member was Madame Pauline Vanier, wife of Governor General Georges Vanier, appointed in 1967. At her first meeting, the story is told, she and her fellow directors were studying the balance sheet. After a few minutes, she whispered to chairman Arnold Hart: "How am I doing so far?" "Fine," he replied, "but it goes like this." And he leaned towards her and turned her sheet around. She had been reading it upside-down. The story is still recounted with chuckles, but the underlying message is that banks and their boards remain very much a male preserve.

On the days before a meeting, the secretary's department at each bank does little else but prepare documentation, nothing for days after but produce and distribute minutes. Its whole effort is directed towards gathering information for the board, trying to anticipate even the most whimsical of questions, the most desultory demand. An officer in another department who is scheduled to make an oral presentation on some topic polishes his words and worries. The maître d' sharpens his knife and finalizes his menu for the lunch to follow. The international group pores over its loan report, and the chief accountant crunches his numbers, for the entire bank's performance is on parade.

As recently as ten years ago, at all the banks, board meetings were rubber stamps for action already taken by management. There have been rare occasions when a board has revolted and thrown out a chairman, as the Commerce did when it rid itself of Neil McKinnon in 1973. There have been rare times, too, when the directors have driven a bank chairman's idea back to the drawing board. One such occasion came in the mid-1970s, when chairman Allen Lambert brought a proposal to his Toronto-Dominion board at a meeting held in Edmonton. In retrospect, the amount of the deal was small, in the range of $5 million to $10 million, tiny for a firm that by 1982 had $7.4 billion in debt, but the philosophy at stake—ownership participation in Dome Petroleum drilling in the Beaufort—was unusual. It was that aspect that brought bile to the lips of the three oil company chairmen on the bank board: Arne Nielsen, then of Mobil, Clarence Shepard of Gulf, and Sir Eric Drake of BP. During the ten minutes that followed, the three persuaded Lambert, surprised by their vehemence, to withdraw the concept and bring it back to the board in altered form. In its time, it was an unusual discussion. Today that kind of debate has become more commonplace.

Appointment to a bank board has always been the ultimate cachet for any businessman, the capstone to a capitalist's career. Until the mid-1970s, the meetings were often boring affairs where management's views were rammed through with no discussion. As the current crop of chairmen came to power, however, and directors' responsibilities everywhere were taken more seriously, the meetings have become more democratic. In 1981, former finance minister John Turner compared corporate board meetings to cabinet meetings this way: "The board meetings are a lot shorter. There is less debate and more *discussion* ... less posturing." Further, the 1980 Bank Act revision did away with what former Bank of Montreal Chairman Fred McNeil has called the "stupid concept" of board approval even for small loans. Now the executive committee of the board does most of the approval work, and at the Big Five banks, loans must be $50 million or larger before they require full board approval. In reality, if management needs to move quickly to finance a take-over, board approval comes after the fact.

Some board candidates are more sought after than others. When Conrad Black became marked as J. A. (Bud) McDougald's successor at Argus, both the TD and the Royal wanted him on their board. When Black told McDougald, who was on the Commerce board, McDougald arranged for a third invitation, which was accepted—from the Commerce. There was initial trouble because of a rule that said no corporate director could become a bank director where one-fifth or more of the company board was already on the bank board. Argus was already up to its quota on the Commerce, so McDougald simply enlarged the Argus board to get around the rule. Beaten out, the TD invited Black's older brother, Monte, onto its board in 1978.

When Ontario premier John Robarts left politics, all the Big Five banks offered him director status. The decision was easy; his father had been an old Imperial banker, so he joined the Canadian Imperial Bank of Commerce board. He claimed to be not much impressed with his function there. "You don't accomplish much," he was known to say, "but it's sure a good lunch." Many past board appointments were made simply because that particular person's firm had a lengthy relationship with a bank. The assumption was that the business would stay with the bank, since switching could prove embarrassing. Today, with more and more firms splitting their banking among various institutions, the links are not as strong, although some appointments are more automatic than others. Successive Imperial Oil chairmen — for example, Bill Twaits, Jack Armstrong, and Don McIvor — have all been named Royal directors during their terms at Imperial.

Fees are the smallest carrot among the enticements to accept a bank board appointment. At best, if a director attended all the meetings, he'd receive about $15,000 a year, plus expenses. The opportunity to comment thoughtfully on major financial issues is also limited. At the height of the take-over activity in 1981, when up to $1.5 billion in loans could be approved by a bank board in twenty minutes, lengthy debate was almost impossible. There is a requirement that directors must absent themselves from discussions when loans to companies with which they have a connection are considered. With the numerous cross-appointments held by most bank directors, the in-and-out traffic between the boardroom and its anteroom, monitored by the board secretary, makes the place look like a busy airport washroom.

Board members are pampered with attention by the respective banks. Spouses of newly elected Commerce directors receive gold medallions; gifts are often handed out at Christmas or at annual meetings. At the

1977 annual meeting of the Bank of Nova Scotia, for example, each director received an AM–FM radio. Fruitless hours were spent trying to devise a way of gift-wrapping the radios in Toronto with the dials pre-set for a suitable Halifax station (where the meeting was held) so that the radios would work immediately upon being unwrapped and turned on.

Directors, of course, are sworn to secrecy about all matters relating to the bank's dealings. Nevertheless, the contacts they make are essential, the participation in the Establishment club is agreeable, and the information gleaned is invaluable. "It's the best show in town," says Sydney Hermant, chairman and CEO of Imperial Optical and a Commerce director who missed only one meeting in twenty-two years. Says Fred Eaton, a TD director: "It is esoteric in a sense. It is like the ayatollahs sitting around in Qum." Commenting on current requirements that loans must be $50 million or more to require board approval, compared with the previous limits of $1 million, Eaton says: "Nowadays—I can't believe I'm saying this—a million isn't very much money. There are credits that get serious questioning, but a director *is* dealing after the fact. The credits have been reviewed by the management already, but when a director comes in with a lot of questions, a director gets a lot of answers. A director's job is to make sure that a bank is well run. A director who has no confidence in management has to remove management."

The bank boards are closed societies, and access by journalists is rare to the point of being nearly non-existent. Under the federal Bank Act, information is secret; directors are regularly sworn. The CBC did some filming at a Royal Bank board meeting for the series *The Establishment*, but the footage was never shown. A 1983 CBC–National Film Board co-production, *Prisoners of Debt*, showed snippets of a Bank of Montreal board meeting. But the report in this book is the most complete documentation ever made public of any bank board meeting.

A six-foot-high Sorel Etrog bronze statue called *La Stretta* stands to the left of the sliding door that leads to the Toronto-Dominion Bank boardroom on the fifty-fourth floor of the TD Centre tower. A sliding door, operated by a wall-mounted button, glides noiselessly open to reveal on the right a seven-by-nine-foot painting, just back from a Paris retrospective, by Jean-Paul Riopelle. Done in 1952 in the heavy impasto style favoured by the artist, it was recently restored and is valued at $200,000.

Awaiting the arrival of the soldiers of fortunes, the empty, silent thirty-by-sixty-foot room speaks no secrets. The north wall is floor-to-ceiling windows, the other three walls are veneered in English brown oak, all taken from a single tree. A panel on the east wall hides the screens for slide shows and audio-visual presentations. A low-rise set of cupboards runs the full length of the room, forming a hallway on the south side that leads to another meeting area beyond. On the wall away from the window hang half a dozen glowering portraits of turn-of-the-century presidents. This room, the two reception areas on the floor, and the bank's executive floor were all designed by architect Ludwig Mies van der Rohe for the building's opening in 1967. Unchanged since, they remain a living museum, sparse and clean in look, gargantuan in size.

The board table is a monster — forty feet long, ten feet wide in the middle, narrowing down to four feet at each end. Consisting of half a dozen gleaming, almost seamless sections (the tapered ends were just recently added to accommodate more attendees), it is surrounded by thirty-four leather chairs, fifteen on each side, two at each end.

As ten-thirty approaches, May 27, 1982, the directors gather like a flock of birds, roosting in the fifty-fourth-floor aerie, their grey and blue worsted plumage a distinctive marking of their breed. They settle around the table like migratory game at a sheltering pond to feed on figures and collect kernels of information. Above all else, they have been lured here by the opportunity to congregate in an assembly of the élite. They are as aware of who was *not* allowed in, excluded by fiat of the flock, whose purity is protected by an invitation that no amount of inveigling could produce for the wrong person. Each owes his or her presence to position elsewhere, and the bank offers membership in this fiduciary parliament of fowls, where they can see and be seen, hear and be heard, as well as maintain their status in the world beyond.

Because of a lengthy executive committee session, the meeting begins ten minutes late, at 10:40 A.M. Says chairman Richard Thomson, "Good morning, everyone, I'm sorry we haven't got a better morning. In Vancouver, where I was attending the International Monetary Conference, the weather is fantastic. One hundred and seventy-five bankers from around the world are enjoying three days of sunshine and no wind. That should help Canada's credit rating."

"While there are serious problems still," he continues, his eyes sweeping the twenty-nine men and one woman seated around the table, "I was interested to find that the Americans are very optimistic, more so than in '74 or '75." His gaze stops at the man sitting across from him. "Bob, do you have anything to add to that?"

Silence for a few seconds as all eyes turn to Robert Richardson, a Canadian who is executive vice-president of Du Pont in Wilmington, Delaware. "The Federal Reserve won't change its policy on M-1 and it's got the industrial sector on its knees. I think the bankers' optimism is misguided," Richardson replies.

In that brief exchange of diverging views, neither man wins or loses, because the topic is not a matter of bank policy or management performance. But it sets the tone for the two and a half hours to come, when all sides and every opinion are heard, all questions put, any topic is raised. The board is not an undergraduate debating society, but it is equally not a rubber-stamp babble of senile senators, approving whatever is thrust under their noses.

Of the thirty-four board members, thirty are on hand, representing both the geographic and the industrial diversity of Canada. They include: Norman Anderson, chairman and CEO of Cominco; Monte Black, president and CEO of Argus Corporation; Jean de Grandpré, chairman and CEO of Bell; Fredrik Eaton, chairman, president, and CEO of the T. Eaton Co.; Leo Kolber, president, Cemp Investments; Lorne Lodge, chairman and president, IBM; John Stoik, president and CEO of Gulf. The lone woman at the table is Mona Campbell, president, Dover Industries.

The minutes of the previous meeting, May 13, are dispensed with quickly and Thomson follows up on some topics discussed at the previous meeting. "The situation in Poland is basically the same." Referring to Quebec's provincial budget that week, he says: "[Jacques] Parizeau has begun to tackle the problem of a very highly rewarded civil service group, but the deficit remains a real concern." No comment comes on either observation so Thomson presses on with the next item on the agenda, the report of the bank's operations for the second quarter of 1982, the period ending April 30. Thomson nods to president Robin Korthals, sitting to his left, to roll out the numbers.

"Just before he begins," Thomson stops with a smile playing across his face like a shaft of sunlight on choppy waves, "he might explain why he looks like he's been out collecting loans." There is an explosion of guffaws around the table. Korthals removes his glasses and swings his head from side to side. The laughter is replaced by murmurs when they see the right eye ringed with a purple bruise. Korthals explains his collision with another cyclist: "I was out for a quiet morning ride and I met another fellow who was out for a quiet morning ride. He won and I woke up in Western Hospital."

Korthals goes on to fill the air with numbers as the board members sit quietly, heads bowed, hands unfolding the printed statements that will be released to shareholders once the board has approved. Earnings are up, assets constant. There are agreeable murmurs. There is more disclosure on losses — $66 million at the half-way point in the year, 108 per cent higher than the previous year. Korthals is asked why more information is being voluntarily disclosed. Thomson cuts in: "The really good analysts can figure it out anyway," he said. "We're being besieged by questions these days. We bit the bullet in 1974 on real estate investment trusts and revealed our losses then. People like [McCarthy Securities Ltd. analyst] Robin Cornwell are sending out missiles every day, and usually their estimates are high." The remainder of the news is grim; almost all the benefit gained in the first quarter (which ended in January) has been wiped out by the next three months. Spreads have narrowed, interest is being reversed on other loans, non-interest expenses are up 17 per cent, salary costs are up 20 per cent (partially because of increased numbers of staff), personal loan demand is down 10 per cent, mortgage amounts are unchanged, and customers are moving low-paying deposit accounts into higher-paying daily interest accounts, thus driving up the cost of money to the bank.

Comments Korthals: "People are managing their money a whole lot more carefully. It contributes to line-ups, and we don't charge for transfers between accounts. It's a problem for the whole industry. Current accounts from small business are way off, too, reflecting the economic times."

Leo Kolber fires a few bullets from the end of the table about the 17 per cent increase in internal costs and is finally satisfied by Thomson's assurance that non-interest expense (salaries, benefits, frauds, stamps — literally everything except interest costs) will be down to a 12 per cent year-over-year increase within six months.

Next, more numbers on another sheaf of papers, a report on the bank's $3.1-billion securities portfolio, which includes $260 million in common and preferred shares, $1.2 billion in term-preferreds, $300 million in small business bonds, and $1 billion in Government of Canada bonds and treasury bills.

Maurice Young, chairman and CEO of Finning Tractor of Vancouver, picks up on an item about interest recovery, and a discussion ensues about the $20-million item a year earlier when past-due interest and full principal payment was repaid by revolution-torn Iran after the American hostages had been released. The money represented payment in full for loans under the Shah. "Really," says Young, leaning over the table from his vantage point at the room's east end, "aren't you just taking distortion out of a quarterly report?"

"Yes, you're right," responds Thomson, "but how far back do you go?" The tone suggests both fair question and final statement. "Our accountants are convinced this is the way it should be reported." Another dart steered away.

Loan losses, up sharply over the previous year, are estimated by Korthals for the twelve months ending October 1982 at $134 million. Of that, $87 million will come from demand loans in domestic operations, $26 million will come in international, $21 million from personal instalment loans including Visa.

With earnings up only modestly, the dividend is not increased from 50 cents a share. No one disagrees, particularly when the hard times are underscored by an announcement Thomson makes at 10:54, after a slip of paper has been handed to him. "We've just been informed that the National Bank has suspended trading and has called a press conference for twelve-thirty." There is the sound of breath being sucked in around the table. "We'll keep you posted, perhaps at lunch." (The National lost $8 million that quarter, an improvement from the $28 million during the previous quarter, but suspended its dividend amid recurring rumours of chairman Michel Bélanger's departure.)

The TD's net income is up 9 per cent, and as figures for the other banks come out over the next few days, the TD's is the best performance among the Big Five, with Scotiabank also up by 9 per cent, while the Commerce dropped 24 per cent year-over-year, the Bank of Montreal, 25 per cent, and the Royal, 32 per cent.

Thomson calls on Korthals to report on the current Parliamentary hearings in Ottawa into bank profits. "They're better than the Bank Act hearings," Korthals begins, a tinge of relief in his voice. "They have some advisers this time, the questions are better, but the ten-minute [questioning] system is clumsy. The focus has quickly changed from bank profits to capital adequacy and loan losses. The committee's concern is with the large loans. The media haven't found much to be critical about. The members were quite surprised by the [complimentary] Consumers' Association brief." As for the individual MPs on the committee, he notes that Vancouver Conservative Pat Carney was the sharpest. On some matters, he says ironically, "we were not able to convince her that she was wrong."

His words continue to drip with irony as he concludes: "They'll solve all our problems for us. The perception is that we aren't as tough on the larger loans as the small. That may be true with Massey," he admits. "I guess that the Commerce today would rather have seen it go [under] the first day. It's cost them a lot of money. There is the feeling [among parliamentarians] there is absolutely no competition in the financial community. And if that's what you want to believe, it's hard to change your mind."

In all, it's an honest assessment that hides nothing and does not try to be a "best face" report. Discussion flows about TD's decision not to testify at the Ottawa hearings although the other big four banks are sending their top shooters. Thomson climbs into the debate to point out the peer pressure they have already avoided. "Rowlie [Frazee] made a decision that he would do it, then Mulholland had to do it, the Commerce followed, and everybody was in."

Chips in director Gordon Osler, chairman of Stanton Pipes Ltd.: "If we are the only one to make more money this quarter and we're the only ones not to appear, won't that look odd?"

Thomson considers the question for a moment and then points out that the decision not to appear was taken some time earlier. "I don't think it will matter," he concludes. "The hearing is no longer about profits."

Next come the large loans for approval. Anything over $50 million must be brought to the board, each with its individual sheet of legal-length paper detailing the amount, the borrower, the security, the purpose, as well as rates, related loans, and a repayment schedule. Only eight loans are considered by the board this day, a sign of tighter times. A year earlier, at the height of the expanding economy, it would have been fifty. Of the eight, six are shared with Canadian banks or are interbank loans, and therefore low-risk. The seventh is to Mexico's National Credit Institute, the eighth a direct loan to the government of Indonesia. Neither of these is very risky and they are approved without comment. An additional eight loans are tabled, for a further $109 million, but not referred to individually, except one loan to Cunard. Two of the company's ships, the *Queen Elizabeth 2* and the *Atlantic Conveyor*, have been commandeered that month by the British government for use in the Falklands recapture. The *Atlantic Conveyor*, reports say, has been hit. Cunard, however, was not liable, although insurance was suspended, because the British government took over responsibility.

Loans to Argentina, says Thomson, are up to date, even during the hostilities, although there was some delay in interest payments. "Shades of the Iranian situation," he adds. "Argentina is paying everyone but the English banks, and the English banks are claiming a *pro rata* share of the funds received by the other participating banks. We're saying no to that."

Gordon Osler proves to be the most regular questioner this day. At this point, referring to the loans before them, he asks about Mexico, where the country's total indebtedness to banks is a worrisome $70 billion. Responds Thomson: "Mexico's looking to refinance a short-term loan — the Bank of America is leading it — but we're staying out because we had none of the short term. We see no reason to refinance someone else's problem."

Du Pont's Richardson asks about the unsecured loan to Singapore Airlines. The response comes from vice-chairman Bob Dickson. "It's unsecured, but we regard it as having government backing." Adds Thomson: "It has had a terrific record. And we regard it as a government airline." No further assurance is needed. With sovereign backing, the likelihood of a loan going sour is nil.

By 11:49, the fog outside has lifted, bringing some colour to the cityscape. With the hint of sun and the end of the international credits in sight, those in the room shift in their seats both in expectation that the next presentation will demand less effort and because the meeting, like any long session, possesses rhythms. The pace vacillates between foot-slogging and forced march, but throughout there is always information in the air, floating about like the tiny water droplets suspended outside, ready to be soaked up by the minds around the table, for information is the aqua vitae of business. Each person around the table had some to dispense; everyone has a lot to absorb.

At each meeting, some industrial sector or geographic region is presented in detail, to give the directors a vista beyond the individual deals. At this meeting, vice-chairman Bob Dickson discusses ASEAN — the Association of South-East Asian Nations — Indonesia, Malaysia, the Philippines, Singapore, and Thailand. TD's market share of Canadian bank business in the ASEAN countries, he reports, is 20 per cent, with particular strength in Indonesia (where most loans are to the government except for loans to Inco and the Shell group). Dickson cites various gross national product numbers, inflation rates, and debt-service ratios (a comparison between total debt and the interest charged). In all, a good place to be doing business, he concludes, and an area of the world where "we're pretty relaxed about our exposure."

After hearing these low debt-service ratios (Singapore 1 per cent, Malaysia 5 per cent), Donald Sobey, president of Empire & Co. Ltd., is intrigued. "What," he asks, "is Canada's debt-service ratio?" Dickson had tried to get the figure that morning, knowing the question might come up, but couldn't. "I'll get that for you," he assured Sobey, of Stellarton, Nova Scotia, whose family is one of the half-dozen broods who dominate Atlantic Canada. (Canada's debt-service ratio is 7.9 per cent.)

Thomson cites the International Monetary Conference meeting in Vancouver again and the worry expressed there about ever-escalating country debt. "That's the problem of inflation," he says, "and we're there." TD has already been retrenching on foreign loans, says Dickson, away from sovereign-risk loans in lesser developed countries to corporate and sovereign-risk loans in industrialized countries. The plan, he told the directors, is to stay in the traditional strong borrowing countries (U.S., France, England, and Japan) and expect more growth in U.S.-based corporate accounts. Says Dickson: "We're opening offices in the U.S. and closing others around the world."

By this point in the meeting, the black leather folders in front of each director are surrounded by a litter of paper created as each finishes with successive items. Next in the pile are loans that may not have been above the $50 million required for the usual board scrutiny, but in which bank directors present that day have a corporate connection with the borrower, either as officer, director, or major shareholder.

Vice-chairman Ted McDowell peers through his glasses, strokes his grey hair, and announces: "Next, director-related credits involving Messrs

Gray, Thomson, Lodge, and Kolber." Without further comment, the four (Gordon Gray, chairman and CEO of A. E. LePage; TD's Thomson; Lorne Lodge; and Leo Kolber rise and leave the room. One of the loans, for example, is to Canadian Gypsum; Thomson is a director. The four need not have bothered, for no one has any comment to make on the five loans totalling $60 million up for review. Within two minutes, they are summoned back, as McDowell continues with a report on non-current loans. (A non-current loan is one on which either interest is not being paid or the borrower's financial condition is deteriorating to the point where management regards it as non-current.) The net amount of domestic conventional business loans on which interest is not being taken into income is $240 million; net international loans in this category are $118 million, for a total of $358 million — plus $60 million in consumer loans. Not something, Thomson tells the board, to worry about, not like the recently reported $135 million after-tax loss by U.S. bank Chase Manhattan when Drysdale, an investment house, went under in New York by, in effect, advancing Chase credit to insufficiently worthy customers. "We're absolutely convinced," says Thomson, "that we did not get involved in those kind of practices. It certainly was a major problem for Chase."

Again the pace changes abruptly with discussion of an art acquisition — ninety pieces of Inuit sculpture and ten etchings — brought before the board for approval. These pieces, from the personal collection of art consultant Melville Francis (Budd) Feheley, were chosen by the Smithsonian Institution for an eleven-city U.S. tour in 1981. To be added to the TD's already sizeable collection of a hundred pieces — assembled with Feheley's advice as the bank's 1967 centennial project — the additional pieces will cost $275,000. By comparison, the current collection of a hundred pieces (little changed since 1967) cost "considerably under $100,000," Thomson informs the board. In a memo describing the purchase, bank curator Pat James points out that the merger "would produce the finest collection of modern Inuit art in the world."

Of the ninety new pieces, fully half are early works from the 1940s and 1950s by artists in ten Eastern Arctic settlements, including Panta, Johnnie Inukpuk, Davidee Sheokjuk, and Joe Talurunili. In explaining the purchase deal, Thomson is quick to point out that the cost was "a very modest amount for those pieces." And, referring to the Smithsonian tour, he adds: "We get the packing boxes, too."

As the directors flip through the booklets that describe the purchase grouping, Thomson talks more about Feheley. "He really regards our collection as partly his." He points out that in the recently announced fourth tower, a $100-million addition to the present three-tower TD Centre, there may be display space on the mezzanine level. If the City of Toronto agrees to designate the mezzanine as a museum area, it would allow an additional floor to be added to the building to make up for the rental revenue lost on the mezzanine. With space renting at $35 to $40 per square foot, the extra floor is an important consideration.

The $275,000 expenditure, says Thomson, will be spread over three years in order to stay within the art acquisition budget. "We won't likely announce it until next year because we don't have a place to display it, although word will leak out in the art world because there were several other interested parties." He looks around the table, expectantly, but there are no comments or questions. "OK? Thank you very much." Approved.

It is 12:20, but if any of the directors is getting restless, the next item rivets their attention. Urban Joseph, senior vice-president for human resources, joins the meeting and takes a seat at the table's end. Thomson nods to him to begin and he plunges nervously into a prepared statement. "We always had the ability to absorb marginal performers at salaries beyond the duties they were performing," he reads. Ears prick up around the table. "We have a number of individuals demoted and in a surplus capacity. We haven't been very successful in encouraging these employees, so a separation policy has been prepared." Joseph goes on to explain that forty-eight long-service employees, and perhaps as many as ten more — 1 per cent of the management group — would be "terminated." At the far end of the table, Monte Black turns to Fred Eaton and whispers: "Is that the same as fired?"

Joseph plods on, telling the board that thirty-five of the employees will be told June 15 and turned over to the consulting firm of Murray Axmith & Associates, a firm known as "de-hirers" for their expertise in handling the recently fired. He outlines the severance pay — four weeks' pay in lieu of notice, plus two weeks' for each year of service up to ten years, and three weeks' for each year over ten. Minimum amount to be paid any individual is six months' salary, with a two-year maximum. The average age of the employees is forty-eight; average annual salary, $34,000; average settlement, $46,000.

He is peppered with questions by the directors. In response, he tells them that there are eighty-five management firings in a normal year, half for performance and half for other causes. Some 250 clerks are fired each year for performance reasons. Someone wants to know if there have been warnings to the group of forty-eight. Yes, Joseph replies, pointing out that some have already had, at bank expense, use of outside consultants. Still, he admits, "It will come as a surprise." Adds Thomson: "Some have just assumed that we'll find something for them. There is an argument that it is humane because it allows them time to find a new career."

The settlements, Joseph continues, meet and exceed any court requirements. "The laws today," says Thomson, "don't allow you the latitude we used to have in a paternalistic way."

Another question, this one from IBM's Lorne Lodge: "What if I'm sixty, have thirty years in the bank, and want the same deal?" Not available, he is told. Further discussion about the settlement amounts results in the board's consensus that it is slightly, but not overly, generous.

Next, director Mona Campbell, chairman of the board's pension fund committee, reports on the bank's holdings in its pension fund, totalling $278.6 million. With the stock market continuing to slide and a further "two-or-three-hundred-point TSE [Toronto Stock Exchange] drop to come," she tells the directors that the fund will not be buying equity — after selling heavily six months ago — until the market bottoms out, in perhaps six weeks. She reports that 40 per cent of the fund is in mortgages, 30 per cent in cash, 18 per cent in Canadian equities, with the rest in foreign equity and bonds. The fund, she reports, had a return in the top quartile among 400 pension funds measured.

At 12:45, the next agenda item is the recent visit of the inspector-general, an annual check done as part of an ongoing review at each of the chartered banks. This year, the usual five-day audit was completed in three, reports secretary Glenn Bumstead. William Kennett, the inspector-general, expecting no major problems, designated his assistant, D. M. Macpherson, to do the audit. "Earnings are the best of the Big Five," Bumstead quotes from management's report on the inspection. "Information systems are second to none." And finally, "The visit was a pleasant experience despite the economic times."

Dick Thomson smiles: "I think we can say we hope he's right."

The final item is donations requests; all bank charitable donations over $20,000 must be approved by the board. Up for study is a $5-million campaign at Trent University in Peterborough, Ontario. Bumstead outlines the university's size and history, refers to charts in each director's binder that show donations from each of the Big Five banks to the three previous Trent campaigns in 1963, 1969, and 1975. "The Commerce will be giving $65,000 over five years," reports Bumstead, "and that reflects their special interest in Trent. We are recommending $22,500 over five years."

The amount is approved, but from down the table booms the voice of John Poole, president of Crestwood Developments in Edmonton, his glasses and grey hair bobbing: "I can't resist commenting that there is nothing west of Brandon for the last five years." Bumstead and Thomson both grin, a bit sheepishly, but say nothing. It's obviously not the first time he has drawn this neglect to their attention.

Just as things are about to wrap up, Gordon Osler calls attention to the remark in the report on the inspector-general's visit about a loan amount to a single borrower — Dome. The company is the best-known debtor in the country, with its estimated $7.4 billion in bank loans debated in public for weeks.

"There really is no news on Dome that hasn't already been made public," says Thomson. "There are negotiations [to sell properties] in Indonesia and in the North Sea. The firming of the world price [by OPEC] has set a better climate. But there's no doubt there would have been better times for a disposition programme."

Osler presses on, staring straight ahead, not looking at Thomson to his left. "The chairman of another bank, I guess the lead bank [Russ Harrison of the Commerce], has said that he's not convinced that [Dome president Jack] Gallagher sees that the banks are serious."

"That has been Jack's problem for some months," agrees Thomson. "He's very reluctant to sell what he's built. I've talked to him as strongly as I know how. We are in no position to provide additional funds, and we told him so eight months ago." At the bank's request, the amount Dome owes TD has been reduced. Along with the other largest loans to single borrowers, it was discussed at the executive committee that morning before the board met.

Before discussion continues, Thomson announces the next meeting for Edmonton on June 10. Mona Campbell asks if government people will be invited to the reception following the meeting. "Some civil servants," replies Thomson, "but not political people. Too many problems. They don't come on time and they cancel at the last minute."

The reception will be at the Edmonton home of John Poole "You *be* there," Maurice Young calls to Poole from the other end of the table, causing laughter all round. At an April meeting in Vancouver, the reception was held at Young's house and he was called out of the city. The reception continued without him.

The meeting is suddenly over. Some, such as Fred Eaton and Leo Kolber, have left early. Jacques de Billy, a Quebec City lawyer, has spent most of the meeting called away to the phone. The rest, including Arne Nielsen, who hasn't been home to Calgary in more than a week, troop down the hall to a buffet lunch in the West Room, where curried shrimp and a veal loaf are served by tuxedoed waiters in front of an original tapestry designed by Jean-Paul Lemieux and woven in St. Cyr, France.

There, along a table with directors ranged on both sides, the talk turns to a gaggle of topics: baseball, flight plans, holidays, the U.S. economy, and a $10-million fraud at a Commerce branch. There is further inspection of Korthals's black eye and of two protrusions on Dick Thomson's forehead where "sunspots" were surgically removed the previous week, at his doctor's advice.

Each director, a leader in his or her own field, a boss in another organization, had, for a few hours at least, set aside competitive instincts and corporate infighting. Around the massive oak table, all were equal. Each demanding and well-fed ego had been checked outside the door like pistols at a Western saloon. Professional hostilities were forgotten, personal gain forgone.

While no one had differed sharply with management, there had been solid discussion and sufficient debate. All questions were answered, no views were dismissed. Management may run the bank, but the board lends a certain discipline to the life of an institution. Material must be assembled, numbers need to be defended, answers prepared even if the questions don't come. Just as a schoolboy cannot function well without regular examinations, no institution could long carry on without all systems on display, every soldier in the regiment inspected minutely for bravery or failure. Those who were found wanting were fired. Campaigns on foreign soil had been reviewed and approval given for continued action. Where losses occurred in other battles closer to home, slowdown was ordered, withdrawals were suggested.

Once done, the corps dispersed. Their own rank had been reaffirmed, their position in the pecking order maintained. Back in the barracks, the spit and polish began anew. For in two weeks' time, each number and every long-range plan would once more be trotted out into the revealing glare of the parade square.

TEN

A QUICK HAND, A QUIXOTIC HEAD

Dick Thomson

CHAIRMAN, THE TORONTO-DOMINION BANK

IT WAS 1978 and Dick Thomson was out with the boys in the Florida Keys. The group included Thomson's Toronto pals Gordon Gray, chairman of A. E. LePage, and Neil Wood, former president of Cadillac-Fairview, who now runs his own development company. The three of them were whiling away the sunny hours with pro golfer Jack Nicklaus and generally knocking about Nicklaus's place, the exclusive Cheeka Lodge at Islamorada. They played five holes of par three golf; Thomson's tee shot was closer to the pin than Nicklaus's every time. Thomson was on a roll when they decided to do a little fishing.

This was no ordinary group looking for trout in a country stream: they were after the elusive bonefish. Found only in the Keys, the bonefish not only is rare, but, when found, spooks easily and is almost never caught and landed. As their guides poled the boats quietly through the shallow water of the Florida flats, they were cautioned that the slightest noise could scare away any bonefish in the vicinity.

Thomson had never done any spin casting before, so the guide showed him the rudiments of putting the rod behind his head, snapping it forward, and sending the line spewing out from the reel. As the rest prepared to await patiently the unlikely arrival of a bonefish, they talked and banged about in the boats, forgetful for the moment about the admonition against noise. Thomson gathered his rod about him, took his first practice cast, and *fwack!* A bonefish took the hook and Thomson reeled it in as if it had been waiting for the master's arrival. It was the only one caught all day.

Life's been like that for Richard Murray Thomson. Buttressed by buddies, ready with the bait, eager and aggressive, he is a man who enjoys no small measure of fortuitous timing and good luck. As chairman and chief executive officer of the Toronto-Dominion Bank, the smallest of the Big Five banks, Thomson is the youngest and most interventionist of the Big

Five CEOs. Thomson inherited a well-run and lean machine from his predecessor, Allen Lambert, after a lengthy grooming and transition that began in 1963 when Thomson, at the brash young age of thirty, was appointed assistant to the president. Under the gentle guidance of Lambert, who left the home fires to be tended by others as he travelled the Pacific building the bank's international business, Thomson gradually took over. Named president in 1972, he became chief executive officer in 1977 and chairman in 1978. As transitions go, it was as smooth as a kitten's wrist.

The son of a banker — his father, Harold, was a vice-chairman of the Canadian Imperial Bank of Commerce — Thomson is a man who is always in control, both of himself and of the circumstances. He sports the biggest, most imposing office of all the bankers. With as many square feet as the average bungalow, it is lit like a night-time tennis court. There is no mound of papers, no morass of open files; it is a tidy place, as befits a man with a tidy mind.

Thomson's tall frame, pushing six-foot-three, is topped by curly black hair. Bespectacled, he looks like the studious kid you grew up with in high school who always carried a briefcase and was days ahead with his homework. But in the modern era, where savvy and backbone count, this is no fragile scholar. Dick Thomson is a drip-dry paladin, active in downtown redevelopment, spotting corporate haemorrhaging before anyone else, piloting a bank that is, bar none, the best-run of the Big Five. Its earnings record is top of the heap even though there are no more people on the executive floor than there were fifteen years ago.

In 1982 the American magazine *Institutional Investor* polled 160 bank chief executive officers world-wide. Richard Thomson was among the handful, and the only Canadian, who received an honourable-mention award as banker of the year. The article read: "The [TD] bank was the first to bring U.S.-style unsecured, cash flow lending to Canada, and it soon emerged as the country's most energetic lender to burgeoning communications and real estate companies. When Canadian institutions became itchy for assets south of the border, Thomson made the TD the country's biggest take-over bank; it lent more than $1 billion to finance such deals. Thomson, however, was more than just a single-minded expansionist, and there is no better proof of that than the bank's performance last year. As Canadian banks piled up assets at a feverish pace, TD was the only one in a position to finance its expansion through retained earnings. And when the economy began to turn sour, TD was the first big bank to pull in its horns."

Thomson personifies the new breed of Canadian banker who plunges into deals before others will, constantly testing his instincts against their outer limits. When Robert Campeau took his run at Royal Trust, it was Thomson who adopted a leadership role and manned the Establishment barricades to corral shares in Royal Trust, thus keeping ownership from changing hands. He will often take the unpopular view, too, confident enough of his capacity to know that even as a loner, he can survive. When Canada Development Corporation took over Aquitaine, it was Thomson who counselled the CDC to stand off. And when the foreign banks were looking to land in Canada, Thomson was the solitary figure who said no. He was the first, in the face of relentless pressure from church groups, to abandon phony tactics and admit his bank had loans to South Africa. He was also the first to say that such loans would cease. When Olympia & York went after Abitibi, Thomson saw a chance to forge new loyalties and gain new business as he attempted to round up another bidding group to join with magnate Ken Thomson (no relation) and his International Thomson Organization to outbid the Reichmanns.

Thomson, the fighter, has his share of scars. On Royal Trust, the bank lost $650,000, on dealings in stock for its own account. CDC pushed ahead with the Aquitaine deal after TD dropped out of the financing, and some CDC business was moved to other banks in retaliation. When the United Church moved its account from Scotiabank in 1982, it chose not the TD after its high-profile stand, but the Royal. Finally, today fifty-five foreign banks are in Canada in strength, and few of them will deal with him or his bank, because of his strong views opposing their presence.

And yet, through it all, his bank has prospered. The TD has the best earnings growth and the shortest lines of communication. Of all the bankers at the top, he has the best balance in his life. He will often depart a party early (even leaving his wife behind), rarely staying out later than midnight even on the weekend, for fear that his response time will slow or that he won't be as clear-headed as he wishes. With business in ninety countries and 1,005 branches in Canada, the TD under Thomson has doubled in asset size to $45 billion while at the same time adding only 6 per cent to its eighteen-thousand-member staff in the last five years.

Perhaps he has done so much so quickly because there are two Dick Thomsons. One is in such tight control of himself that he might be following Mackenzie King's dictum: "Few men have ever suffered in public for what they did not say." The other knows when he can take a high-profile stand and survive. He is not the type one invites to a frivolous lunch, yet give him a yo-yo at a party and he can and will demonstrate all the tricks he learned while selling the toy at Eaton's in Winnipeg as a teenager. His guardedness protects him not from enemies, but from false friends and sometime associates. He can go nowhere — except with a very few close acquaintances like John Tory, Neil Wood, Gordon Gray, and Teleguide general manager Barry Thomas—without being asked for something. It might be a plea for a donation (the bank gives $1 million annually to charity), or the right name to phone for a loan, or a job prospect for a nephew, or his presence at some event.

At fifty, he has another fifteen years at the top. His friends worry that he'll become bored, yet he shows no signs of restlessness, and why should he? His annual salary is about $425,000; he owns $675,000 in TD stock that pays him an annual dividend of $30,000; he can afford to outfit his wife, Heather (nicknamed Hedy or Old Head), in metallic evening outfits by Ferré; he has a three-storey Georgian home with a pool in stately North Toronto; a ski chalet near Craigleith, Ontario; a ranch-style bungalow in Florida; a chauffeur-driven silver Cadillac Fleetwood. He travels the world in style, spending half his time away from his Toronto office, often touring with his wife, squeezing in sightseeing with the zinc mine tours or having a holiday as he did after watching the Telesat satellite launch in Florida last year with his young son, Richard.

There is no other job that could offer him the lifestyle to which he has grown accustomed. In fact, he may just now be growing into his role even though he's been tipped for the top or at the peak for twenty years. He occupies his post like a highly trained technocrat with an encyclopedic memory. Says TD president and number two man Robin Korthals: "He knows dates, times, and roles of people in deals for years back. His mind is a matrix." As a result, he makes decisions quickly and wants complete and competent information to pour from those around him. According to senior vice-president and chief economist Doug Peters: "He grasps things almost too quickly. Even when I came to the bank [in 1966] and I wanted a decision, that's where you went. Dick would give you a decision in a quarter of a second. You'd better not tell him a half-truth, or he'll nail your hide to the wall." Still, he had his failings in those days, foibles he's growing out of. "He wasn't sophisticated," says vice-president Alan Hockin, "but he is developing right now. He is beginning to gain a new dimension."

It is that new dimension that may speak to those who worry that Thomson will get bored long before retirement age. When his friend Neil Wood left Cadillac-Fairview in 1981 at fifty to strike out on his own, Thomson saw him at lunch that day. "I'd like to be your partner," Thomson said to Wood. "Let's talk." Taken aback, Wood at first thought Thomson meant that he wanted to join with Wood personally. A later meeting cleared the air. It was the TD that Thomson was offering as partner; he wanted the bank to put some money into Wood's new operation. "I wouldn't think of leaving here," he told Wood. "I just can't imagine what it's like to make that kind of step." For all his courageous stands and lonely views, Thomson could only have succeeded within the confines of an institution. As an entrepreneurial figure, he can only function within the vast support system of the bank. It is there he wants to build his reputation and leave his mark upon the corporate cairn. Says Bryan Vaughan, a former chairman of the advertising agency Vickers & Benson: "Dick wants to make his own career a memorial to his father."

Harold Thomson was a gentle man, an old Imperial banker in Winnipeg and Brandon during the Depression years who passed his solid prairie virtues on to his sons. Some of the most vivid early memories shared by Dick and his brother, Tom, now a vice-president with Imperial Oil in Toronto, include drives in the 1940s with their father to inspect the dust-blown and abandoned farms that the bank had taken over during the Depression years. Many were in southern Manitoba, with dirt piled up to their window-sills, the land being worked by a neighbour. "He was working hard to get the farms back into the hands of the farmers where he thought they belonged," recalls Tom. "I remember the intensity of those discussions."

Dick was born in 1933, his younger brother two years later. In Winnipeg, Harold Thomson was senior accountant, then assistant manager, at the Imperial branch on North Main. On Saturdays, the boys would visit the branch, perch at the desks, punch out figures on the calculating machines, and play at being teller. They moved to Brandon in 1944, where their father was manager of the branch, and back to Winnipeg in 1946, when their father was made manager of the main branch.

In addition to his summer yo-yo demonstration job, Dick also golfed (his father belonged to St. Charles) and spent time on the farm near Arcola, Saskatchewan, where his mother had been raised. He also, in turn, delivered newspapers, was a drugstore delivery boy, and made banana splits at Brown's drugstore, a teenage hang-out.

Banking was a long way from Dick's mind as a career, but he was impressed by his father's knowledge of the community and its people. Although his father had left school after Grade 11 in Fort Qu'appelle, Saskatchewan (Dick's mother had attended university, an unusual occurrence for a woman of the era), he could reel off poems and vast chunks of memorized Shakespeare as dinner-table entertainment. If he were looking at a new branch site as the bank expanded after the war, or touring a sugar-beet plant, he'd often take the boys along.

In 1950, Harold Thomson was transferred east to Toronto, where Dick finished high school and enrolled in engineering at the University of Toronto. He had not been the kind of youngster who built or invented things. The closest he got to mechanical tinkering was the time at the age of thirteen when he took apart an outboard motor and successfully put it back together. There being no lake handy, he tested the motor in a rain barrel.

At U of T, the course, now called industrial engineering, was a tough one and combined engineering and business studies. Of the seventy students who started first year, only forty graduated four years later. Thomson lived at home, joined a fraternity, and was active on students' council; he was junior badminton champ and editor for two years of the engineers' newspaper, *Toike Oike*. Thirty years later Thomson would still describe himself as "a frustrated writer." Says he: "My ambition was to be the editor of the *Globe and Mail*." He always placed among the top three students and when he wrote the exam that screened students for entry into U.S. colleges, he placed at the top end of the first quartile. His summer jobs while at university, working in assembly-line operations making electrical controls, convinced him that he did not want to be an engineer for the rest of his life. More appealing, he discovered, were the accounting and economics courses he took in the third and fourth years that led him to continue his schooling at Harvard in the two-year Master of Business Administration programme.

He flourished in the Harvard programme and didn't think about a career in banking until second year. A friend of his father from the Commerce, George Currie (later chairman of MacMillan Bloedel), was attending an advanced management course at Harvard and invited Thomson out for dinner one night. During the meal, Currie asked Thomson about his future and suggested: "Why don't you consider banking?" Thomson pointed out that he couldn't imagine that the banks would be interested in an MBA graduate when he finished in 1957. He said he'd seen the American banks aggressively recruiting on campus, but there were no Canadian banks in sight. Currie noted that the Commerce had hired a Harvard MBA two years earlier and that he was doing very well.

Thomson liked the idea and told his parents about his newly discovered interest in the "family" business. His father was stunned, his mother adamantly opposed, pointing out that it was unusual to attend university for six years only to end up as a bank clerk. Dick's mind was made up, however, and his parents finally agreed. The only stipulation Thomson's father made was that his son should not come to work at his bank, the Commerce. He directed him instead to the Toronto-Dominion Bank, just created as a result of a merger in 1955.

The Toronto-based TD traces its history to beginnings amid bread and booze. The Toronto Bank was founded in 1855 by a group of millers who felt poorly served by the Bank of Montreal. As Upper Canadian businessmen, they wanted to be rid of the Montreal establishment and felt that the grain farmers of Upper Canada would follow their lead. The distillers soon followed as well and two families, the Gooderhams and the Wortses, became involved. James G. Worts was named vice-president of the bank in 1857, and in 1864, William Gooderham, Worts's uncle and senior partner, became president.

The Dominion Bank didn't open its doors for business until 1871, again with high-powered Toronto families involved. Among them were James Austin, founder of Consumers' Gas; Henry Pellatt (whose son would later build Toronto's only castle, Casa Loma); and Edmund Osler (older brother to Sir William Osler). Gooderham's son, George, set an amusing style for the other directors of the day. The board, the story is told, was made up of penny-pinchers who would extinguish the coal-oil lamps to conserve fuel. The meetings would continue on in the dark. One such meeting was interrupted by noises coming from Gooderham's direction. Since no one could see well enough to know what was happening, someone asked Gooderham what he was doing. "Just taking off my pants," he replied. "If nobody's going to see them, might as well save wear and tear on the seat."

It was a hierarchical system these men established, one that set indentured apprenticeship as the standard for future promotions in the years to come. Clerks would spend long hours slaving on stools, working through lean times before receiving promotions. In the early years of both banks, many young men were eventually rewarded for their toil with a seat on the board and a lifetime of security.

In 1954, six months of secret negotiations between the two banks led to an amalgamation proposal. The Dominion Bank had been looking for a deal; discussions with the Commerce had fallen apart when no agreement could be reached on the name. Both the Toronto and the Dominion realized they were too small to compete against the larger banks, and the gap was growing wider. The Dominion Bank was active in textile loans; the Bank of Toronto was more involved in forest products and mining. Rather than fall behind, or become small, specialty banks, they proposed to amalgamate their 449 branches (more than half in Ontario). The minister of finance gave his consent, the shareholders approved, and the Toronto-Dominion Bank came into being February 1, 1955, with assets of $1.3 billion. Executives of the Bank of Toronto quickly took the upper hand, and the following year, Allen Lambert was appointed general manager.

A fresh-faced Dick Thomson visited Lambert in the spring of 1957, armed with his business degree and a technocrat's mind in an age when both were becoming highly praised and highly priced commodities in some sectors. The bank, however, was not quite ready for the modern era, its institutional mind still mired somewhere in the past. Thomson was interviewed by Harold Burns, head of the personnel department, who wondered out loud why Thomson had chosen to attend an American university. He also allowed as how he couldn't understand why Thomson would want to join a bank with his higher education. Eventually convinced of Thomson's patriotism and interest, Burns hired him on probation for $325 a month. After three months, if he worked out, his salary would increase to $375.

Thomson spent his first week at the King and Yonge branch in downtown Toronto observing, followed by three weeks in a classroom training programme about branch banking. Then he was posted to another downtown Toronto branch as an assistant accountant, thus skipping the position of teller. It was a leap that saved him two years of slogging. The promotions would continue with the same rapidity for the next twenty years. It had taken Allen Lambert thirty-three years from the day he joined the Bank of Toronto in 1927 to become president. Even though Lambert was a young president for his day, Thomson's climb would be even shorter; he would achieve the president's chair in only fifteen years.

There were a few tough days on the way. In the fall of 1957, as a branch accountant, Thomson was ill-prepared for the onslaught of customers for Canada Savings Bonds. He recalls: "Anybody who's waited on the public soon learns that there is a real knack to giving good service. It looks easy if it's done right, like anything else, but if you haven't got the practice and you don't know where the right forms are, you haven't prepared yourself for the day's opening, once business starts at ten o'clock and that door's opened and it's a busy day, you can't recover if you get hopelessly behind. The more frustration you have dealing with a customer, the more the thing starts to go downhill." He barely survived, and only because the manager came out to the counter to rescue him, showing him how to organize himself and get through the day.

His next major posting was to downtown Montreal's St. James and McGill branch, where he was senior assistant manager. By then, he was married to Heather Lorimer, a nurse, and was seen as a serious young man, with little time for relaxation. His next appointment, assistant to the president in 1963, was, in effect, his last. After a mere six years at the bank, he'd been chosen for the top, designated to succeed Lambert when the time came.

Because the top job was his to lose, he was like an overgrown boy to whom exertion and excitement are the same. He constantly reminded himself that the eyes of the business world were on him. There were others within the bank who had been there longer than he — much longer — who had plied their apprenticeship roles diligently with, so far, insufficient reward. They were gunning for him, waiting for him to stumble and fall on his face.

His enemies were disappointed. Thomson was satisfied to submerge his ego in the institution, do Lambert's bidding, and see his time as part of a continuum that was moving at a much faster rate than any previous rise to the top. He was a full generation ahead of himself, and began receiving promotions he should not have had until he was fifty. As he beat his colleagues up the ladder, other pretenders to the throne fled, leaving the executive shelves barren for a time. A director at thirty-eight, he joined an ancient club, but joined as one of the few bankers given to wearing something as exciting as a striped shirt rather than the uniform, starched white style.

In spite of a taste in clothing that might have seemed *outré*, Thomson still projected a guarded nature. Says one who has known him from those early days: "Everything must have a purpose. He's always looked occupied. Even twenty years ago in Montreal he looked occupied." Even his best friends, those few with whom he can relax, are in awe of his control. Says John Tory, president of International Thomson: "He's very much in control of himself. I think, at times, that irritates Heather a little bit."

"He has gained much greater personal confidence and poise," says Neil Wood. "Then, he was so anxious to succeed. On social occasions he really wasn't relaxing. He wouldn't laugh, or enjoy a joke, or be at ease with people." Golfing buddy and Burns, Fry president Jack Lawrence sees a growing dichotomy: "As the years go by, he becomes more and more worried about where he is seen in public. He even worries about being seen dancing with his wife. Heather likes a bit of fun, she likes to swing."

Thomson rarely gets angry and when he does, it shows only in the tone of his voice as the timbre changes; a careful listener can detect a note of disappointment, nothing else. Friend Gordon Gray, of A. E. LePage, explains it this way: "Losing your temper is to lose control, become irrational. I've never seen him lose his temper. The strong, silent types lose their temper; he is open and democratic."

Others disagree. "Dick Thomson is a very defensive guy," says one director. "I think he's quite insecure. If anybody questions him, he draws back. With Lambert, everything was open to discussion. Dick's shy. The best thing he's got going for him is his wife, Heather. He's an automated robot as far as I'm concerned. Instead of entertaining people, he's at the Cambridge Club running and having a salad by himself."

Indeed, the Cambridge Club is a favourite haunt. While all of his predecessors and many of his contemporaries at the other banks prefer to sup at the Toronto Club, where stowing away deep-fried smelt is about as risqué as things get, Thomson is part of the young, entrepreneurial squad who frequent the health club three blocks north of his office. He tries to get there two or three noon-hours a week for a twenty-minute run on the outdoor roof track, followed by twenty-five to thirty minutes of light work-out on the bench and with weights, maintaining a fitness programme designed specifically for him. But he doesn't brag about his top fitness rating. Jack Lawrence, one of the initial club investors, once approached Thomson to be photographed and featured in a club membership mailing along with Bill Wilder, deputy chairman of Consumers'-Home, and several other members. Even with much cajoling, Thomson refused: he just did not want anyone to know that he was running the track rather than hustling business.

Holidays are important to Thomson, as he tries to preserve a rhythm in his life that includes relaxation. It is almost as if he's holding something within himself in reserve against unknown professional agony or personal anguish that will require strength to survive. In 1981 he bought a white stretched bungalow in an exclusive palm-lined compound at Lost Tree near Palm Beach, Florida. Five miles away is Seminole, Ben Hogan's favourite course, and one of the top ten courses in North America. Thomson is a member, one of a handful of Canadians allowed to belong. He skis, but carefully; Heather will take more risks. In Vail, Colorado, where they skied on holidays with a dozen other couples a few years back, the final night's dinner was held at a Greek restaurant complete with gyrating belly dancer. As a joke, Thomson was named by the group as the "most improved" skier. When he opened the gift, his prize was a Bank of Montreal tie. He good-naturedly put it on over his ski sweater and wore it all evening.

If Thomson's mind is a computer for remembering all the deals, his body is a shrine to be preserved. He doesn't smoke, drinks little, and never over-eats. *Mens sana in corpore sano*: a sound mind in a sound body. Getting out of control is something that runaway economies do; getting out of shape is for reckless executives.

The sky hangs suspended like a grey corrugated metal roof — dark, low, and noisy. Below, on the first tee of the Glen Abbey Golf Course in Oakville, Ontario, spots of rain land on the marshal's hat as he makes his announcement. "From Grenelefe, Florida, and the winner of the 1981 Doral Open, Andy Bean." "1982," comes the drawled correction. "Y'all get the news a year later up heah?" The Georgia-born Bean tugs at his sleeveless vest and continues. "Hell, Jack wasn't there, Tom wasn't there, they just went and gave it to me." The announcer presses on. "Your amateurs are Jack Lawrence, Ralph Simmons [a regional manager for London Life Insurance], and Dick Thomson." Pro-Am day at the 1982 Canadian Open, with fifty-eight pros from the Tournament Players Association, each teamed up with three amateurs, every one of whom has paid $1,600 for the pleasure of a round with the big boys. Ahead of this foursome, Bobby Clampett, a $200,000 winner the previous year; and Don Halldorson, top Canadian money man on the tour. Yet to come, more names: Nicklaus, Trevino, Crenshaw, Weiskopf, Player — and the man who became Canadian Open champion the following Sunday, Bruce Lietzke.

Dick Thomson lines up with his playing partners for the official photographer. As the flash lights up Thomson's yellow pullover sweater, beige and blue checked pants, black golf shoes, and his Rosedale Golf Club sun visor in his hand, it catches his grin, silly and forced as befits such a staged show. His teeth are slightly uneven beneath the parted lips, and the lower jaw possesses a slight forward thrust, giving his face a determined look that lasts long after the smile is gone. As he walks over to the markers at the first tee, his shoulders show signs of rounding, the only portent of his creeping age. He tees up his ball and looks languidly down the fairway towards the green, 369 yards away. He settles in by bobbling back and forth on his firmly planted feet, takes a practice swing, then a slow and methodical backswing, then *swaaak*, a perfectly respectable first tee shot 175 yards out and just into the groomed short rough on the left-hand side of the fairway. Another wood shot and he is near the sand trap in front of the green. An approach iron clears the bunker and hits the back of the green. On, along with Bean, in a respectable three. Thomson cleans off the ball and with little wasted time bangs a 35-foot putt to within eighteen inches of the hole. Ralph Simmons, also on in three, strokes a 25-footer that heads for the hole just as though it has eyes. "Go in, go in," comes the directive from Thomson. It does. "Way to go, Ralph," shouts Thomson. The team, taking Simmons's birdie as its best ball score, goes one under par. Better than Bean, who takes a bogey five after his putt for par rims the cup.

Thomson is beginning to feel loose now. He flaps his arms out from his sides, parallel to the ground, and flexes his fingers. It is his first Pro-Am, and he is doing well. No reason not to, for although it is only his sixth time on the course, he shot an 83 on the par-72 6,200-yard monster four days earlier. There is, however, some special pressure. "It's always easier in the practice round," he says. "Just like the second putt. It always goes in when you take it over again." Just the same, he starts well, scoring a par on the third after hitting the green on his first shot over the pond. On the 452-yard fifth, his 225-yard drive outdistances Bean. "Way to go, man," he hollers when Lawrence retrieves a par on the tricky seventh. His solid game fades on the ninth, when, after a 225-yard drive, he lobs his second shot into the water hazard just five feet short of safety. "I lifted my head," he explains; "it's so easy to do."

He grabs a soft drink and heads for the back nine as the sun struggles out and the sweaters come off. His drives are becoming almost pneumatic in their consistency — 225 yards out — except for the eleventh, where the tee is elevated 120 feet and a drive must carry 220 yards just to reach the fairway. He steps up to his ball, teed as usual near the left marker, takes his customary stance with the right foot dropped back behind the left, and storms out the drive of the day — a towering 300-yard hit.

He charges down the hill, pleased with the hit, joshing with his partners as if being on a golf course brought out the boy in him. He might be back in Brandon, Manitoba, playing with borrowed sticks, for he is all gawky looks and gangly limbs. On the course, the professional banker's reserve disappears. Gone is the tight walk of the head-office corridor, so controlled that the arms barely swing. While he moves there with silken ease, there is a protective shield that fends off the arrows of others and ensures that the secrets within cannot be breached. Here, on the golf course, his arms are in motion even when he is not shooting. He is open, almost vulnerable, his guard down, all corporate systems relaxed, the jangle of the phones gone. When someone else makes a tough putt, his shouted cheer is punctuated by raised arms in a traditional exuberant victory salute.

Today Thomson does better than Bean, who picks up in disgust on the tenth hole and plays the rest of the round without keeping score. For Thomson and his amateur buddies, their best ball score for eighteen holes is 62, about in the middle of the pack. Throughout, Thomson battles well against the course, through rain squalls, sun showers, and soggy ground. As he readies himself for the fifteenth hole, he looks back at the fourteenth, where he'd three-putted after being on in two shots. He had spent five minutes, along with Bean, replaying the putts.

"Those damn greens are so tough, you can't just aim for the pin." His eyes cloud over with concern as he looks up at the fifteenth green, elevated 12 feet above the tee, but only 115 yards away, the shortest hole on the course. "Look at this bugger," he sighs. He selects a ten-iron, takes a practice swing, then hits the ball. The arc is perfect and the thump as it hits the green, 20 feet from the pin, is audible at the tee. Applause issues from the spectators sitting on the sloping hill around the green. "That's not a bad shot," Thomson says with satisfaction. Without missing a beat, Bean adds, "For a damn banker."

The three black towers of the Toronto-Dominion Centre rise like spikes driven in from on high for some godly game of quoits. Designed by architect Ludwig Mies van der Rohe, dreamed up by New York developer William Zeckendorf, they exist today only because of the daring of Allen Lambert and the drive of the man he turned to — Dick Thomson. Since the building of the Royal York Hotel and the Bank of Commerce tower decades earlier, downtown Toronto remained largely unchanged until the 1960s. At thirty-nine storeys, the Commerce building was for years the unchallenged holder of the title of tallest building in the British Commonwealth.

Today, it is all but hidden in the canyon created by the other bank buildings that followed in a crazy race to erect the tallest monument. First came the TD at fifty-four storeys, then the Commerce tower at sixty, and finally the Bank of Montreal at seventy-two. But back in 1960, when the idea was first presented to Lambert, no one was even sure where downtown Toronto would be in ten years. Some wanted to move it north towards the new City Hall, others even farther, to Bloor Street. The man who, more than any politician, created the reborn core and picked its site was Allen Lambert.

Lambert's sad blue eyes stare from sunken pockets, hung with heavy lids that give a cast to the outside corners and create a kind of downward mobility that makes his face look as if at any moment it will begin slipping away from both sides of his skull. There is a hound-dog look to him that is only broken when the slightest of smiles splits his face before being papered over again. Two jug ears are clamped to his head and his hair rolls in two waves above the smooth sandy beach of his forehead. It was he who propelled the TD on from its 1955 merger so that by the time he retired, twenty-two years later, shareholders and employees had tripled, assets had grown by thirty times, and non-Canadian deposits had increased by a factor of 180.

When Zeckendorf first approached Lambert in 1960 with a redevelopment plan that would include both the Commerce and the TD, Lambert rejected the models Zeckendorf brought that showed a single twenty-five-storey tower on the current TD property and a higher-rising building across Bay for the Commerce. Lambert turned to Cemp Investments Ltd., a Bronfman investment firm, which agreed to a three-tower complex, then the biggest office project in the British Commonwealth. Under the deal, the TD tower land and the land on which the bank pavilion was built would be owned by the bank and leased to a partnership company owned equally by Cemp and the TD. After ninety-nine years, ownership will revert to the bank, at which time it will share ownership of the other buildings and land.

Gordon Gray, then president of A. E. LePage, did the land assembly. It took two years and $15 million to buy thirty-eight parcels of land in an operation filled with intrigue and ingenuity. A variety of real estate firms and lawyers were used in order to hide the fact that a single buyer — presumed to have money to burn — was behind all the interests. LePage, to confuse things further, even spent $75,000 to renovate one newly acquired building to fool nearby hold-outs into thinking no development was planned. The building was razed after the assembly was finished. Construction took three years, 1964 to 1967, and the complex gained national prominence as the site for the Confederation of Tomorrow conference, hosted by Ontario premier John Robarts. Lambert allows: "You have to be a bit visionary."

It was this man — who went to China looking for business for the first time in 1956 and worked his way all over the Pacific and Far East nations building the bank's international base, who assembled the bank's collection of three hundred paintings and the largest group of Inuit carvings in the world — who picked Thomson as his assistant and protégé in 1963. Attracted to Thomson by his ability to size up situations well and quickly, Lambert designated Thomson the bank representative at all negotiations on the TD Centre. Others on the team were Gordon Gray and Leo Kolber of Cemp (both were later named to the TD board of directors). For Thomson, it was a chance to shine in several areas. One evening, for example, he heard that the investment firm of Pitfield, Mackay, Ross was looking for new quarters. He was on the phone at a quarter to nine the next morning, pitching the building to PMR chairman Ward Pitfield. The firm signed up.

The early successes were welcome. The size of the project was mind-boggling. The old Commerce building had one-third of a million square feet. The first TD tower had 1.25 million square feet: there could have been a lot of empty offices. However, the complex proved itself to be a good business deal, and created a cashbox for the bank that is paying out to this day. Initial rents were $6.35 a square foot; now charges go as high as $40. And while the management costs have risen, debt costs have not. The whole development had been financed by fixed-term debt, well removed from the vagaries of volatile interest rates.

When the building was finished, it wasn't enough for Thomson that it was a success, that the provincial premiers came, that Princess Alexandra paid an official visit: it had to *look* successful, have the right bearing to spread the TD name. One of the deals that had been negotiated by Gray was the roof-top installation of television antennae to serve a local cable television licensee, Rogers Cablesystems. Gray had negotiated the deal for so long that owner Ted Rogers had finally asked Gray to join one of the Rogers boards. The antennae system was quite a coup — and paid a handsome fee. But the first day the television towers were erected, Thomson took one look at them, found them unsightly, and announced: "They have to be removed." Rogers immediately complied, and the towers eventually found a home atop the Bank of Montreal headquarters across the street.

The successful venture of the Toronto bank complex led Thomson to do other similarly lucrative deals across the country. As a result, he has had a hand in fashioning downtowns right across Canada. The TD owns half of the TD Centre in Toronto; one-third of Vancouver's Pacific Centre; 20 per cent in the Eaton Centre in Toronto, the largest shopping centre in North America; 30 per cent of the Edmonton Centre. According to a report by Alfred Bunting Co. Ltd., the replacement value of the four centres is $750 million — a total soon to be increased with the completion next year of a thirty-five-storey fourth tower for the Toronto TD Centre.

The bank's holdings are not limited to real estate. It has been actively acquiring equity interests in several companies over the years. They include 5 per cent of communications company Maclean Hunter Ltd.; 15 per cent of real estate giant A. E. LePage; 20 per cent of Talcorp Associates Ltd.; 40 per cent of Oxford Development, a $1.4-billion real estate development company. TD also has just under 10 per cent of Trilon Holdings, the new financial services arm of London Life Insurance, and stands to pick up ownership pieces of two more of its customers, Costain Ltd., a real estate development firm, and Whonnock Industries, a West Coast forest products company. Both companies have been in trouble during the recent recession and, as their banker, TD has taken shares in the companies as part of the work-out agreements.

TD is not just a passive investor. President Korthals sits on the Talcorp board, and Thomson takes an active interest in the corporate health of companies the bank has an interest in. In 1981, he and his wife were among a busload of revellers off to see the production of George Bernard Shaw's *Too True to Be Good* at Niagara-on-the-Lake, about an hour and a half from Toronto. Just after the group was under way and the glasses of wine had been poured, the bus passed a Talcorp subsidiary, Reichhold Limited, its neon sign blazing red in the darkness. Talcorp president Bob Smith was also on the bus and proudly pointed out the sight. Ever the banker worried about red ink, Thomson quipped: "I hope the colour doesn't mean anything."

Dick Thomson does not like the smell of losers. He likes to sit back, identify winners, then get close to them. When communications and newspaper magnate Roy Thomson, Lord Thomson of Fleet, was alive,

Dick Thomson put Roy's son Ken, who later inherited both the title and the fortune from his father, on the TD board. As a result, the banking business of the world-wide Thomson empire, financed by North Sea oil, is split between the Royal and the upstart TD. There was a similar divide-and-conquer scenario with the Black brothers. When Conrad was appointed to the Commerce board in 1978, Thomson quickly offered a TD board position to brother Monte. The TD became the number two banker to the burgeoning Argus empire. Seagram's Charles Bronfman is on the Bank of Montreal board, but his number two man, Leo Kolber, is a TD director, thus sending some of Seagram's business to TD. Not a bad strategy for the number five bank to become number two to corporate giants.

Thomson was also among the first bankers to foresee the customer demand for automated services. Starting with fourteen "Green Machine" automated tellers in 1979, the bank has 250 now. He took early initiatives to get out of unprofitable retail banking outside Canada, selling off TD's share in Midland and International Banks as well as its 26 per cent interest in a California bank, in order to focus on wholesale operations, where overhead was lower and profits were higher. His capacity to see trouble coming was demonstrated in 1982 when he announced that the TD would limit risky Third World loan exposure to a maximum of 15 per cent of loan amounts outstanding each year.

Even with its huge Dome loan of $1 billion, the TD is the least exposed of any of the Big Five banks to troublesome oil and gas credits. They were once expected to be profitable forever, but stagnant energy prices have meant the rush to nab such business was ill-advised. It's not just their knack with numbers that kept TD in better shape than its competitors. "At the TD," says Jack Lawrence of Burns, Fry, "they seem to let ego get in the way of decisions the least of all the banks."

TD is further aided by its organizational structure. Even a branch manager is only one reporting level removed from the president. The reduced hierarchy makes the place easier to run than some of Thomson's top-heavy competitors with expensive branch systems. Thomson has seen no need to layer on a level of spear-carriers with little to do but watch someone else. Instead he has recruited and promoted carefully. Says Tom Kierans, president of the investment firm McLeod Young Weir: "Allen Lambert allowed Thomson to create an organization built on brains."

Of no small assistance has been the historic location of TD's business in Canada. Sixty per cent is in Ontario, with 60 per cent of that amount located in Metropolitan Toronto. Thus, when recession hits, the TD suffers least, because it has little representation in the hardest-hit areas, such as the Maritimes.

For Thomson, whether the times are good or bad, the appeal of banking is that it offers an entrée to many industries. The young man who did not want to become an engineer after working summers in a plant still cherishes variety. "You're in a different business every day. It's fun. You're not stuck in one place in one plant in one part of the city for the rest of your life. The senior banker in any community in the country is right in with the senior people in the community, whether it's in Barrie or Saskatoon or Toronto." While the job may offer professional freedom, there are some personal constraints. There is, for example, the constant fear of kidnap and extortion. In 1972, a man forced his way into the Thomson home early one morning and trussed Heather and their two-year-old son in an aborted ransom attempt.

The personal misfortunes have been few, however, allowing Thomson to focus on his work and achieve the kind of results that keep shareholders content even in the bad times. Last year, return on average assets (a measurement much liked by the analysts) was 0.68 per cent, well ahead of the competition. Closest that year was the Bank of Nova Scotia at 0.51 per cent. The TD always seems to do well, sharing "best performance" accolades with a different bank every year.

The Republic of South Africa, with a population of about twenty-four million people, is perched on the southernmost tip of the continent. Its ruling white citizens are outnumbered by the black population about five to one, but this minority has a firm and exclusive grip on economic and political power. No other nation's internal policies—except perhaps interest rates set in the United States—have so plagued Canadian bankers as South Africa's white supremacist laws. Foes of apartheid, especially church groups, have tried to pressure Canadian banks to stop lending money to South Africa. Noisy demonstrators have gathered outside annual meetings of bank shareholders, accounts have been closed in protest, and lobby groups have peppered bank chairmen with questions in public and in private for the last decade.

Thomson is not a crowd-follower, either of the noisy folk in the street or of the boardroom apologists. In 1979, the interchurch Taskforce on the Churches and Corporate Responsibility seemed to be making some headway with the banks, getting them to agree to make no more loans to South Africa. In the face of that changing mood, Thomson and the TD approved a loan for a coal-fired plant run by South Africa's Electricity Supply Commission (Escom), a huge producer that generates 90 per cent of the country's electricity, which amounts to 60 per cent of all the electricity used on the continent. The bank had made no loans to South Africa during the previous three years, but this one, argued Thomson, appeared different. "They were going to increase the electrification of all parts of their country," Thomson explained, "including Soweto. We thought it was for a very good reason." Thomson was out front and out of step, but confident in his position.

The protests quickened and proof that the loan was "for a very good reason" was not forthcoming. In 1980, he changed his mind again and ruled out further loans unless for specific commercial purposes. Unlike other bankers, he was willing to admit his mistake and explain his thinking. "It's very difficult when you make a loan to a government agency to follow the loan as to how the dollars are used. This is why we had second thoughts. We changed our mind. The loan was made and made with good intentions. You try to do something and if it doesn't work out, you don't do it again."

Lambert did not approve of the return to a no-loan stance and voted against it at the board meeting where the decision was taken. The outcome was a sign of Thomson's strength and his capacity to impose his view. It was also a sign of Lambert's magnanimity in letting his successor get on with the job as he saw it. There were others on the board who agreed with Lambert and thought Thomson was wrong to bend to the pressure groups. Argues director Fred Eaton: "Cutting off loans to South Africa just hurts the blacks. I don't understand why these ginger groups say it's perfectly moral to lend to the Chinese or other regimes run by thugs. It's highly selective, and I'm against selective moralism."

In the end, if business considerations were Thomson's reason for halting loans, little came of it. The demonstrations died down and the protesters trained their volley of words elsewhere. At the 1982 annual meeting, there was only one question from the floor on the topic; in 1983, there were none. But in 1982, when the United Church of Canada moved its account from the Bank of Nova Scotia, it chose the Royal Bank even though the TD had firmly stated that it would make no further loans to South Africa. The Royal, for its part, reserves the right to consider loan requests, but has said only that "under the current circumstances" it will not make general-purpose or balance-of-payment loans to the South African government. Thomson's understated reaction to the surprising switch by the church to which he belongs: "I sure thought they made a mistake."

That pragmatism extends to corporate charitable donations. The bank gives about $1 million a year, with the board approving any donation of more than $20,000. Publicly, such donations are offered as an example of corporate social responsibility; privately they are also seen as a method of cementing business relations. Thomson takes a close interest in the larger sums as a committee sifts through all requests. The first question often put about a request from an organization that has not applied before is: who is their banker? Although there is a bank rule against donations to private schools, sums are sent anyway, particularly to schools where the executives have placed their own children: Havergal and Crescent for the Thomsons; Bishop Strachan for Korthals.

Thomson's interest also extends to such minutiae as the bank's long-established liquor policy. In Lambert's time, at regional meetings of the board of directors held outside Toronto, there were always complimentary bottles of rum and Scotch placed in each director's hotel room, a nod to the representation of liquor companies on the TD board. Thomson ended that practice, arguing it was an unnecessary expense, causing some grumbling among directors who saw one of their perks disappear. He did not, however, alter the careful balance of liquor labels at TD receptions — Seagram's 60 per cent, Hiram Walker 35 per cent, and Gilbey's 5 per cent — to reflect the long-time shareholdings of the various companies and their resulting clout.

The ratio and the labels have been known to become a *cause célèbre*. On the occasion of Allen Lambert's fiftieth anniversary in the bank, TD director Cliff Hatch, president and CEO of Hiram Walker–Gooderham & Worts, would not even register in the hotel where the gala was being held, the Four Seasons in Vancouver, because he knew the hotel did not usually buy from his company. In charge of proceedings was Graham Miller, who worked out of Edmonton in branch development. In addition to his regular duties, Miller was a trouble-shooter, the kind of guy who could be counted on to get something done the way the top brass wanted it. Prior to the reception he waded in and told the hotel staff, in no uncertain words, what to do with the booze from the wrong distilleries: "You get that crap out of here or I'll break every bottle in the place." The right brands were served.

In Bill Richards's office at Dome Petroleum, the style is the man himself. Its nine windows permit him to watch the world to the south and west, a wild panorama of Calgary winds and watch-towers with the blue Rocky Mountains humping along the skyline. The Dome president is glassed off from the city as he peers down on it like a ranger looking for the first sign of fire in the forest.

In 1981, however, it was Dick Thomson who saw the first sparks of the blaze to come. Dome was simply too clogged with debt. When Richards and chairman Jack Gallagher came back to the Canadian banks to finance the second half of the Hudson's Bay Oil and Gas purchase, it was Thomson who said no. He had been nervous enough about the $2 billion Dome borrowed from the banks in May 1981, a ten-year floating loan with no principal payments for five years. It was well secured, he admitted, but with interest rates going up and oil prices stagnant, Thomson argued that Dome could afford no more. Richards had once said that the U.S. banks were only good for petty cash, but Dome had to turn to them, and set up a further (U.S.) $1.8-billion credit line with a consortium of twenty-nine banks from North America, Europe, and Japan. It was the last time Dome would have such pull with the bankers.

About the same time, Thomson began urging Gallagher to get cash by selling off some of Dome's assets. He also insisted that Dome begin to pay down its loan to TD, which was over $1 billion at that point — the largest single corporate loan on the bank's books. Gallagher didn't listen to Thomson's advice about selling off assets — not until he had to put some of Dome's corporate holdings up for sale six months later as part of the negotiations with the federal government — but Dome did begin to pay down the TD loan. When a banker like Thomson wants his money back, even a dreamer like Jack Gallagher must comply.

In the summer of 1982, as negotiations continued among Dome, the government, and the four Canadian banks (the Royal, Montreal, Commerce, and TD), TD was odd man out. Thomson did not want a bail-out, but he was torn and did not want to see Dome go under, either. TD president Robin Korthals was a hawk on Thomson's shoulder. "We should take our lumps and return to the discipline of the marketplace," he said in July, as the deal was being debated. He worried that there would be "a different kind of banking world" as a result of the Dome deal. He felt that the Massey bail-out, for example, had been a mistake: "They should have let that one go."

Korthals and Thomson understood the rationale for preserving Dome — energy self-sufficiency based on oil in the Beaufort — but they were dubious. "If it turns out well and there's oil in the Beaufort," said Korthals, "then it will have been a brilliant investment. If it doesn't, it will be a turkey."

That kind of thinking put Thomson at odds with the other bankers, particularly Russ Harrison at the Commerce, who would curse Thomson in private. But the advice Thomson was receiving from the likes of Arne Nielsen, the TD's senior western Canadian director (he's been on the board a dozen years) and chairman and chief executive officer of Canadian Superior Oil Ltd., was not reassuring. Said Nielsen: "Canadian Superior has got 2.8 million acres in the Beaufort, and much and all as I'd like to find something there, the geology just isn't as good as Hibernia — it's a good field right now. I wish we had 5 per cent of it. I was with Mobil when we put it together." Nielsen, who lives just five houses from Gallagher on Calgary's Britannia Drive, wasn't just offering the view of a competitor; his was the position of an admirer who stood to profit from the Beaufort.

"Jack's the eternal optimist," said Nielsen; "that's how he built Dome."

In the end, it was that optimism that swung TD into the bail-out deal. Dome, admitted Thomson, was "the national dream." The other admission, made in a speech to bank analysts the day after the Dome deal was announced in September 1982, was even more profound. "We made a mistake," he said; "we shouldn't have got so heavily involved. I regret it." Yet Thomson—ever pragmatic—could be sanguine about the whole deal. "We're going to have to get into bed with government from time to time in this country because we have such big deals going on." He pointed to that other national dream, the CPR, and cited an 1885 deal whereby the government bailed out the Bank of Montreal by guaranteeing a loan of $20 million, an amount greater than the total government revenue at the time. "That was a good decision," he argued. "Don't we need a large private-sector oil company in this country, if for no other reason than to be a check to Petro-Can?"

There is a sizeable group on the TD board that has been concerned by Thomson's maverick position on other deals. Commenting on Thomson's Labour Day weekend activities in the Royal Trust affair, TD secretary Glenn Bumstead remarked wistfully to a colleague: "We have to figure out a way to get Dick out of town on long weekends." In another incident, Sam Belzberg, president and CEO of First City Financial Corporation, bid for Canada Permanent Trust, and Thomson agreed to finance him even though the pursuer and the pursued were both TD customers. He made the decision to back Belzberg without going to the board first for approval. Some on the board were aghast. "I was horrified," recalls one director, "because Canada Permanent and the bank had been closely knit together. Didn't they realize the account would be lost?" The director spoke out at the meeting when Thomson told the board what he'd done, but the opposing view received only lukewarm support from two or three other directors. After the meeting, away from the watchful eye of the chairman, a dozen directors spoke supportively to the director who had opposed Thomson. It was too late. Recalls the director: "I said, 'Where in heaven's name were you?' "

While the director did not call into question the right and responsibility of Thomson and management to do deals and then seek board approval, there was the view that financing a take-over of a company such as Canada Permanent was unethical. "After Royal Trust," maintains the questioning director, "a lot of outside people said, 'Why the hell didn't you fire him?' "

Another director agrees that there was "a certain amount" of feeling that Thomson had ridden rough-shod over the board on the Belzberg loan approval. "There were people who were opposed to the loan," says the director, "but a board can't second-guess management. You have to let management wheel and deal. You can't involve the board, that's just too many people."

Whether they always approve or not, most directors do see Thomson as being out on the firing line, gunning for business. "He's deal-oriented," says director Monte Black, "and likes to get involved in take-overs and play a role beyond just being a lender. Even when he gets caught out on something, he has that funny little grin and laugh that are endearing, and he gets off." Gordon Gray describes Thomson's style this way: "You pick from the opportunities that are put before you. The spectrum goes from old loyalties to new connections. He thinks things through quickly and has the courage to do it. The easy thing to do is nothing, to turn down deals."

If there is one thing that Thomson does not do, it is take the easy route. He was alone among senior bankers, for example, in his position on the foreign banks. Beginning in the early 1970s, the Bank of Nova Scotia, among others, began to agitate for regulation over the so-called suitcase bankers. These interlopers, it was argued, came to Montreal or Toronto or Vancouver, briefly set up shop in a hotel room, arranged loans with companies operating in Canada, then booked them with the bank's head office in the U.S., the U.K., Japan, or half a dozen other countries. Overheads were nil, there were no reserve requirements or other central bank rules to follow, and the foreign banks could undercut the Canadian banks because their costs were close to zero.

"If we were a fifty-first state," Thomson argued, "New York banks wouldn't be operating here, just like they don't operate in Illinois. Look at Philadelphia, Baltimore, or Boston: they've all lost strength as financial centres because they haven't protected themselves. Chicago, on the other hand, has very firm rules and has maintained strength." He wanted to protect Toronto from becoming a financial backwater.

Further, he argued that the TD had offices in the U.S. to do business with everyone, while the U.S. banks, for example, would come to Canada only to serve U.S. companies in Canada; Japanese banks would cream off the business of Japanese companies operating in Canada. "It's like arguing for reciprocity on a one-way air route," he maintained.

"Someone had to take that stand," says Korthals. "He *is* a moderate nationalist. The foreign banks could have just come in here and taken over. We didn't get the collar on them that we wanted, but we did get *a* collar. He's very happy with the outcome."

Still, the action that even Korthals admits was a "suicide mission" had its price — a boycott of the TD by the foreign banks. Also, venerable banking relationships have been cancelled. Typical is British-based Midland

Bank. In the salad days of the British Empire, Midland was the world's largest correspondent bank. It maintained connections with local banks in most countries around the world rather than opening its own offices. For years, the association with Canada was with the TD. Thomson's position caused Midland to switch to the Bank of Montreal.

The continuing solo flights seem to strengthen Thomson's resolve. After the difficulties of 1982 and early 1983 over Crown Trust, Greymac, and Seaway Trust in Ontario, the limit on the amount deposited in an institution by an individual that could be guaranteed by the Canadian Deposit Insurance Corporation was increased from $20,000 to $60,000. Most applaud the new ceiling and say it was long overdue. Not Thomson. It was too hefty an increase, he insists, bringing it out of the realm of the small saver "into the realm of those who should be aware of the risk."

Dick Thomson would be the last to regard himself as a crusader, yet of all the senior bankers, he takes the most individualistic positions on issues. At the same time, he doesn't seek the spotlight for his own aggrandizement. While he returns most calls from journalists himself rather than sending inquiries the long way round the public relations department, Thomson makes few speeches to promote his views, contenting himself with the odd news conference or interview opportunity. Explains vice-president Alan Hockin: "He underestimates his own power of communication. He feels inadequate talking to politicians, the newspapers, or civil servants. He draws in upon himself. His training is so technical — engineering and business — and he's not an economist, not a political scientist. In a debate where art dominates science, he just closes up." Thomson also suffers from the lack of a consistent perspective, an ideology into which he can place his views. One time, he gave a newspaper interview that he later told a colleague was "easy," not realizing until it was printed that he had claimed to be a fan of a free market — then in the next breath had called for government to halt the influx of Japanese-built automobiles.

Another reason that he shies away from public speaking is that he dislikes working with prepared texts. Although he has a basso profundo voice worthy of a broadcaster, he feels he needs to rehearse a speech several times before giving it. By the time presentation day arrives, he has grown sick of his own words. At that point, he'd rather speak without notes at all, but he fears that if he did, he might deviate even slightly from his intended meaning. "He finds speeches time-consuming," says vice-president Doug Peters. "It's not a challenge. It becomes a performance and he doesn't like to perform. He's got a job where he doesn't have to do what he doesn't want to do — so he doesn't do it. Why should he do something he finds boring?"

For the most part, he is genuinely happy doing his job. "I love it," he says. "Bankers feel on the inside. It's an exciting thing to be involved in." While he can afford to take the lonely view on public issues, he stays away from solo operations at the bank. "We're not," he insists, "a bunch of high-wire artists working on an independent act." Instead, he lets others handle most multimillion-dollar deals, preferring to dip into three or four that may be on the go at any one time, just to keep his hand in.

During the last year, with more deals coming apart than being put together, he has become more involved. He honestly sees banking as a personal business, a trait he inherited from his father. He knows that customers become and remain loyal for the slightest of reasons. He has often retold a favourite tale of his father's, about a man who had a large cash balance in an account that was paying no interest. When Harold Thomson urged the man to move his money into a different account where he could earn interest, the customer replied: "I feel an obligation to this bank. You don't need to pay me any interest."

Another lesson his father taught him was never to give bad news over the telephone or by letter — always deliver it in person. Thomson recently spent most of an afternoon trying to work out a bad loan with a customer. At $10 million, it wasn't a large loan, but Thomson worked out the problem himself. "He's had a difficult year," says friend Bob Smith. "He's had to do things to friends and acquaintances that I guess he'd rather not have done."

It was former U.S. secretary of state Dean Acheson who once said of Prime Minister Lester Pearson that he had parlayed a small country into a position of much greater influence than its size would justify. So, too, with Dick Thomson. His bank has half the assets of the first-place Royal, but the little guy is lighter on his feet, can move more quickly and act while others are dithering.

After all, wasn't that how he caught the bonefish? It is stuffed and mounted now, hanging incongruously in his ski chalet hundreds of miles from salt-water. Never mind that it looks a little foolish against a backdrop of corn snow and cordwood; never mind that Heather keeps threatening to take it off the wall: it is a symbol of his quick hand. Only a weekend fisherman dwells on the one that got away. The mistakes are hidden behind a shield of self-control; the trophies are hung for all to see.

ELEVEN

NOT EVERYBODY WINS

Sad Scenes from Corporate Life

MOST OF THE PEOPLE in this book are winners. They have survived in the corporate world and risen to the top. Such success takes a certain brand of stamina, for it is easy to get stuck in one place, be passed over or tossed down. Politics and pot-shotting in the banker's executive suite have always been a commonplace phenomenon, as this incident from the late 1940s illustrates. Jack Mackenzie, of the investment firm Elliott and Page, was investigating a career with the Bank of Montreal. About the same time, he was invited to a party at the home of Jimmy Muir, chairman of the Royal Bank. Mackenzie told Muir that he'd been talking to the Bank of Montreal. A waste of time, said Muir, and urged him to join the Royal. Mackenzie pressed Muir for details about how he might progress in the job. Talking of the bank as a ladder, Muir replied: "As you get a lead on a guy, you stamp on his hand so he falls back a bit. Then you catch up to the next guy and stamp on his hand." Incredulous, Mackenzie asked if the same was true at all the banks. "I don't know," said Muir; "it's certainly true at the Royal."

From the outside, with their solid doors, secure locks, and proper ways, banks appear to be above all that. From within, the reality is quite different. Careers can collapse in a moment; people can crumble in a morning; others simply come up short. Here, then, are nine vignettes of people (some anonymous) who have suffered in some way at the hand of the system and come up as corporate losers.

Stan Davison has a slight squint in his left eye, as if he's just a little incredulous at what is going on around him. A mousy man, his small, brown head is perched on a stooped six-foot-one frame. Except for a fringe of white hair, he is perfectly bald. His lackadaisical air makes him look more like a small-town parson than a Calgary banker. "Banking," he says, "is surprisingly personal, even at the corporate level." If so, this meek man who is the Bank of Montreal's highest-ranking officer in Calgary — a vice-chairman — may be out-hustled by local competitors such as the Royal's gregarious vice-chairman, Hal Wyatt.

Davison has all the perks of power and substance: the title, the corner office, the $225,000 annual salary, the chauffeur-driven Cadillac, the memberships in Calgary Golf and Country as well as the Petroleum Club — but behind the trappings lurks a surprising truth. Many consider him a man promoted beyond his skills.

Born in 1928, Davison joined the bank in 1947 and held various positions in British Columbia, Alberta, and Quebec. First made a vice-president in 1968, he was an executive vice-president for domestic banking by 1971. By 1978, as executive vice-president and chief general manager, he was running the bank on a day-to-day basis for hard-driving president Bill Mulholland. As Anglos left Quebec, and head offices moved from Montreal to Toronto, Davison was part of B of M's westward surge. Chairman McNeil would go to Calgary, Mulholland would become CEO in 1979, staying in Montreal, and Davison would move to Toronto to watch over the 80 to 85 per cent of the bank's domestic business done west of Quebec. Says Davison: "It didn't seem to make a great deal of sense to have all of us in Montreal." It was expected that when McNeil retired three years later in 1981 and Mulholland became chairman, Davison would be Mulholland's number two.

When 1981 came, however, the man at the right hand of Mulholland was not Davison. It was deputy chairman Grant Reuber, an economist from the University of Western Ontario and deputy minister of finance in the Joe Clark government. Reuber ran the staff groups (personnel, comptroller, financial, economics), and Bill Bradford became the new number three and president — carrying out the duties of a chief operating officer. Davison was dispatched to Calgary as vice-chairman. Kicked upstairs, as the parlance would have it. From the man slotted to be number two, he had become number four and falling.

Davison's problem came when Mulholland began to pile on the responsibilities and found him coming up short. Says Stelco chairman and B of M director Peter Gordon: "Bill [Mulholland] fed him as much as he could possibly stand and finally recognized that that wasn't Stan's position. He was, in fact, slightly over his depth, and the sooner they recognized that, the better." Like many others he has worked with, Mulholland chewed through Davison, found too little juice for his liking, and spat him aside.

According to Fred McNeil, who along with Mulholland made the decision to hoist Davison: "He didn't have the breadth to be president. There's a real quantum jump at the top one or two jobs in any institution. It's *requirement*. There are a helluva lot of guys that can do a job that'd be fine, but the strategist often doesn't come up out of a line activity. A lot of people just top off, so you've got maybe half a dozen guys you hope have that potential, but, God, they fall off fast." Says Gordon: "He's an example of the Peter Principle; he was promoted beyond his ability to perform."

Davison himself knows he didn't have the fibre for the final push. "In every organization," says Davison, "when you are building something, you need good architects and good general contractors. We've got both. I look at fellows like Mulholland and Reuber as very good architects."

When word spread of his appointment as vice-chairman, some job offers came forward in Toronto from people assuming he was being pushed aside. He turned them down, willing to try the West, knowing that it would take time to become accustomed.

"I'm really doing the things the chairman would do if he was here. He's said to me, 'You're sort of my arm out there.' I could interfere as much as I want to in operations, but I don't really intend to. I'm here for consulting, if they want to consult with me. I participate in all the committees at head office, and I can be there as often as I want. It's a role you can be very busy at or do nothing at." In the end, that's all he's left with, the power to choose between the two. The shelf he sits on, however, remains the same.

J. had finished the final draft, polishing it as carefully as a jeweller placing stones in an eternity ring. It read well; he knew it. He knew it would restore his standing with the vice-president. The fall from grace, after all, couldn't last forever.

J. had accepted the change in his reporting relationship with some hope. It was a sideways move, a little of the old soft-shoe perhaps, but one that gave him a chance to rehabilitate his status and stature. The fact that he was given a chance to write this message to shareholders at all must have meant something — didn't it?

Damn right it did, he answered his own question as he looked over his hand-written copy, laboriously redone at the kitchen table early that grey morning. He reread it with satisfaction, knowing that every word was right. Approval by the vice-president would be perfunctory, the paper would be whisked on to the president untouched. The ten-minute speech for the annual meeting had just the right balance of pragmatism and vision.

By early afternoon, there was still no word. But any moment, the phone would ring and it would be the president, his brash congratulations spilling warmly from the earpiece.

Three o'clock. Could he leave the desk long enough to go to the washroom and risk missing the call? As he passed the vice-president's office, he asked the secretary to watch his line. As he paused to speak to her, his eye was drawn to three words in capital letters at the top of the page poking from her typewriter: MESSAGE TO SHAREHOLDERS.

—Is that for him? he asked, nodding towards the vice-president's office.

—Oh no, it's for the president. It's from down there, nodding towards the marketing department.

He walked towards marketing, hardly believing what he knew had happened.

—What's with the president's message?

Marketing threw his hands up to protest his innocence, but his mouth formed into a mocking grin.

—Don't ask me. The veep brought me your draft this morning and asked me to fix it. It's being typed now.

Crushed, he strode back towards the vice-president's office and barged in.

—Why didn't you return it to me instead of sending it on to be reworked, as if it were on a route slip?

A dismissive wave.

—I fooled with it, marketing fooled with it, if you have anything more to add, go ahead. If you're worried about pride of authorship, forget it. I lost mine long ago.

—I don't understand.

—I don't have to explain that or a whole lot of other things to you.

J's mouth opened to respond, but no words came.

Barry Zukerman was rejected by the banking system just as the human body might reject an organ transplant. After all, in the quiet corridors and hushed reception areas, he was an outsider: he was a Jew. Even the early backing of Dick Thomson, later to be Toronto-Dominion chairman, was not enough to change the system's bigotry. Over lunch at a job interview in 1972, Thomson had said to him: "We'll get our money out of you and if we can't keep you happy, and you go, it's our fault."

At thirty-one, with successful positions at Canadian Pacific and two brokerage houses behind him, Zukerman joined TD as superintendent for investments, a lofty title for the time, and he was the youngest to hold that rank in the bank. The status was an initial positive signal. "That was important," says Zukerman, "because a lot of my friends said the bank was WASPish and anti-Semitic."

There were no signs of that in the beginning, however, and he moved into his role running the bank's pension fund and stock market purchases with a vengeance. It was Zukerman, in fact, who plunged all banks into term-preferreds, a form of financing that gave corporate borrowers lower interest rates and the banks lower tax rates.

"It was the TD, me really, who thought up term-preferreds. In 1972, the government allowed deductibility of interest to buy shares. Dividends in Canada have always had 100 per cent exemption between public companies. We modified the criteria to limit the risk [thus] matching rates and the termination." It was Zukerman who asked a three-fold question: Why couldn't companies buy back the term-preferreds? Why couldn't floating rather than fixed rates be used? Why couldn't the risk be limited, because they were of lower quality? There was, it turned out, nothing to stop the banks from doing all three. In the next two and a half years, Zukerman did seventy such after-tax deals, some as large as $200 million, and TD's domestic income tax rate fell from over 40 per cent towards the teens, thereby bringing unexpected profits to the bank.

Zukerman was a hot commodity and was soon managing fully 10 per cent of the bank's multibillion dollars in assets. By 1979, his salary had increased handsomely to $50,000 a year, but there was no progress towards his real goal: being the first Jewish vice-president of a Canadian bank. In fact, his job title had remained frozen throughout at superintendent. And that other important measuring stick, his corporate reporting relationship, hadn't altered either. He continued to report to an assistant general manager. He began to realize that while his friends may not have been right about bigotry at the bank, he wasn't able to prove them wrong.

It was an amicable departure. The bank was even kind enough to lend him $615,000 — at going rates, of course — to buy a stake in HCI Holdings, where he landed with financial whiz Andy Sarlos. While the value of Zukerman's 435,000 shares has bounced around badly with the market, he doesn't need anyone's pity. The bank did give him a boost, which he acknowledges readily, towards his current position. And yet: they wouldn't let him grow. For Zukerman, the reason was clear. "I'm sure it wasn't 'Who's that pushy kid?' It was 'Who's that pushy Jew?'"

C. has a grey and lifeless face. Even with an outside wall that gives his office the status of a window, there isn't enough light to brighten his eyes. He walks with a slight stoop as he shows off his department. Well, not so much shows it off as points it out. It is difficult to know whether the desultory flick of the wrist as he motions towards something is due to modesty or indifference. In his office, he seems more secure. With his back to the wall, the buffer of a desk separating him from his visitor, he looks almost ensconced.

"How *is* Mr. B.?" he asks the visitor. Thinking that the query is mere chit-chat, the visitor fills the air with some trivial stuff until he realizes that C. is hanging on his every word, no matter how irrelevant. He is starved for news from the executive floor and, he hopes, they for news of him. In his heart, however, he knows they aren't. Not since that day five years ago when he'd crossed Mr. B. Afterwards, no one could recall exactly what happened — or no one wanted to, it was hard to tell. The only certainty was the banishment to a position of little clout in a department of no consequence.

"I'm still waiting for the other shoe to drop," sighs the dispossessed, "and when it does, I don't know if it will be up or out."

On May 12, 1981, at three-thirty, Arnold Agnew, general manager of public affairs at the Toronto-Dominion Bank, telephoned his stockbroker, Barbara Danuke, of McLeod Young Weir. The conversation took no more than a minute, but the consequences reverberated long after. Agnew knew in advance, as he often did about such announcements, that when the stock market closed at four that day, the bank would announce it was buying back, for $24, all shares of TD Realty, then trading for about $21. During their casual chat, he made passing reference to a realty meeting and indicated there might be an announcement. Twenty discreet years as a source-protecting newspaperman and ten years as a confidant to bank chairmen momentarily forgotten.

Danuke, a thirty-six-year-old rookie broker, immediately connected that slipped tidbit with something she'd overheard in a bar four days earlier, when two men talked of the banks buying back their real estate operations. Her excitement infected her boss and two of the three colleagues who shared her desk. Before the market closed, about twenty minutes later, three of them had bought 3,200 shares for themselves and two clients. Total worth, some $67,000. Possible profit, about $10,000.

The Toronto Stock Exchange surveillance crew (also aware of the pending announcement) was alerted by the activity in the stock, which normally trades about five hundred shares a day, as it surged at the close on orders from one firm. The Agnew–Danuke link was established the next day, evidence gathered, and a public hearing ordered by the Ontario Securities Commission, the first inquiry into registered representatives, as brokers are formally known, trading on insider knowledge.

Agnew, then fifty-six, decided his own fate by resigning from his bank job when he learned of the investigation the day following his one-minute call. His reason was simple and easily put, as he describes his indiscretion: "One doesn't say these things." He further agreed not to trade in securities for six months.

It was the first public misstep in a high-profile and high-performance career. As editor-in-chief of the *Telegram*, he is universally remembered as an honest soldier who handled staff with care and compassion, attempting to find jobs for many when the Toronto newspaper folded in 1971. After twenty years in the newspaper business in the U.K. and Canada, he joined the TD, and for nine and a half years offered his savvy to successive chairmen. As a banker, he was a man of manners and morals.

The OSC found the McLeod staffers guilty and gave three-day job suspensions to Danuke and her desk-mates, James MacDonald and Donald Scott; a five-day suspension to her boss, William Seitz—a wrist-slap compared with the lifetime suspensions that could have been imposed. For Agnew, nearer to the close of his career than to the start, the price paid was higher than any debt owed. Although he alone had sought no personal gain, in a world where the public hearing has replaced the public hanging, he suffered most.

Rumour, Mark Twain said, is half-way around the globe while truth puts on its shoes. Ironically, in the stock market world, where rumour is the staff of life, the OSC sought to stamp out truth. Securities training was upgraded and the brokerage industry put on notice that *any* information from within a company is not to be used. So if a broker gets a hot tip from a good source, it's taboo. A rumour that runs about with no home, however, is OK. It may be totally fair, but not a little foolish. And to achieve this wonderful standard, for Agnew and the McLeod four, justice, it is said, was done. And a career was snuffed out.

M. seemed the perfect mentor. He had a small office that was a comfortable jumble, almost a personal place amid the austere cubicles hung with rented art occupied by the others. He was unlike them in other ways, too. He was a sharer, telling all he knew. He walked the halls with the equanimity of a man who knew himself and his place in the world. He feared no one. Perhaps, as it turned out, because he had nothing they wanted, except the tranquillity that comes, if boredom can be beaten back, from operating with expertise far beyond what was required of his function. He was treated with the deference that might have come with his age, but not with the fawning awe that should have followed his status. The job was clearly so far beneath his talents, why was he wasting away there?

—He made a mistake once. He authorized a deal above his lending limit and it went sour.

—When was that?

There was a pause.

—Next month, it will be twenty-three years.

The west branch of the Don River gurgled contentedly outside the window at the foot of the backyard in the fall of 1981 as Charles M. Laidley, late of the Canadian Imperial Bank of Commerce, drew thoughtfully on an early-morning cigar. The former bank vice-chairman looked about his recreation-room office in his North Toronto home—complete with covered billiard table and unlit pinball machine—sent a plume of blue-grey smoke towards the ceiling, and admitted: "You miss the excitement of being involved. You read about it in the paper now. Before, you knew about it *before* it was in the paper. There was a lot of power in that position."

Yet, after twenty-nine years with the bank, fifty-year-old Chuck Laidley, the man they called the "credit czar" at the Commerce, walked away from it all. In June 1981 he turned his back on the $175,000 annual salary, the Cadillac and driver, the use of the bank's DH-125 to fly wherever he wanted, the club memberships, and the low-interest executive loans. The story put out for public consumption was that he just wanted a change, that if he was going to start a new career, now was the time. Yet six months after leaving the bank, he still had no prospects other than two honorific positions on boards of smaller companies. (In May of 1982 he became chairman of Grindlay's, a small Canadian subsidiary of a British bank.)

Lost from sight, he had gone to ground and been difficult to find. The phone book turned up a Charles Laidley on Dundas Street East. My call was not the first this other Mr. Laidley had received looking for the ex-banker. A Calgary-based oil company had also called this Mr. Laidley and offered him a seat on its board. "When I told them I was a truck driver, they said, 'Oh sorry, I guess we've got the wrong one.'" Laid off a few weeks later after twenty-three years' employment, the trucker was tempted to mention the offer on his UI application along with other attempts to find work.

Banker Laidley needed no UI cheque, but there was a faraway look in his eye when I told him of the misdirected Calgary call. Several months had passed and no such offer had come to him. Still, apart from the wan look around the eye, he remained a handsome man. There was no outward scar to show what had happened; his wounds were internal, all healing hidden. His grey hair, slightly freckled complexion, and erect manner made him look like John Kennedy.

Chuck Laidley joined the Bank of Commerce as a young whipper-snapper with a commerce degree from the University of Toronto in 1952. The bank had just begun to hire university grads, but didn't know quite what to do with them. "The myth was that you couldn't become a banker unless you began by peddling drafts," he recalled. A management training scheme put in place for new employees like him enabled him to become a branch manager at Yonge and Charles streets in Toronto while still in his twenties.

The training programme also brought his first fight with the system that would eventually do him in. One of his customers, Tom Beck, had a small firm called Beck Electric (later to become Noma of Christmas-light fame). Laidley saw the potential in Beck, but had a terrible time convincing the head office credit department that a loan would be safe. The argument flowed back and forth, the credit people refusing with new reasons for every argument Laidley put forward, until finally the man from head office, with the ultimate in logic, demanded: "What if Christmas doesn't come?"

There were close calls, too. In New York, Laidley almost got drawn into what later became known as the DeAngelis food-oil scandal. Approached by Anthony (Tino) DeAngelis with a clutch of warehouse receipts for salad oil stored in New Jersey and contracts for sale of the oil, Laidley had all but agreed to float DeAngelis a loan. DeAngelis was even willing to pay more than the going interest rate for the money, saying he'd go one and a half points over prime for the $10 million he wanted. When Laidley's supervisor heard about the deal, he wondered: "Why are they willing to pay such a high rate?" Laidley began a further check and before he completed his investigation, on November 20, 1963, a commodities scandal broke on Wall Street and two firms were suspended from membership on the New York Stock Exchange. One of them, Ira Haupt & Co., went into liquidation a week later. DeAngelis, it seemed, had borrowed millions of dollars and pledged various oils as security, but only a fraction of the oils existed. He'd bought on margin in the hope of sales, prices fell, and his firm couldn't meet margin calls. Total losses were at least $100 million, and DeAngelis went to jail. One timely question had saved Chuck Laidley and the Commerce from being caught up in the costly scam.

His career continued upward as agent for the bank in New York; executive vice-president of a bank subsidiary, California Canadian Bank; head of an Ontario region in 1969, and vice-president in 1971. Throughout, however, his progress mystified him. Promotions were one sign, but, he maintained: "You really never knew how well you were doing. It wasn't really until the last five or six years that I knew. By then I was one of the top five or six in the bank. There comes a time, you know, when as long as you don't make a fool of yourself, you are going to progress."

Senior vice-president in 1973, executive vice-president in 1978, he survived the atrocities of the Neil McKinnon era, when politics dominated the executive suite. Laidley did not play politics and that strategy contributed to his downfall. In a world where you not only need to be tough, but you need support from other tough nuts, Laidley often did not recognize the games that swirled about him. There were times, after social events, when his wife would chide him that all the innuendoes of the evening had just gone over his head. After McKinnon was ousted as chairman, the bank was run by a triumvirate, Page Wadsworth, Russ Harrison, and Don Fullerton. While it was an awkward arrangement, Wadsworth did calm the place down. After Wadsworth retired, the triumvirate became a duumvirate of Harrison and Fullerton.

One less boss, however, did not help. After all the corporate machinations the Commerce had been through, no lessons had been learned and leadership remained unclear. Said Laidley: "Russ and Don never really came to an agreement as to who was to do what." Harrison would delegate authority, but then ride herd so that responsibility was never really passed. Finally, when Fullerton tried to press for more power, Harrison beat him back. In that final shuffle, destined to be Laidley's last, Harrison created three second-in-commands. Fullerton lost his chief operating officer title and was made vice-chairman in charge of international; John Hilliker was named vice-chairman in charge of domestic business; and Laidley became vice-chairman with responsibility for corporate lending.

Harrison announced the changes with some glee in August of 1980, his own position now secure. Laidley, he told anyone who would listen, would cover "all aspects of credit in the bank. To put it simply, he will be Hilliker's and Fullerton's alter ego." While Laidley's problem of knowing who was boss had been solved, loan losses and asset–liability mismatch (when it costs more to raise money than the bank charges to loan it out) became his bailiwick. The Commerce wrote off a $100-million loss on Massey-Ferguson. Other bad loans were beginning to bubble beneath him, although this was before Dome Petroleum and Turbo Resources became public dilemmas. Chuck Laidley had been given an impossible task.

Worse, along with the known new pressures came something that was totally unexpected: wider and more onerous responsibilities. Said Laidley: "You can manage a *part* of the operation the way you want to. When you get to be vice-chairman and a member of the board, your responsibility is to the *whole* organization." The work-load became ever heavier, its weight unwelcome. "It was 8:00 A.M. until 6:00 P.M. every day and a whole lot of work at night. Any idea that people have that the work gets easier as you get near the top, with all the perks, is wrong. You're not master of your own time at all."

He also became increasingly frustrated and unhappy with the bank's planning process. "Every time we sat down to plan, we were planning from the bottom up. You need clear direction from the top. We could never really get around to that." Also, there simply weren't enough strong horses to pull the load. "The executive suite at the Commerce was woefully undermanned. The people at the top were expected to know far more than could be reasonably expected. We were short of good people at the top."

As the office pressure built, the policy disagreements grew, until he could stay quiet no longer. "I expressed some dissatisfaction with the way things were going. That triggered the suggestion that I would leave." But no departure is simple for an employee at so high a level, nor is it inexpensive for the employer. Said Laidley: "I wasn't just going to close up my desk and walk out. I couldn't do that financially." There was some fencing between him and Harrison about a settlement, and they discussed a move to Calgary. The move was, however, never a real option for him, more of a face-saver. "If I wanted that," he told friends, of the other position, "I'd stay here." Instead, Calgary became part of the negotiations towards a golden handshake, legal gobbledy-gook so that Laidley could say to Harrison, "You're changing my job," and receive a settlement. Observes Commerce director Sydney Hermant: "The bankers look after themselves."

Harrison and Laidley worked out a deal in March and April of 1981 whereby Laidley would stay on staff until the end of June, then leave with a fistful of cash, plus a paid-up pension that kicks out $24,000 a year starting in 1996. When Harrison informed the executive committee of the board of directors, he seemed honestly sorry, even bewildered, to report that Laidley was leaving. "I just wish," he said, "I could tell you that there was something I could do about it."

After the announcement, there was some belated hand-wringing. Among others, Hermant called on Laidley to see what had happened, hoping for some second thoughts. Hermant asked Laidley: "Has pride become so involved that you can't walk the twenty feet of carpet [to Harrison's office]?" Laidley assured him that he was relaxed about his decision.

But, in the end, it was pride in self, as well as the plain fact that he was repelled by the corporate pressure, fed up with his role, and frustrated by the way things were done. The power he'd attained wasn't worth the trade-off. "That's a bit of an ego trip," he said. "I've satisfied my ego. I got to the very senior level in a large corporation. Now I can enjoy life."

There is, however, one final worry, a small corner of him that recognizes the professional failing, sees the personal foible. He watches one last plume of cigar smoke and sighs: "I never really resolved in my mind whether or not I wanted to be chief executive officer."

Just as individuals can be losers, the system can suffer, too. Nowhere have the banks lost more than in their dealings with women. Although they make up 75 per cent of total employment at banks, women have been kept out of management positions for dozens of reasons, all of them wrong. In 1979, Commerce chairman Russ Harrison proudly pointed out that a woman was about to be named an assistant general manager, two levels below a VP, but the highest rank attained by a female to that point. "But don't say that," he cautioned me; "she'll know who she is." That any one woman could be so obvious out of more than twenty-five thousand people spoke eloquently about how many women the bank had brought along.

In 1982, when the Royal Bank, at the stroke of a pen, made every officer with the title of assistant general manager and higher into a vice-president, the number of VPs was immediately doubled to 190. The number of women included in that executive net: one. Even at the branch manager level, growth in number of female managers is slow. The Bank of Nova Scotia, first of the big five to appoint a female branch manager twenty years ago, has made only marginal progress since. There are female managers in fewer than 7 per cent of its branches.

This is just one all-too-typical story of how the system cannot cope with a bright and educated woman who wants to succeed.

Linda Duguay was born in Rhode Island and grew up in Connecticut. During her high school summers, she worked at the Peoples Savings Bank, a twenty-four-branch savings and loan institution in southwest Connecticut, moving up from teller to a position where she sold personal pension plans. She sped through school with such ease that she was ready for university at sixteen. Instead, she judged herself too immature and spent a year in Brazil, as a Rotary International Exchange student. There she quickly learned Portuguese; she later mastered Spanish and French.

Her French-Canadian heritage and her interest in languages took her to McGill University in Montreal, where she completed a degree in French literature, hoping to become a translator. She eventually decided such work was too solitary, and was drawn instead to business through campus contacts with other students in the Master of Business Administration programme. McGill uses both theory and the case-study method, so Duguay found herself working outside the classroom as well, consulting with other students on a project for Pascal's hardware chain, and on Golden Eagle Oil, where they studied a new private-brand gas-line antifreeze through customer research and retail analysis. The group's final report, an inch-thick document, was so convincing that Golden Eagle launched the product.

The course was a gruelling one, particularly because she had little background in mathematics, but she worked hard and finished in the top third of her class. After a year of travelling, while she waited for her visa to work in Canada, and armed with two degrees and four languages, she took job interviews with four of Canada's big five banks.

Personnel officers at two of the banks (Bank of Montreal and TD) asked the classic question put to female graduates, but never to males: Can you type? At the Royal, however, marketing manager Jake Thun seemed different from the rest. In November 1980, Duguay was hired, at twenty-five, as an analyst in Toronto, to develop training aids (films, written material, and other internal programmes) for fellow bankers in the international department.

It was, she thought, a high-flying and auspicious start, with a boss who understood her hopes and an institution that appreciated her talents. Until, that is, the day very soon after, when she discovered that the people using the programmes she was developing were also recent MBA graduates with similar backgrounds to hers — and, at $27,000, they were earning much more than her $21,500. Still, she plunged along gamely for four and a half months, then was moved into marketing analysis under a new boss, Ram Angod, manager of market planning, who reported directly to Mike Baptista, vice-president of commercial marketing, Ontario District.

A few months later, without warning, one Wednesday afternoon at five, Angod informed her that the department was being folded and she would be shifted into another area, cash management, although she had previously made him aware that she was not interested in this area. "I didn't like the job. I didn't want the job," she said. No wonder. Until then she had been classified as a Level 13 (an internal ranking that meant she was at the first management rung); she would be dropped to a Level 7 in the new role. It was, in effect, a clerical job, although her pay would not change.

When she protested the demotion, Angod said, "Don't worry. It's only for a short while." She was not convinced and telephoned the personnel department for further explanation. The officer there, Keith Hogunbaum, seemed to care more that he hadn't been informed than he cared about the impact it would have on Duguay. "You can't be transferred," he kept saying, "I don't know anything about this." Hogunbaum must have called Baptista, for within thirty minutes she was summoned to the vice-president's eighth-floor office. "Now Linda," he began soothingly, leaning back in his chair, "what *are* you so upset about? Why did you go to personnel?" Although he, too, seemed more interested in her approach to the personnel department than in what had happened to her, he listened while she explained her frustration and lack of interest in the new post — the third in less than a year without a raise. "Within six months you'll be out of that job," Baptista assured her; "it's only for training." After twenty minutes of such soothing talk, she was calmer. "If you have any problems," he said, "be sure you call me."

Her new boss was George Dickson. The position, distinctly clerical;

the surroundings, definitely sexist. At one point during a meeting, coworker Bill MacKenzie made a facetious comment, suggesting that Duguay probably wasn't any good in bed. Stunned that he would make any such overt remark and angered that Dickson, who was chairing the meeting, didn't tell MacKenzie to keep quiet, Duguay said nothing until she was alone with Dickson in his office, where she complained vociferously.

Boys will be boys, he explained, although he sympathized by saying: "You know I agree with you, but ..." "But nothing," she interrupted; "you run this department. If you don't stop them, who will?" She found her male colleagues' attitude towards secretaries chauvinistic, also. At one point, within earshot of a long-time secretary, colleague Mike Craft commented: "Male secretaries aren't called secretaries, they're called executive assistants and are paid more money." The secretary was amazed and asked: "You mean if I were a male, I'd have a different title and be paid more money?"

Even when remarks were not directed at Duguay or other women, the men she worked with persisted in using locker-room jargon. During one meeting, when Dickson was speaking about a marketing campaign, he enthused: "We've got to get some balls into this campaign." "Well, George," Duguay added icily, "how about some ovaries? I'd like to contribute what I can."

Most of the time, however, she couldn't hold her own against the onslaught in a job she didn't like, among people she did not respect. By Christmas of 1981, she was distraught and beside herself with frustration. "When I started crying at *Laverne and Shirley*, I knew something was wrong." She set an April departure deadline (when she would have finished the Canadian securities course she was taking in the evenings) and tried to precipitate action. A telephone call to vice-president Baptista was returned by Ram Angod, who said he'd see what he could do. All that brought was a phone call from someone else who told her she shouldn't have phoned Baptista.

She then contacted Ann Lamont, the equal employment officer in Montreal, and told Lamont about her Level 7 position. "Omigod," Lamont responded, "how did you ever get into that job?" With Lamont's help, Duguay flew to Montreal for an interview with Bob Watson, a head office personnel officer. She told him she wanted to be transferred to the international training programme. "Try again," he told her, "when you get a better job review." She pointed out that her reviews had been fine, considering she was in a job for which she wasn't trained and was overqualified. He claimed the bank was not hiring in the international programme at the moment. She knew they were on campus recruiting graduates.

Message received. She began actively looking for another job in May. When word spread she was looking, a promotion was suddenly proffered. She was to be called an assistant manager, but there were two catches. First, there was to be no increase in her salary; second, she was to keep her promotion quiet from her colleagues. The title could be used externally, but would not be put in the bank directory. It was listed briefly, then expunged, in the word processor that stored the telephone lists for her floor.

The insult simply added to her growing insight as she weighed job offers from two other banks, finally choosing a U.S. bank with offices in Toronto. She resigned from the Royal in June 1982 to become an account manager trainee at $30,000 a year. She was careful to ask and receive permission to interview others in the U.S. bank before accepting the job and, burned by the Royal, remained suspicious in her new role, waiting for chauvinism to erupt. It never did. "I'm being treated as a person, not a male or a female," she says, and that's exactly how she wants it.

The difference between the American and Canadian banks, she suggests, is both the state and a state of mind. The U.S. banks have been positively affected by equal rights legislation for a decade. The place of women has been assured, the battle long won. There is no such revolution in sight in Canada. Nor is there likely to be an evolution, either, for Canadian management is more hidebound, less likely to welcome any woman other than a wife, who is trotted out like some hackney pony on all the right occasions.

At the Royal, Duguay says, "They choose people who are characteristic of the system, people who won't rock the boat. Senior officers don't want flak. They're very conservative, and they're huge institutions to move. I'd never work for another Canadian institution. No way."

It is six o'clock on a dark November night, and the regulars have gathered at Hy's piano bar in downtown Toronto. No matter how harassed the broker's face, or how frumpy the woman's body, the rosy glow of the room and the liquids poured in it are great levellers. Sex, said Noel Coward, is essentially a matter of lighting. And, he might have added, a modicum of liquor. It is here that loud-mouths from the law courts and the braggarts from Bay Street come to celebrate the ego-massage of success or to wallow in the self-pity of failure.

The surroundings can only be described as nouveau decadent. A group of red velvet stuffed chairs and sofas are clustered around low glass-topped wooden tables. Waitresses swish about in long skirts with waist-high side slits and clinging silk-like tops. Around the grand piano at the back of the room are arranged bar stools, and beyond, on the back wall, hangs a saloon-style painting of a naked and reclining woman. One arm is folded behind her head, pillow-like, the other is languidly draped on her crotch. The room is filled with the smoke and the sound of comers and might-have-beens along with a smatter of those who never were.

Holding forth from a two-seater couch in the middle of the room is Clarence W. (Peter) Cole, executive vice-president of the Canadian Imperial Bank of Commerce. With him, an old friend, Murray Sinclair, founder of Guardian Growth Fund, and Barry Gordon, vice-president of the investment boutique Brown, Baldwin. Across the table, three women, the object of their imprecations, are ranged in another sofa and chair. At this point, any courting among the group is kept to sidelong glances. Even the cheques are separate, a sure sign nothing overt is happening.

Cole's six-foot-three frame is clothed in a grey checked suit; he is scrunched into the two-seater with Sinclair. Cole's receding and greying hair is pulled across his scalp. His incongruously jet-black eyebrows tilt up and away from the bridge of his nose to give him an impish devil-may-care look that renders his next move unpredictable. Will he roll a punch line or throw a punch? Right now, his hand is occupied with a drink, the first of several he will stow away over the next four hours, without apparent effect. His mood, however, is ebullient one minute, morose the next, and he will switch back and forth between the two all evening long.

He is telling a joke. "A farmer goes to get a bank loan so he can drill for water on his property. 'How many cows have you got?' the banker asks. 'Two,' the man replies. So the banker comes around, inspects them, counts how many tits they've got, and uses the cows as collateral on the loan. The well is drilled, but instead of finding water, they strike sticky black stuff." Cole hunches forward in his seat, his face reddening with pleasure. "The farmer is fabulously wealthy, and so the banker comes around again and says, 'Why don't you put all that money you're earning on deposit with us?' And the farmer says: 'How many cows have *you* got?'" There is much laughter all around as Cole adds: "*That's* what banking is all about."

His merry mood quickly darkens as he launches into a pessimistic description of something else banking is all about these days: worrisome international debt. A recent session he attended in Washington for bankers, diplomats, and government officials from both the West and the developing nations left him gloomy about the future because of heavy worldwide debt and zero banking liquidity (the amount by which assets exceed liabilities), according to the Washington gathering. No solutions were found, but there will be another meeting in two months' time. Like the United Nations, the banking system can keep going as long as people talk about keeping it going.

Clarence W. Cole (only his mother calls him Clarence) is, at forty-six, the man in charge of the liability side of the Commerce (deposits and anything else that the bank *owes* to customers), and it has been his job during the last four years to reduce the mismatch (when the terms of loans and deposits don't match, causing spreads and profits to disappear) from $6 billion down to zero. One of five executive vice-presidents, he is often mentioned as a possible successor to chairman and chief executive officer Russ Harrison. He joined the bank eight years ago and has carved out a name for himself as a tough nut, someone Harrison listens to. Cole is an extroverted *bon vivant*, and some of his escapades are legendary in the circumspect world of banking. No one likes to tell stories about Peter Cole more than Cole himself.

A natural raconteur, he is recalling one typical night of partying he shared with Sinclair in London. Cole had travelled to Britain in 1978 to close the deal when the Commerce joined with Hambros Bank Ltd., one of the largest merchant banking groups in the U.K., to hold a majority interest in a new international investment banking company called CIBC Ltd.

"The night before," he reminisces, "I got mixed up with some *baaad* company. You were there, Sinc. Remember we went in a taxi to that club? Roddy Llewellyn, Princess Margaret's friend, was the doorman. The Earl of Athlone or someone was playing the piano. The place was filled with dukes and duchesses. We finally left about four in the morning, pissed to the gills. There were eight of us in the cab and on the way back to the Dorchester, we got it rocking. We'd get it up on two wheels on the one side, then up on two wheels on the other. The taxi driver didn't give a shit, he was drunk, too. We'd kept him waiting outside the club all night and kept sending him out drinks. We got back to the hotel and the party carried on in my room until seven. I was supposed to close the Hambros deal but I thought, the hell with that — I'm going to bed. I crawled in between the mattress and the box springs with the bedspread pulled around my head so I couldn't hear the phone ring when they tried to reach me. I slept right through the day." He ends with a hoot of laughter and wipes tears from the corners of his eyes.

Cole is more than just some jokester who loves high jinks, although once, at a going-away party for a Greenshields colleague, Cole did a running dive onto a table, sending glasses and crockery flying. He is a man who desperately wants to succeed. He was born in Picton, Ontario, where his grandfather had run a cooperage. The grandfather died, in debt, when

Peter's father was fourteen. Peter's father was somewhat more successful, eventually owning the Picton *Gazette*. Peter left home to attend Ryerson Polytechnical Institute in Toronto and was two years through a three-year course in retail merchandising when he joined Greenshields, a brokerage house, as a messenger in 1958. The starting pay was such that all he could afford was $6-a-week lodgings in a rooming house, and he spent more money on beer than on food. He caught on quickly at Greenshields and was soon a bond trader, moving up the ladder before joining another investment firm, Cochrane, Murray (now Walwyn Stodgell Cochrane Murray), eventually becoming a partner and 9 per cent owner in the firm. In 1975, the Commerce went looking for a replacement for Ted Avison, who had been running the investment department.

"If I'd stayed, that 9 per cent would be worth $3 million today. I agonized over leaving, but I wanted to take a shot at the top. My grandfather never travelled further than a hundred miles from home, my father never got further than two hundred miles. I just want to *be* somebody." So he was hired and quickly made a name for himself among the stuffed shirts as a maverick with good advice and the ear of Harrison.

The pay, at $185,000 a year, is acceptable, but what he really wants is Harrison's job. He hasn't given up, he feels he deserves it, but the fight for the top is bitter and he fears he's losing. He knows that colleagues Don Fullerton and Warren Moysey rank ahead of him in the view of the board. "Weston and Conrad and Mulroney and Dougie Bassett — those fellows get along with Moysey." Chimes in Sinclair: "The old school tie." "That's right," says Cole. "He's *their* kind of guy. He's the white-haired and blue-blooded boy. I'm just an asshole."

Cole is separated from his wife, who lives in the west Toronto suburb of Islington with their seven-year-old daughter, Jennifer. His marital status hurts Cole's chances for promotion at the bank, and he knows it. He cannot entertain the out-of-town bankers as Moysey does. Nor is Cole even allowed to bring a woman to bank functions when wives attend. "You know how bad it is? Let me tell you how bad it is. After the annual meeting there's a dinner and dance. I get the word not to bring anyone. I'm told to come stag. The IMF [meeting] comes along. There are three lunches and three dinners. I host a table at all the lunches; I'm invited to none of the dinners." He knows that if he sought reconciliation with his wife, he'd be better thought of by the higher-ups, but he refuses, saying: "That's not what life is all about. I don't want to be chairman that bad."

And yet he thinks he deserves the top job and scorns Moysey's perceived success in the bank. "I'm the one that's made them the money. I took the mismatch down from $6 billion to zero. There's about $280 million in profit this year that's due to me. How many people has Moysey hired? None. I've hired 250. There's a lot of genius under me." The world outside is beginning to recognize that Cole may not succeed Harrison, either, and sees him as a talent to be lured away. During the previous year, he's been turning down job offers — including CEO at Canada Permanent (before it went to Hilliker) and president of Royal Trust — even as the signals grow stronger around Moysey. With the departure of Hilliker as vice-chairman, Harrison has given Hilliker's domestic responsibilities to Moysey. Worse, from Cole's viewpoint, Moysey, who along with Cole had been an executive vice-president, will be called *senior* executive vice-president. That one word signals to the world without and the watchers within that Moysey has pulled ahead of Cole in the sweeps. But it is more than a week after the appointment was confirmed by the board, and there has been no public announcement. Not the least of the reasons for the delay is Cole's anger.

Cole was in Palm Springs, California, the week before, golfing with Edmonton Oilers owner Peter Pocklington and former U.S. president Gerald Ford, when Harrison decided to elevate Moysey. Cole returned to Toronto and made his displeasure known to Harrison, emboldened by an offer in his pocket that would have taken him away from the Commerce and, he claimed, made him $1 million. (A title matching Moysey's was conferred upon Cole four months later.)

It is the clout he wants, the class that comes with the position, not just the money. At the time, Cole despaired of the self-described "high-rise hovel" in which he lived. He has since bought in Rosedale on the strength of his new job, but he'd also like a place in Florida where he could escape for the odd week in winter. Meanwhile there *is* golf in California, marlin fishing with his pals in Bimini, and sailing in the Azores with Michael Davies, owner of the Kingston *Whig-Standard*.

Suddenly he becomes the articulate pleader for the top job. "I want to change the system," he begins. "I could take the Xerox marketing programme through that bank and make it hum. Do you know how many different savings accounts we've got? Two hundred and four! How's anybody on the counter supposed to remember all of those? We spend all kinds of money telling that we're a friendly bank! What a waste!" he shakes his head in amazement. "We waste more money. Why not put a screen up in each branch outlining the services, so that the people know what they are?"

His mood, which has been veering between venom and vision, changes again. Now he is the global pessimist, down on banking. "It's all smoke and mirrors. A sham." He denies that his corporate success is any indication of prowess. "Banking is easy," he scoffs. "I do well because everybody else is a dummy." Then he turns on himself. "I sometimes drink to excess." He looks across the table at the writer who has spent the evening with him. "If you write this, I'll kill you."

He turns in his seat and calls to the pianist: "Linda, play my favourite songs." She smiles and begins to play "I'll Be Seeing You." "Aren't you going to sing?" he shouts. "You always sing the words, Peter," she replies. As if on cue, he bounds from his seat, places a hand on the piano, turns to face the room, and sings the Second World War song of sad separations between lovers.

Cathedral bells were tolling
and our hearts sang on.
Was it the spell of Paris
or the April dawn?
Who knows if we shall meet again?
But when the morning chimes ring
sweet again:

I'll be seeing you in all the old
familiar places
That my heart and mind embraces
all day through.
In that small café, the park across
the way,
The children's carousel,
the chestnut trees, the wishing well.

I'll be seeing you in
every lovely summer's day.
In ev'rything that's
light and gay, I'll always
think of you that way.
I'll find you in the
morning sun, and when the night is new,
I'll be looking at the moon,
but I'll be seeing you.

He sings with his chin raised, the words projected above those left in the bar as if he were reaching for the far balcony, but few listen. He finishes with a flourish and withdraws back to his chair. A final drink, a single, is downed to the tune of his other favourite song, "The Old-fashioned

Way." The music mellows him and he changes his mind about the evening's conversation: "I don't care what you write, just be honest." He falls silent, for the first time in the evening. Gordon long ago left, Sinclair does not leap in, and Cole cannot let the silence last. Finally, he says, quietly, "I'm never going to be chairman of the Commerce." It is a summation of the evening, perhaps an epitaph to his career.

He doesn't stay still long enough to ponder it, however; there is a flurry of activity as he and Sinclair make for the door, hail a taxi and head to another bar for more carousing. He raises a clenched fist and shouts down the street, "Tell it like it is," then climbs into the taxi and lurches off into the night. If the good life at the top is not available, good times will have to do.

TWELVE

HOT MILLIONS

Scams, Ransoms, and Computer Theft

A SCENE IN THE 1951 FILM classic *The Lavender Hill Mob* neatly portrays both the hierarchical structure of the banks (it still exists more than thirty years later) and the fear that is endemic — theft. In the movie, a twenty-year bank employee, played by Alec Guinness, has the job of overseeing the daily gold bullion shipment. His participation in the robbery of £1 million in bullion is so artful that he is seen by his employers as the hero who tried, valiantly but unsuccessfully, to protect his employers' gold. He is summoned to receive congratulations from his supervisor, who takes him on to an office down the hall bearing the door plaque announcing the rank of the next man up — chief cashier. He ferries them both on to the office of the deputy chairman who, in turn, leads the threesome to the chairman. All niceties observed, the final door is closed and congratulatory laughter can be heard from within.

In the end, of course, the law catches up with Guinness, who is living a life of luxury in a southern clime. The closing scene shows him being led away in manacles. In these more permissive days, a film thief such as Peter Ustinov in *Hot Millions* gets away with his theft — by computer — of several millions. Not all of life imitates art, however. The banks haven't changed: Canadian banks continue to be run by an entrenched hierarchy, and employee theft is reviled everywhere. The latter is an even more terrifying prospect as new technology has increased the potential for inventive scams and the amounts available have sky-rocketed. Bank employee theft even has its own name — "defalcation" — a word spoken in hushed tones or sometimes shortened to the secretive "D," as if it were some perversion that dared not speak its name.

By far the most spectacular defalcation was of $10.4 million found missing from a Toronto branch of the Canadian Imperial Bank of

Commerce last year. According to police, the sum disappeared over a two-year period — much of it gambled away in Atlantic City casinos — unnoticed by the bank. The scam was uncovered when Toronto police began investigating a book-making ring that led to the alleged fraud. Bank loans had been made to legitimate companies, unbeknownst to those companies, and immediately transferred to fictitious companies, then on to Atlantic City bank accounts. A man was arrested in connection with the fraud just after he stepped off a private plane that had deposited him at the Toronto airport on a flight from Atlantic City. Brian Patrick Molony, an assistant manager at the branch, faces charges of fraud and possession of property obtained by crime.

Even a $50,000 reward offer has yet to produce any leads in another bank bilking. The scam began on December 3, 1982, when a woman phoned the Bank of Montreal's main branch at First Canadian Place in Toronto. She knew all the proper internal codes for the transfer of funds to a man using the name of David Lugo, of Grand Cayman Islands. The money, some $700,000, was to be drawn from Barclay's Bank, in London, England, and transferred to the Bank of Montreal. Lugo had approached a Toronto law firm, Goodman & Goodman, the day before, asking the firm to act as trustee. On December 6, a representative of the law firm, acting on Lugo's instruction, bought thirteen 100-troy-ounce bars of gold — worth $742,700 — from the main branch of the Bank of Nova Scotia and put the bullion into a safety deposit box in the same bank. Later in the day, Lugo emptied the box, carried out the ninety pounds of gold — and it was a full month before anyone realized there was no money coming from London.

If there is one thing that bankers fear as much as personal failure in their career path or professional fault in their credit performance, it is facing a criminal. The bank teller lives with the possibility that a stick-up artist will poke a gun across the counter and demand cash; the branch manager worries that a spouse or a child will be held to ransom; the senior executive worries about kidnap. They have reason to be nervous: incidents do happen. That's why bankers like low profiles in the community and across the country. Ransom demands such as those in 1982 on Edmonton Oilers owner Peter Pocklington and John Irving, one of New Brunswick magnate K. C. Irving's sons, just add to the fears of business heads in general and bankers in particular. Low profiles mean fewer problems. "It's visibility," said one senior banker after the Pocklington incident. Wanting to remain invisible himself, he quickly added: "And don't quote me."

Tellers often need counselling after a robbery because of the resulting trauma. According to Marie Brisebois, head of the Employee Counselling and Assistance Program for the Bank of Montreal: "They remain fearful for some time. The first week after the robbery they're even suspicious of customers. However, what is most hurtful to them is having had their pride hurt by the robber. It's as if someone had robbed them of their own money." Often professional help is required to avoid a psychological carry-over known as second wound phenomenon.

While statistics on bank robberies are readily available (1,249 robberies in Canada in 1981, 1,085 in 1982), stories about threats against bank executives are kept hidden. There have been at least two, however, in the last decade. In the mid-1970s, a well-dressed man with a polished appearance and an athletic build presented himself at the reception desk on the executive floor of the Bank of Nova Scotia and asked to see Gordon Bell, then chief general manager. As is the custom, he was ushered to a nearby reception room (dubbed the slumber room around the bank), and Bell was summoned to join him there. As Bell approached, the man extended his hand for the traditional handshake greeting and said: "Mr. Bell, so nice to see you again." As the unsuspecting Bell drew closer, the outstretched hand suddenly revealed a revolver. The visitor's left hand flashed behind Bell's neck and pulled his head forward. At the same time, the right hand thrust the gun into Bell's mouth and down his throat. He told Bell that he and an accomplice knew the whereabouts of Bell's wife and two teenaged children. The demand to avert foul play: $1 million.

He marched Bell downstairs to the main Toronto branch where, with the help of the manager, Bell convinced him that a request for $1 million in cash would alert everyone that something was afoot. They talked him down to $50,000, which they paid, and he fled. There was, it turned out, no accomplice. Because the bank was able to reconstruct the money package given the man, the banking system was alerted to watch out for certain serial numbers. Within days, some of the pay-off notes showed up at a Bank of Montreal branch in Montreal, deposited by a retailer. The thief turned out to be an American pianist, down on his luck, who had taken drastic steps to get money to buy himself a piano. Armed guards were added to the Bank of Nova Scotia executive floor, and visitors now come under close scrutiny.

The security system is not as elaborate as the one at the Bank of Montreal's new First Canadian Place offices in Toronto. Several floors there have television monitors in the reception area, manned by a guard who controls access to the offices. On the executive floor, just finished and occupied in 1982, an armed security man sits behind bullet-proof glass eyeing three television monitor screens that give him a view of many locations on the floor, including the "trap" reception room that leads from the elevators to one of the groups of offices. There, visitors can be held for final approval behind doors that can be automatically locked.

Bankers' wives must take precautions, too. When Fred McNeil was chairman of the Bank of Montreal, his Montreal home was regularly patrolled by security and his wife never answered the door without carrying a hand-held device to summon help if needed. Heather Thomson, wife of TD chairman Dick Thomson, had no such device in her hand when she answered the door early one morning in 1972 and a man pushed his way into their North Toronto house. She was alone with their youngest child, then a baby. The intruder tied them both to kitchen chairs, took photographs, and headed downtown, saying he was going to demand money from her husband on the strength of the pictures. After he left, she managed to bump the chair to a phone and, using her tongue, dialled for help. The assailant never arrived at the office and was never apprehended. As is typical in such cases where bankers are involved, the incident was hushed up, although police patrols were increased on the street. Word finally leaked out several weeks later and a story was published in the *Toronto Sun*. For his part, Thomson took no additional precautions beyond removing his home address from *Who's Who*.

Other protective methods adopted by most bank executives include panic buttons on their desk and in their cars, as well as evasive driving courses for their chauffeurs so they can shake pursuers. Driving routes and times are varied in order that no one can establish a regular pattern. Still, with all the precautions, says Royal chairman Rowlie Frazee: "It is very worrisome." As for kidnap: "If someone were clever enough, he could do it."

Although the boss gets priority treatment, by far the most "guarded" is the bank's computer centre. There, stored on magnetic tapes, are all transactions with every bit and byte of information on every customer. Paranoia is so great that steps are taken against such unlikely sabotage as someone entering with an electromagnet strapped to his body to jumble the precious tapes. Data centres, scattered in locations across Canada, invariably have no outward identifying marks linking them with the bank. Tours, other than by employees, are rare, and locations are kept secret for fear of terrorist attack or ransom attempts. One banker describes his concern this way: "We've got two and a half miles of line to Bell from the data centre. It goes underground, through backyards, et cetera. Someone could climb down any one of eighteen manhole covers, saw through the line with a hacksaw, and put the on-line network [in the branches] down for two weeks."

The data centre entry could belong to a department store. There is no designation, no corporate logo. But the four revolving doors can be activated only with the appropriate Honeywell system ID card. Inside, the correct card, with its various encoded levels of security, allows only a select few into the holy of holies — the main computer room. This day, however, four floors up, security is not the only thing on the mind of Bill Free, manager of the Toronto-Dominion Data Centre. Among the cheques that were cleared through here the previous working day was one from the Canadian Commercial and Industrial Bank in Edmonton. Intended to be a $5-million payment to be held by the Bank of Canada as part of CCIB's no-interest reserve, the cheque was mistakenly made out for $50 million. Duly processed by the data centre, it created a $45-million overdraft on the Canadian Commercial and Industrial Bank's account in Edmonton. To correct the error, CCIB suggests the cheque be put back through. "I don't think we can," says Free. Unsure what to do, he telephones the Bank of Canada, but they are also at a loss as to how to correct the error. Finally someone suggests that the CCIB write a $45-million cheque drawn on the Bank of Canada and put that back through the system as a way of cancelling out the mistake and eliminating the overdraft.

That cheque is among the $2 billion worth pouring in this day after being collected from various TD branches, then shipped via plane and truck to the centre's below-ground loading docks. There, under the watchful eye of low-light television cameras, courier drivers (who are not allowed inside the building) load the cheques contained in the green TD bags into eighteen-inch-deep grey bins that hold forty pounds of cheques. From there, data centre staff send them up a dumbwaiter system to the fourth floor, where they rattle on noisy rollers to the middle of the room. Next, each cheque is encoded (by adding the amount of the cheque to the row of numbers already at the bottom of the cheque) by operators using NCR 775 twenty-pocket machines, each worth $25,000. If all the cheques are legible, an operator can process twenty cheques a minute. Then they are batched into piles of 250 for high-speed reading on a $600,000 IBM 3890 that processes 90,000 items per hour. This machine stamps, codes, and microfilms all the cheques, then sends them along a belt at twenty-two miles per hour towards thirty sorting pockets. From there they are collected and sent on to other banks or back to various TD branches for return to the issuer.

The daily volume of this data centre averages one million pieces. Only one-quarter of one per cent of those items are valued at $50,000 or over — but they represent 85 per cent of the daily dollar value. Because of their value, and because clients want such items credited quickly for interest, each is handled separately. "I don't want them buried in the system," says Free. After processing, any lost cheque can be replaced because it has been microfilmed and will be stored on another floor for at least a year—longer if there is a dispute. Data on tapes is more transitory. All of today's transactions will be kept on five to seven hundred half-inch tapes; yesterday's tapes (called "father") are retained in case today's are destroyed or stolen, for in Europe there have been cases of magnetic tape being held for ransom. Tape from two days previous (called "grandfather") is also retained. Three-day-old tapes are erased and reused. Three days, three generations, and the ancestors are eliminated.

Most computer centres have equally elaborate security and other precautions, but perhaps none is so refined as the Bank of Montreal's new $40-million centre in Scarborough. Its sophisticated technology includes bullet-proof glass, man-traps between sections, and a control room with no windows (although there is a skylight in the three-storey room) to prevent bomb attacks. A three-stage sprinkler system and gas cylinders stand ready for fires. Finally, constant power is assured, provided by feeds from two municipalities and a twenty-cylinder back-up diesel generator. The largest ever built in Canada, the generator has the capacity to supply a city with a population of 100,000. Even the back-up has a back-up. Because the generator could take up to ten minutes to reach full capacity, there is a standby rack of batteries that can supply thirty minutes of power. That's enough, as they say in the trade, for a "soft landing" that damages neither the equipment nor the stored information. In fact, disruptions are more likely from other sources. On December 3, 1971, a courier from BDC Ltd. was on what's known as a "round robin" in Montreal, picking up cancelled cheques from all the banks en route to a data centre for sorting, coding, and distribution. The driver stopped for coffee, and while he left the truck, it was broken into. Eleven bags, stuffed with $50 million in cancelled cheques, were stolen.

The thief made contact with Mike Ballard, director of security at the Canadian Bankers' Association in Montreal, and demanded ransom. One of the banks, which had no back-up microfilm records of what it had lost, wanted to pay the ransom; the rest refused. In the end, no ransom was paid, the cheques were not returned, and all transactions had to be painstakingly reconstructed from branch records and (where available) microfilm. A year later, a prostitute picked up by police in Quebec City was discovered to be carrying several cancelled cheques dated December 3, 1971. A detective on the Quebec City force who had been working in Montreal at the time of the original heist recalled the theft. A deal was made with her, she fingered those involved, and the cheques were belatedly recovered in a locker. "We do not," insists Ballard today, "pay ransom."

Such incidents are all too possible in a national clearing system such as Canada's, with some 1.5 billion cheques worth $5.4 trillion processed annually by the chartered banks. A cheque drawn on a Victoria bank and deposited in a Halifax account will usually be credited immediately and charged to the customer's account in Victoria within one day. In the U.S., cheque-clearing can take up to eight days. During the twenty-four hours the cheque makes its way from Halifax to Vancouver, it will be handled by up to fifteen people, three courier services, and two data centres; it will travel across the country along with twenty tons of cheques and other data shipped daily by the banks via air courier services.

Such streamlining, while efficient, is also open to disaster. In Halifax, in 1979, a bank courier plane crashed, killing the pilot and the co-pilot. The fifty-nine bags aboard, containing $30 million in cancelled cheques, were reduced to less than four pounds of ashes. The ashes were sifted for months by RCMP and forensic experts who vainly attempted to identify the transactions. Reconstruction of all the transactions, paid for by insurance policies held by the courier, took months to complete at all the Maritime branches involved.

More common than major disasters, however, are minor diversions by employees. At the TD's Toronto Data Centre, for example, a woman who operated an encoder machine set up a system that would regularly divert $100 deposits made at a particular branch into her own account. As with any such scheme, it only worked because the branch didn't verify that the deposit had been properly credited the next day or someone at the branch was in cahoots with her. In any event, the system has since been changed so that each encoder operator deals with different branches all the time.

Clearly, the intricate bank security system relies heavily on individual integrity. At most data centres, particularly in the top security areas where key operators operate the system from glassed-in control panels, employees have obtained the jobs only after supplying as many as three references, followed by careful screening for any unsavoury political involvement or psychological quirk that could hint at future sabotage or theft. "The whole system works on various levels of responsibility and a lot of trust," admits Free. "If a programmer slipped something through that would put one cent per transaction into his account, well ..." His voice fades away and he shrugs his shoulders. "There's got to be an easier way for the underworld to pick up a few bucks than by holding a computer centre up to ransom. The real threat is the disgruntled employee. If somebody up there wants to screw me tonight, they can do it royally by pressing the wrong button."

But it is not just within the walls of the bank's data centre that information is potentially available. According to Peter Campbell, detective inspector with the Ontario Provincial Police, the information that banks send on Bell Canada lines is also very exposed. "It is physically visible to a great many Bell employees. Given a reasonable level of expertise, they could disrupt it or alter it. You don't have to go to the banks to extort information. You can get it within the Bell telephone environment." Ed Birce, product manager for Dataroute, Bell's private-line network for the banks, admits that such activity is possible, but "highly improbable." Says Birce: "If one of our employees really wanted to, he could go in and monitor that channel, and he would see a bunch of encoded signals." No employee, Birce insists, would understand the coding, but he stopped short of denying the potential for abuse by saying it would be "virtually impossible to extort it and practically impossible to alter it."

Everyone in the industry is equally wary because stories about computer fraud are as common as mushrooms after a rain. The largest electronic bank fraud in the U.S. was disovered in 1981 when California's Wells Fargo Bank found that an employee had used the bank computer to embezzle $21.3 million. The amount was half the total take of all U.S. bank robberies in a year. In another incident in 1978, Stanley Mark Rifkin, who had been a computer consultant for the Security Pacific Bank in Los Angeles, visited the bank's wire transfer room and obtained the electronic funds transfer code. Later, posing as a branch manager, he phoned in and used the code to send money to Switzerland. By the time the bank's computers caught up with the fraud, Rifkin had flown to Switzerland and converted the money to diamonds and returned to the U.S. Only when he boasted of his feat was he caught and convicted.

The fraud story most often heard—and least likely to be true—cites a bank computer operator who programmed the system to take portions of cents from various accounts and siphon them off into his own account. Every time interest was calculated on any account and the resulting interest payment worked out to a number that ended with less than half a cent, the interest payment would be rounded down to the nearest cent and the programmer would sweep away the shaving. According to the stories, the amounts gathered from these round-off frauds have reached $200,000. In a study of future economic losses caused by computers, thirty-four computer specialists said they believed thirty-six such thefts would occur each year, with an average loss of $110,000 per theft. There is, however, no firm proof that losses anywhere near that size have happened. In fact, in a 1980 study, *Computer/Law Journal* spent seventeen pages and used intricate mathematical formulas to prove that no such fraud had yet occurred. Even in banks with millions of accounts, such a crime would take eight years to accumulate $200,000, and be spotted long before the eight years passed, the study maintained.

None of the Canadian banks has so far admitted major computer crime of any sort. The Canadian Bankers' Association swears that none has happened. However, it may just be a matter of time, as a group of computer-wise pre-teens from Manhattan's private Dalton School proved in 1980 when they gained access to a number of corporate and institutional data systems (no banks) in Canada. No funds were diverted, but some damage was done to data files.

To date, most of the known illegal entries have been more for fun than to defraud. Typical is the 1981 infiltration of a computer system in London, Ontario. The company, Masterfeeds, is in the feed, grain, and farm supply business, with branches from Alberta to Newfoundland. The firm has a Prime 400 computer linked to the outside world by Datapac, a sub-network of Bell Canada's telephone system. That system allows North American users to dial a local number, type in an eight-digit code, and gain access to any computer on the network. Every computer comes from the manufacturer with the same access number, and every user is supposed to change the number to make its individual system secure. Many don't.

Daniel Zuckerman, a twenty-year-old college student from Albany, New York, became familiar with the Prime computer at school and programmed his own Radio Shack TRS-80 to try each eight-digit address, looking for a system where security was so lax that the original entry number hadn't been changed. His computer could try hundreds of numbers, even when he was sleeping. Finally he discovered Masterfeeds and spent about twenty hours in the company's system. According to F. E. Eisan, Masterfeeds controller, "Daniel was not trying to defraud Masterfeeds, or even vandalize us, he was simply furthering his education — at our expense." The firm discovered the invasion when they started work on the computer one Monday morning and a message flashed up on the screen: "I am the random glitch, catch me if you can." Catching him turned out to be easy, since only one trunk connects Datapac with the Telenet and the Tymenet networks in the U.S. All transmissions pass through the National Control Centre in Ottawa, so the call from Zuckerman could be traced easily. There was, however, no law under which the FBI could make an arrest.

According to the OPP's Campbell, "There's an incredible potential for computer abuse. There is a considerable amount of anecdotal evidence that would suggest there is a lot going on." To date, any admitted fraudulent activity that has come to light has been with automated teller machines (ATMs). In Calgary, for example, a man opened a Royal Bank account with a $50 deposit and obtained a card for the bank's ATM. He then proceeded to withdraw his limit each day ($500) until he had run up an overdraft of $15,000. He was charged and convicted of fraud and sent to prison for six months. The Royal says that its units were not "on-line" originally; the particular branch had to do manual checks daily and failed in this case. Now, claims the bank, units are hooked directly into the computer, rendering such fraud impossible. Insists Campbell: "Most banks have some similar kind of flaw in their system. The amount they are likely to lose will cost less than the amount they are likely to spend to stop it. It's a trade-off."

Twenty other methods to loot ATMs are contained in a six-page brochure published in Alamogordo, New Mexico. Entitled *Automated Teller Machines*, the brochure had the industry in such a tizzy when it came out last year that the respected New York-based newsletter *ATM Report* even urged banks to band together to buy the silence of the pamphleteer, John J. Williams. The newsletter claimed he would cease publishing his brochure if he were paid $50,000. Williams has published a number of similar brochures, including one called *Toilet Trainer*, which describes how to flush special exploding devices down corporate toilets, thus rendering skyscrapers useless for months.

In his ATM booklet, his ideas range from the wacko (build a false front for an ATM that includes a holding compartment to intercept withdrawals by users, who would assume the machine wasn't working) to the supertechnical, such as three techniques to tap ATM phone lines, record transaction data, and then loot the machines by playing back the recorded material. That, writes Williams, is the best way to "get the banking world by the balls." The simplest extortion method he suggests is to open an account with $10,000, keep it clean for several months, then as soon as a monthly statement is issued, make regular withdrawals until the account is empty. When the next statement arrives, rush into the bank claiming that someone has stolen the funds. Lie detector tests are rare, he insists.

Most ATM fraud, like credit-card abuse, occurs after cards have been stolen, often in the mail on the way to new applicants. The banks, under pressure for a while to use registered mail to send credit and ATM cards to customers, have returned to using regular mail, for cost reasons. At one time, bank security personnel estimated that 60 per cent of credit-card losses were caused when cards were intercepted in the mail, sold for $50 to $100, and used fraudulently. There are also cases, however, of surprising honesty from the post office. Once, a two-ounce gold bar was shipped from an Ontario bank branch to Toronto head office in an ordinary

No. 10 envelope. The envelope arrived in Toronto with a hole in it where the bar had shot out. A few days went by and a call came from the post office: "Did you lose any gold?"

As banks move towards the cashless society, relying more and more on machines — including access to accounts from home terminals — the probability grows for massive fraud or disruption. In his book *The Cashless Society, EFTS at the Crossroads,* August Bequai cites a variety of computer thefts including one where robbers, presumably with mob connections, diverted more than two hundred freight cars from the Pennsylvania Railroad Co. to a small railway terminal in Illinois. "The sabotage of a key EFT [electronic funds transfer] system could bring about political and economic chaos in any of our large cities, where the populace would find it difficult to conduct its everyday financial transactions." Wiretaps on bank data lines are so simple that demonstrations using $1,000 of equipment, purchasable from any computer store, have become part of a Motorola sales pitch intended to scare bankers into buying the company's hardware to defeat such theft.

All the while, computer systems continue to grow in size and complexity. The Society for Worldwide Interbank Financial Telecommunication (SWIFT) links nine hundred banks in forty countries with more than three hundred thousand messages sent daily. While security is tight, any computer expert will admit that absolute security is impossible. The other point on which everyone agrees is that no one knows how much computer crime there is, or how much money has been lost. The U.S. Chamber of Commerce puts the annual loss from electronic theft at $100 million, but most specialists agree that the true figure is considerably higher. Computer manufacturers are responding with more sophisticated programmes to prevent unauthorized access, as well as an advertising barrage to increase corporate awareness of the problem. Says the headline in one IBM ad: "The computer didn't do it." The ad argues that with proper precautions against human misuse, computers are safe places to keep information.

For Canadian consumers, the issue comes down to trust that their funds are secure. But no one can ensure that a computer system won't suffer the worst potential loss. In public, the bankers claim rock-solid confidence. In private, they are not so sure. Says one former data centre manager, noting the geography around his bank's suburban data centre: "You could come along the creek bed, get a boost up on to the low roof, leave a bag with a bomb behind, and that's it — we're wiped out." The OPP's Campbell agrees with their private worries about sabotage and fraud: "Banks are among the most advanced in computer security, some of them smugly so. I almost wish they'd get stung."

THIRTEEN

The Heirs Apparent

The Next "Big Five" Chairmen

FOR ANYONE SCRABBLING up the ladder at Canada's "Big Five" chartered banks, only one title qualifies as the winner's trophy: chairman and chief executive officer. Nothing is worse than finishing a rung back. While most bankers may not crave high profiles, they certainly want position. The disgrace that comes from a lunge that misses or a fruitless wait gives a man an eternal stench. Unlike superstitious athletes, who don't know where their power comes from, bankers do. For them, position is all.

The next generation of bank bosses chosen from the heirs apparent listed in this chapter will have a roster of talents that their predecessors could not imagine. The world is becoming an even tougher place for money at risk, so international expertise and contacts will be essential. Much of the growth in the next decade will occur in the U.S., so knowledge of that market and its politics will be beneficial. There will always be a place for special pleading, so the man with friends in government will do well. As Canadians move towards the cashless society, an understanding of technology will be essential. So will communications skills, once seen as unnecessary among this elusive breed.

Further, tomorrow's top banker will be less the money merchant and more the proprietor. In addition to an ability to crunch numbers, he'll need to know about marketing, manufacturing, personnel, trade, and the host of details that compose business. He will need this because Massey, Dome, the fisheries — and more businesses to come — will be run by bankers. Those bankers will be chosen from the bright-eyed and bushy-tailed heirs, the crown princes of the Big Five banks. As a group, they are less modest and better equipped than their predecessors for a more public life. Within the banks, they are even now being measured for what former Bank of Montreal chairman Fred McNeil terms, simply, "requirement." It's what Tom Wolfe has called "the right stuff," the inner ability to rise above the rest on a combination of guts, smarts, talent, luck, and the capacity for risk and reward.

The way to the top is not easy. It is littered with the bodies of those who have failed or been beaten. Says McNeil: "There's nothing more unhappy than a guy pushed one step too far. That's the ultimate cruelty. You see him start to break—his health or his family. He feels the pressure, he knows he's not coping."

Getting the successors ready is even tougher. Bill Mulholland, McNeil's successor, puts it this way: "You see it in politics, too. As you get more responsibility, character makes more difference than competence. Character traits get magnified. In business, a middle-level person becomes dominant as he is promoted. Those are the types of things that trip up a lot of people. That's why a lot of otherwise competent people trip over the last hurdle.

"As you prepare people for the next role, the thing is not to worry about technical skills; it's to try and place them in an environment similar to where they're going. You just can't tell how people are going to behave under pressure until you see them under pressure. It's the most difficult thing to do. People themselves don't know how they will respond. A small guy can become a monster." And a crown prince can become a king.

ROYAL BANK OF CANADA

Royal Bank chairman Rowlie Frazee has been actively recruiting at the top. His catch includes Jack Stabback, former National Energy Board chairman; Ed Neufeld, former senior finance mandarin; and John Abell, one-time senior partner in the investment firm of Wood Gundy. All have been layered into an already well-populated executive group.

In fact, compared with the twenty-year term of his predecessor, Earle McLaughlin, Frazee will serve a relatively short term. He was named president in 1977, chief executive officer in 1979, and chairman in 1980; he designated his successor, Allan Taylor, as president and chief operating officer in 1983. Former president Jock Finlayson, the man Frazee beat out for the top, took early retirement in May, thus opening up the position for Frazee's pick.

The tapping of Taylor does not mean, however, that the position of chief executive officer and chairman will automatically follow. "If he doesn't shape up," warns Frazee, "then it might be somebody else."

The choice depended on more than management capacity. As David Culver, president of Alcan Aluminum Ltd., once put it to a meeting sponsored by the bank: "There are twenty people who could *run* the Royal Bank, but there are only four or five who can *change* the Royal

Bank." In the end, even that estimate was high, for Frazee made the choice between only two internal heirs, both born in Saskatchewan: Allan Taylor, formerly executive vice-president, international banking; and Geoff Styles, now senior executive vice-president, international and corporate banking division.

When the Royal Bank opened its new offices in Bangkok last year, Allan Taylor knelt along with the nine saffron-robed monks sitting cross-legged before a small Buddhist shrine. He lit joss sticks and candles and probably muttered his own prayer when the monk sprinkled holy water and ordered: "Now, make money."

Taylor was born in 1932 in Prince Albert, Saskatchewan, in the part of the province that straddles the two realities that make up the Prairies: timber to the north and farms to the south. His father was an electrician with Burns and Co. during the Depression, so his trade and the fact that he worked for a meat packer ensured that the Taylors (Allan was the fourth of five children) never went without. During the war, his father joined the army and built training camps in the West with the engineers. That led to a contruction supervision post with the Veterans' Land Act Administration after the war.

It was a stable life and the family was devoutly Anglican. Taylor's father was a minister's warden for thirty years; his mother was president of the Women's Association. Honesty and integrity were watchwords in the household, and everyone was expected to contribute. Taylor spent his Christmas holidays working at the post office, his summers as a caddy either at the local golf course or at Waskesiu, the resort in Prince Albert National Park north of the town of fifteen thousand.

He did well in high school, finishing at sixteen with a 75 per cent average and a $500-a-year scholarship from the Church of England to attend the university of his choice. He couldn't choose between pharmacy and commerce, so in 1949 he decided to work for a year in the local branch of the Royal Bank, where his brother Bob (today a senior inspector in Alberta) had begun his career ten years earlier. He never returned to school. "I got caught up in the whole thing," he says.

He began by delivering drafts to the local businesses, running the postage-stamp box, and doing all the other menial chores that went with being a lowly junior in those days. He was promoted quickly on to other Saskatchewan branches in Meadow Lake, Lanigan, Oxbow, Moose Jaw, and North Battleford, and became a junior inspector in 1952. During the next two and a half years, he visited eighty-three of the eighty-five branches in Saskatchewan. At one, he turned up a $500 defalcation that led to the firing of an employee. In 1955, he came off the road and was named assistant accountant, then accountant, in Saskatoon.

The big move came in 1957 when he was sent east to the credit department in Toronto, bringing with him his new wife, who had been his secretary in Saskatoon. In Toronto, his mentor was A. P. Murphy, a credit supervisor who taught him not just how to decide which applications should be approved, but also how to turn down the others with good humour. He then served in branches in Toronto and Hamilton before going to New York in 1965 as senior assistant agent.

Although he felt that he was at the very heart of the financial world, he was not over-awed. "When you're from Saskatchewan," he says, "maybe you don't know enough to be in awe." Working at the Royal's New York agency was like working at a small U.S. bank—he got to see all the different departments. He also brushed up against other financiers and felt plugged in to world affairs. Two-hour lunches with the Wall Street crowd at Oscar's made him feel like an international banker. "I could have lived there forever," he recalls. "You were involved with things that were on the front page of the *New York Times*. That really got me hooked."

His next posting was to head office in Montreal where, as supervisor of correspondent banking, he worked with three thousand banks around the world and was involved in the Royal's first Eurodollar loan, a $28-million deal shared among four banks. Although it was small by current standards, Taylor was on the leading edge of the international deals of the day. He became an assistant general manager in international, then was transferred back to Toronto in 1971. As manager of the main branch, he was in charge of five hundred people and realized for the first time that his career might have real growth potential.

In 1974, he returned to Montreal as a deputy general manager in the international division and became executive vice-president for international banking in 1977. Throughout his time in international, he took a cautious view of the other banks' headlong rush to loan money to developing countries. "We looked a little askance at what was going on," he says. "Everybody wanted to get into Bahrain, for example, but we didn't go in there until much later." The Royal didn't do general-purpose balance-of-payment financing. Instead, the focus was on loans for trade or specific projects.

It was a cautious stance that paid off. While the Royal is North America's fourth-largest bank, its loans to the heavily indebted nations such as Mexico, Argentina, Brazil, and Venezuela rank twelfth in total — well behind many smaller U.S. institutions. Loans to Mexico are $1.3 billion, to Brazil, $812 million. "We're not sitting badly compared with other banks," he says, "but that's damn small comfort." It was Taylor who chaired the country risk meetings in the early 1980s, assessing risk in each of the nations where the Royal had loans. He developed an intricate weighting system, which helped the committee decide. If the committee was split, the ultimate judgement was his.

His wavy brown hair and a jowly face put a soft wrapping on thought processes that are carefully compartmentalized. His rapid-fire logic and background arguments are always ready for ordered presentation. As a member of the bank's management committee, he has been involved in the regular Tuesday strategy meetings attended by the senior executive in Montreal and Toronto. Until recently, the ninety-minute meetings were held in Montreal. Now they are conducted by television hook-up, on a secure audio-visual circuit that means Toronto-based executives don't have to waste the day travelling.

Traditionally the bank's strengths were equally divided, with assets split in thirds among international, commercial, and retail business. While in recent years the international side has swung up to 40 per cent of the share, following the purchase of the Orion Bank in England, the balance is likely to be restored in the near future. As a result, domestic experience will be most important at the top. Taylor was seen as having the best background; Styles's career had been too heavily tilted towards international for too long. It was, however, a close call.

Taylor learned of his elevation to president just before Christmas 1982. Less than a month later, it was announced at the bank's annual meeting. Frazee invited Taylor to his house one afternoon and sprang the news to him there. He also informed Taylor that he would carry the title of chief operating officer. The added duties of being responsible for the day-to-day operations of the bank — along with Taylor's posting in Toronto — signalled that the centre of gravity of the Royal Bank had irreversibly shifted. In Toronto, Taylor will have strategic management responsibility for domestic banking, international and corporate banking, as well as other departments, including financial control and administration. "We've got a split head office," Taylor admits. Frazee knew the change had to come. A year earlier, when the Royal's Lockheed Jetstar landed in Montreal one morning, the airport was so quiet that the pilot was able to turn around and taxi back on the same runway towards the terminal. Noting this, Frazee said: "That demonstrates the decline of Montreal as a financial centre. It's like landing at Presque Isle, Maine. Any other big-city airport and you'd have to get off *so* fast."

After the job and location were sorted out, Taylor and Frazee spent the rest of the afternoon, until it grew dark, talking about the Royal and where the other players would fit beneath them. They both knew that the 1982 results were not satisfactory, and they talked about how to turn earnings around. They also agreed that asset growth would continue to be slow because of weak loan demand and that people development must go hand-in-hand with the coming electronic revolution in banking.

Unspoken that afternoon, but present nevertheless, was the knowledge that when Taylor takes over from Frazee in 1986, Taylor will be the first chairman and chief executive officer of the Royal in more than twenty-five years not to have a university degree. At a time when institutions are putting a premium on education and filling the executive suite with MBAs, there is a certain irony in the Royal's reversal. "People could look at this bank, where a lot of MBAs have been hired," admits Taylor, "and say, 'How did that happen?' I don't see that it will make any difference. It doesn't occur to me except when people remind me."

Already his profile has been raised because the position requires regular speeches, numerous interviews, and countless receptions or other honorific occasions where the bank needs senior representation. In choosing Taylor over Styles, the Royal will see a transition without a ripple. "I'm not coming in here and saying, 'My God, I can change things and put Taylor's stamp on this bank.' I've had a voice these past eight years. I can't walk away from the responsibility, so I might as well take the credit."

The bank opted for the traditional figure of a Royal banker as embodied by Taylor, rather than the more entrepreneurial Geoff Styles. Bob Utting, a vice-chairman, who is the size of an automatic clothes-dryer and was, in his day, one of the best foreign-exchange traders the bank ever had, would have made an even less likely choice than Styles. In the end, the Royal stuck with the smooth and the handsome, staying away from a lurch in the ancestral order that has served so well. Also-rans included Joe Regan and A.H. (Mike) Michell. Along with Styles they were named senior executive vice-presidents — all reporting to Taylor.

Styles, fifty-two, has a Bachelor of Commerce degree and started in the bank as a teller and collector of collections in Victoria. Since then, he has worked in Chicago, London (Ontario), Montreal, and Toronto as well as serving two stints in Britain. He wanted the job of president and was disappointed when Taylor was appointed. "My objective has always been one job higher," he said before the decision was announced. "When I started as a teller, I thought if I could become an accountant, I would be happy."

Bank of Montreal

At the bank of Montreal, the successor may well be whoever is still standing when current chairman and CEO William Mulholland has stopped chewing through underlings. At fifty-seven, he still has a few years to go, as long as the bank can keep his attention. An official successor won't be named for three to five years, but Mulholland is ready. "My job," he says, "is to give the directors options. In short, no crown princes. It takes a long time to get someone ready for that role, and getting several people ready simultaneously is a helluva balancing act. I go back to the Bible: many are called, but few are chosen."

If Mulholland left early, the successor would most likely be deputy chairman Grant Reuber. The other major contender is president Bill Bradford. One notch back from both are Dale Parker, who heads Canadian commercial banking, and William Harker, who is in charge of domestic banking. None of the other Big Five banks has such rank outsiders among its current inheritors. That's because Mulholland himself is a newcomer and has rebuilt the place in his mould. As his PR man and vice-president, Richard O'Hagan, puts it: "When Mulholland came here, this bank was a wasteland. I mean, what do you do? Raid Canadian banks? You can only do so much of that. Go after Americans? As an American, he could only do so much of that, too, before filling his quota. So he had to look around in other areas for people. Mulholland is a renaissance man and has done a number of things in his life. He responds to people who have also done a number of things, not just stuck it out at the bank for decades. He likes Reuber and has made him his number two. A lot of bankers are just concerned about the day-to-day; Reuber isn't. He has a lot to learn yet, he's still getting his footing, but he can see the environment, he knows why things are happening and how they've happened before."

Just a year younger than Mulholland, Grant Reuber was raised on a farm two miles away from the small southern Ontario town of Mildmay. He has his doctorate in economics and has worked in the federal finance department, the Bank of Canada, and the Organization for Economic Cooperation and Development in Paris; he also taught at the University of Western Ontario for twenty years, where he rose to be vice-president (administration) and provost. Mulholland hired him for his brains, although he knew that Reuber was green as a corporate strategist — a talent Mulholland admires and requires in others. Says B of M director Peter Gordon: "Reuber is a strong, determined individual who will ride over anybody who is not quite as strong intellectually as he is. Mulholland needs somebody to bounce ideas off, who can stay with him intellectually. Reuber can certainly do that."

Reuber walks on the balls of his feet, almost jauntily, as if ready to side-step any trouble. His head is squat, framed by wiry grey hair and ears that are slightly pointed, giving him the look of a cheery gargoyle high up on a parapet, leering down at lesser mortals. Because he has been in banking only since 1978, he can afford to laugh at the profession. One of his favourite jokes goes as follows: A man due for a heart transplant was given the choice between the heart of a beautiful young woman and a banker's heart. "The choice was obvious," says Reuber. "The banker's heart would undoubtedly be in better shape because it hadn't been used very much."

Reuber was the only student in the one-room schoolhouse to make it to Walkerton High School. On graduation he won a scholarship to the University of Western Ontario in London and had his eyes opened by a campus filled with worldly-wise veterans returning from the Second World War. He lived at a fraternity house, Zeta Psi, did the usual amount of beer-drinking, and graduated in honours economics. After two years at the Bank of Canada in Ottawa, where he did work on price inflation following the Korean War, he went to Harvard for his master's degree and his doctorate in economics. His thesis, on the impediments to British exports, was "largely unread," he laughs, "and perhaps just as well." After study at Cambridge and two years in the Department of Finance, he returned to Western, his base for the next twenty years. "I think I had a reputation at the university for being tough but fair," he says. "I guess I *am* demanding of people." While at Western, he chaired the Ontario Economic Council and spent four summers in Paris writing a paper for the OECD.

In 1978, Bill Mulholland went looking for a chief economist and Reuber took the risky leap into the private sector, but only after arranging a leave from Western, so that if he fizzled at the bank, he could return to the university. A year later he was tapped by then Prime Minister Joe Clark to be deputy minister of finance. Although happy with the bank, he couldn't turn down the chance to go to Ottawa. "One didn't take it for the longevity or the money. You took it on face value, warts and all."

He arrived in September 1979, in time to prepare the ill-fated budget on which the Clark government fell. Mulholland, however, was only too happy to take him back. Peter Kirkham, former head of Statistics Canada, had Reuber's old job by then, so a new one was created: executive vice-president with responsibility for his former department as well as treasury. In 1981 he was made deputy chairman and deputy chief executive and, like Mulholland, he is uncompromising: "I really don't think we want people around the bank who don't want to do what they're doing."

As president, Bill Bradford is the number three man in the bank and is in charge of day-to-day operations. With a mere six people reporting to him, he has delegated responsibilities well. Sandy-grey hair tops a triangular face dominated by large-rimmed bifocal glasses. He is five-foot-ten and at fifty favours suits with padded shoulders that make him look like the former hockey player he is. Not only is he tough enough to do Mulholland's bidding, he's a veteran of two wars under the same boss, first at Brinco and now at the bank.

Bradford was raised in various parts of the rugged northeast end of

Montreal, an only child whose mother died when he was twelve. He grew up viewing French-Canadian kids as the "enemy." Battles were so regular that he would fear for his own safety on his early-morning rounds, delivering the *Gazette*. In high school he played golf (a seven handicap) and a little basketball and made the junior hockey team. As a student, he was lazy and did only enough to get by. After graduation, he was sent off to work in his grandfather's downtown sweatshop for $15 a week. He was cured of thinking he could face the world with only his hands and a high school diploma. His next step, the mailroom at Northern Telecom, wasn't much farther up the ladder, but he also enrolled in night school accounting courses, and during the next five years, he added a credit each year as he worked his way through a variety of low-level positions in the accounting and treasury departments. By 1955, he was married and accounting supervisor, and began to get serious about the twenty-one credits required for his degree in commerce.

When he graduated in 1960, he jumped to Canada Iron Foundries as senior internal auditor, continued to work at night on his certified general accountants programme, and passed his exams in a class where 70 per cent failed. In 1962, he joined Reynolds Extrusion Co. and was quickly promoted to Toronto plant manager. Before he moved his family, personal disaster struck. One night, his wife awoke to the smell of smoke in their Dollard des Ormeaux house. Bradford scuttled downstairs from the upper floor of their split-level home. The playroom door felt red-hot, and when he opened it, the rush of oxygen-laden air into the room caused the smouldering fire to explode and sweep through the house. The family and a visiting friend of one of the children rushed to safety into the cool Easter weather. The home was destroyed. It wouldn't be his last narrow escape.

In 1967, he was approached by Eric Lambert, a former vice-president of Canada Wire and Cable, to join him in a new venture, Churchill Falls (Labrador) Corp. Ltd. As project controller, it was Bradford's job to shepherd the $1-billion hydro job through a myriad of deadlines. The falls inspired an almost poetic response in Bradford: "It was really extraordinary, one of the most beautiful sights in the world. You could actually walk around to a meadow on the far side of the falls so you could face it. There was a huge drop and the mists were all around, sky-rocketing thousands of feet into the air."

In November 1969, most of the management team was at Churchill Falls for meetings. At the close of the sessions, president Don McParland was scheduled to give an evening speech in nearby Labrador City. That day, a surprise high-ranking European visitor arrived at the site, so Bradford and construction manager Harold Snyder were delegated to stay behind rather than accompany McParland as planned, in order to show off the site. Bradford and Snyder saw McParland and his six associates onto the plane and went off to dinner at the company hotel with their visitor. During the meal came the whispered and ominous message: "They can't find the plane." Bradford and Snyder packed their guest off to his bungalow and hurried to the airport for more news. The plane had crashed on final approach to Labrador City, killing McParland and everyone else on board.

It was that crash that brought Mulholland into the Churchill Falls Corporation and Brinco and meant, over time, that Bradford rose quickly in the organization. He was made vice-president at thirty-eight and saw the completion of the project and its take-over in 1974 by the govenment of Newfoundland. Bradford did not want to work for the government and fled to Canadian International Power as vice-president for finance, but it wasn't long before Mulholland was back in his life. Within two months of becoming president of the Bank of Montreal, Mulholland invited Bradford to lunch at the Mount Royal Club early in 1975. After a pre-meal drink, they took a table in the main dining room and Mulholland outlined his preliminary views on what was needed at the bank. Then he popped the question: "Would you consider working at the bank?" Bradford joined and was part of the turnaround that saw many senior executives — both old guard and new — come up short in Mulholland's eyes. The casualty rate didn't surprise the tough Bradford. "It's inevitable that there had to be some fall-out. There were some people who didn't measure up and were encouraged to find other things to do."

Named president in 1981, Bradford has, however, gone about as far as he is likely to go. He was seen to be a better administrator than now vice-chairman Stan Davison, but the members of the board also concluded that Bradford lacked the "sheer fibre" for the top. "There are a helluva lot of capable people who are superb second men," says Fred McNeil, "but not to sit at the top. You have to be a kind of social philosopher, you have to keep alert to what the hell is going on in the world around you ... to have some judgement about it and back those judgements with strategies and policies." Bradford is now overseeing a reorganization in the bank, as the commercial banking functions are centralized and taken out of the branches. Bradford does see himself as a "potential successor" to Mulholland, but he notes wryly: "Whether or not we'll all survive him is another question."

THE CANADIAN IMPERIAL BANK OF COMMERCE

At the Commerce, former paratrooper Russ Harrison has seen three of his senior associates bail out because of the institutional turmoil and because their prospects for advancement looked better elsewhere. Although the jumpers included almost half the higher-ups in the place, none was a likely successor to Harrison.

In 1981, after more than twenty years with the Commerce, David Lewis left his job as senior vice-president for Ontario to become executive vice-president and chief operating officer of Continental Bank, with the promise of the presidency to follow. Lewis had been the key man for the Commerce on the Bank Act revision, which became law in November 1980, and was open to blandishments when Noranda president and Continental director Adam Zimmerman approached him. In less than three weeks, the job had been offered and accepted. The Commerce did not struggle to keep Lewis.

Later in 1981, vice-chairman Chuck Laidley left even though he had no immediate job prospects. He was not fired, nor did he quit, although there was a handsome settlement. Said one director: "Laidley was laid-back, lazy. He was a nine-to-five banker. You can't be like that; you have to work from eight to seven-thirty. He was a good credit man but a poor administrator."

The third senior man to leave was another vice-chairman, John Hilliker. In 1982 he quit to become chief executive officer of Canada Permanent Trust, in a move that was said to have doubled his pay and compensation package to $500,000 a year. While his jump was a surprise around the bank, Hilliker was not a favourite among the other senior Commerce bankers. As one colleague put it kindly: "Hilliker is an implementer of other people's policies." Hilliker, said director Sydney Hermant, was "not an inspirational leader. As they say in tennis: high over the net and straight between the lines."

All of these leave-takings were from a bank with already thin top ranks. Throughout, Harrison brought into a top job but one outsider who could be even remotely considered as an heir apparent — Frank Logan.

Frank Logan doesn't just walk, he surges. He doesn't just sit, he seethes. Now fifty-three, he stands six-foot-two, struggles to keep his weight at 210 pounds, and has the bull neck and shoulders of a full-back. When Laidley left, Harrison recruited Logan from the investment firm of Dominion Securities, where he had been chairman. He got out just at the right moment, when A. E. Ames was being merged with DS and there had been high-flying times on the stock market. Logan owned about 6 per cent of DS, and that interest was bought by four or five others in the firm for about $2 million. Even after capital gains tax, he was a millionaire. He left an annual salary of $125,000, swollen by that year's $200,000 bonus.

Posted to Calgary in September 1981 to corral oil and gas loan business, Logan arrived when the oil patch, along with the rest of the economy, went into a tailspin. Within a year, he was recalled to Toronto and now oversees marketing as a vice-chairman. An avid tennis player and outdoorsman, he hunts ducks, fishes for salmon, and often has his catch served for friends at the York Club in Toronto. A man of some sartorial style, he favours bow-ties and cloaks. Says Brascan chairman Trevor Eyton: "Frank was really born middle-aged. He came into the world wearing a three-piece suit and making speeches." Some of his competitors sourly regard him as no more than a back-slapping buffoon and story-teller, but most see him as a tough business-getter. Argus president and CEO Monte Black calls him "one of the greatest corporate developers this country has ever seen. He's a war-horse and has thundered all over the world." However, the career bankers at the Commerce who struggle for recognition will see that Logan goes no higher. As Harrison told a friend when Logan joined: "I'm going to provide Frank with all the protection I can give him, but in the final analysis, he's on his own—and they're sure out to get him."

There are others near the top who don't stand much of a chance in the sweeps, either, including the five high-ranking vice-presidents. Harrison chose each for his current slot, but none is likely to be picked by him as a successor. Typical is Jim Bickford, who in 1981 was shuffled away from international into administration and replaced by hot-shot Warren Moysey. In November 1982, when Moysey was elevated, Bickford was shuffled back to international. In making the announcement to the board of directors at a time when pay-back of international loans was more important than expansion, Harrison characterized Bickford thus: "We moved him out when we needed somebody more aggressive. Now I guess that's not so important."

C. W. (Peter) Cole, at 46, is a senior executive vice-president and looks after the liability side of the bank. He joined the bank from the investment community in 1975 and has since built a good-sized empire beneath him. He enjoys a particular status with Harrison as the only underling from whom Harrison will brook argument. He also enjoys a maverick position in the community as a lover of high times and high jinks. A man of mercurial moods, Cole can still find himself in the odd bar fight and hangs out with a fun-loving crowd.

In April 1973, Cole joined a group of brokers who had gathered in the Victoria Room at the King Edward Hotel. The market was behaving badly, but more importantly, they had just heard that a friend was dying of cancer. They decided to celebrate life and began drinking double martinis. Cole's friend Murray Sinclair tried his trick of whipping the tablecloth off a fully set table. He didn't succeed that day, because there was a felt underpad under the first table he tried.

The group then piled into several cars and headed for the Oyster Bar in chic Yorkville to continue the party. Sinclair was among the first batch to arrive; not wanting to leave the room while a good story was in progress at his table, he relieved himself into an empty beer bottle and set it aside. When Cole arrived, he was handed the bottle by another reveller, who knew the contents. Cole took a slug, then, realizing what it contained and knowing the culprit immediately, made to pop Sinclair on the chin. Sinclair beat him to it, however, and knocked Cole unconscious. At that point, Cole's wife, Carol, who had been called to join the gathering, walked in. When she saw her husband lying unconscious, she barely blinked and said, "And what's he done now?"

Cole then came to and resumed his attack, only to have Sinclair deck him again. After the second revival, they made up, and they remain great friends and drinking buddies. Sinclair says of Cole: "I wouldn't say he has a drinking problem, but when he does drink, he [sometimes] drinks to excess. It's frustration. He's so bright, the wheels are always turning. He needs to unwind." Whatever the accurate description of Cole's drinking habits, the morning-after indicator is a breakout of psoriasis on his face.

"Cole is a flash thinker," says Jack Mackenzie, of Elliott and Page Ltd. "He's tough as hell and he doesn't give a shit. He doesn't stand on niceties, director relationships, whatever. He just wants to do deals."

Although Cole was elevated to senior executive vice-president in 1983, third in line for the throne, a more likely candidate for Harrison's job is vice-chairman Don Fullerton. His time, however, may well be past. After twenty years with the bank, Fullerton, fifty-two, has spent half of those years one step from the top — and that's not quite the same thing as being a heart-beat away. He can be gracious on occasion, but he can also be a cold fish.

Fullerton has a strangely pointed face that tips upward from the chin to a puckered mouth that suffers from underbite. As a banker, he's an old pro and has been Harrison's man in the trouble-spots. He's been the Commerce representative on the Massey board since 1981, and has also been handling the bank's problems with Dome, Turbo, and some of the sour international loans for much of that time. His day in the sun, however, has passed. "If things turned around tomorrow and the world looked better," says one director, "I'm not sure he'd have very much to do."

As recently as 1980, when Fullerton carried the title of chief operating officer, he was clearly number two to Harrison. He was until then the heir apparent, but he made a tactical error and began pushing for a larger role and a change in title. It was a serious blunder. "That only works," says one who knows the Commerce scene, "when a chairman is in the withdrawal stage." Harrison not only wasn't ready to give up anything, he was disappointed that Fullerton had made his move. Within a week,

Harrison had the unanimous support of the board, and Fullerton was stripped of his CEO title. "The retribution," says a close observer in the investment community, "was swift and savage." If only he had been patient, the top job would likely have been his, but he wasn't and it won't be. Harrison, at sixty-two, has three years for the final grooming of his likely choice — Warren Moysey.

At forty-four, senior executive vice-president Warren Moysey is the bank's best and brightest. He also carries the highest profile in an otherwise secretive group. When the Computer Communications Group ran a series of half-page newspaper advertisements in 1981 promoting its Dataroute services, Moysey willingly sang the praises of the system beside a full-colour photo of himself. It was a blurb for the bank's five thousand on-line computer terminals in individual branches, eight regional data centres, and three Visa credit centres. But it was also a bit of bugling for Moysey, who oversaw the installation of the modern era in more than sixteen hundred of the bank's branches across Canada. Never mind that the Commerce was the last of the Big Five to automate and that everyone else had discovered the mistakes first, Moysey was credited with getting the system up and running successfully.

Moysey was first spotted as a comer in McKinnon's day, was put in charge of the international division in 1981, and was told to beef up corporate loans abroad in what had been a weak area for the bank. There he worked gamely on through the tragic death of his son in 1982. The fourteen-year-old boy had just been picked to become a member of the Ontario Junior Downhill Ski Team and took a celebratory solo run at Osler Bluffs near Collingwood, Ontario. He struck a tree and was killed.

Moysey's social connections are impeccable, although one is a bit bizarre. Along with Scotiabank vice-chairman Peter Godsoe and Continental president David Lewis, Moysey belongs to a golf group that encompasses thirty men. Its sole purpose is to play once a year for a trophy stolen twenty years ago from a Jewish fraternity on St. George Street near the University of Toronto. The plaque, dedicated to one Milton Flugelman, has given the name to the group, and over the years a host of other bric-a-brac has been built up, including songs, jackets, and a crest, with a yellow-and-black colour scheme, an upside-down tee, the initials "MF," and a Latin motto: N*umquam super + in numquam* (Never up, never in). The group plays at Toronto Golf, Miami's Doral, or in Las Vegas.

In November 1982, after Hilliker left, Moysey was elevated to the position of senior executive vice-president. In addition to co-ordinating the activities of the five executive vice-presidents, he became part of the chief executive's office, a group that also includes Harrison, Logan, and Fullerton. Moysey's specific responsibility is to co-ordinate the day-today operations of the bank: chief operating officer—without the title. If energy is required to succeed, Moysey's got it. Says Nick Ross, a CA with Clarkson Gordon and a Milton Flugelman member: "If the word 'hyperactive' had been invented when he was younger, that's what they would have called him."

But to reach the top, patience is needed, too, as Don Fullerton knows. While Moysey is the current choice, that could change while Harrison takes on more and more of the foibles of McKinnon as he gets older. McKinnon liked to pick several successors, then send them packing one by one. Harrison has only worked his way through two. So far.

The Bank of Nova Scotia

Unless workaholic Scotiabank chairman and CEO Ced Ritchie, who is fifty-six, harries himself into an early grave, succession is stalled. If a change were needed very soon, it would be right-hand man and deputy chairman Gordon Bell, who, like Ritchie, joined the bank after high school and slugged his way up. More likely, the next CEO will be either Scott McDonald or Peter Godsoe, both vice-chairmen. In the next echelon down are chief financial officer Bob Brooks; Bruce Birmingham, who runs the U.S. operations; and George Hare, who runs retail banking and is currently on the fast track ahead of Brooks. One of them will likely be number two to Ritchie's successor.

When Gordon Bell was named president in 1979 and told the news to his wife, Charlene, she asked: "Do you get any more money?" "No, I was given a salary increase last month. There isn't another." "Do you get more holidays?" "No," he replied, "that stays the same." "Well," she said after further reflection, "you're sure not any better-looking." Bell's rich brown eyes dance with delight when he tells such a story, but they can grow cold and hard when he's denouncing a politician. He can be almost charismatic in a small group, but he carries a short fuse. His raised voice and sharp tongue regularly send ill-prepared or incompetent colleagues slinking from his office.

Bell joined the bank the day after he graduated from high school in Toronto in 1948, spent time in various branches, was sent out on inspection five years later, and was posted to England in 1955. There, at the Waterloo Square branch, a mailman arrived one day with a parcel, demanding duty of £20, but would not reveal the contents. The bank wanted to know the contents first. Bell was called from his office to adjudicate and he sent a colleague for a hammer. "If he refuses to let go of the package," Bell instructed him, "when I try to take it from his hands, you rap him on the skull." The mailman hung on for a few seconds, then, realizing the bankers were serious, let go. The parcel was opened and found to contain engraved banking forms (a heavily dutied item), so the bank paid. The mailman fled and returned almost immediately with a bobby. "It took some fast talking to get out of that one," recalled Bell. "But you should have seen the look on the mailman's face when he let go."

After London, he served in Halifax, Ottawa, and Jamaica before returning to Toronto in 1968; there he moved up the ladder through personnel and administration to become Ritchie's chief general manager, president in 1979, and deputy chairman in 1982. As the inheritors push up around him with their university degrees, Bell jokes about his "Grade 2 education" and works ever harder. Surgery and radiation for throat cancer in 1981 have left him slightly hoarse. Too bad, for he is the best natural public speaker in the bank, a talent inherited from his father, a fire-and-brimstone United Church minister. A former heavy smoker, Bell quit the habit nearly a decade ago. In those days, he'd rise at five-thirty, climb into the bathtub with the morning paper, drink coffee, and smoke half a dozen Kents before breakfast.

Throughout his career, banking has been dog-eat-dog. "I don't feel power in a deal. I feel god-damned sweaty palms that somebody else out there is going to get that deal. Sure there's the power to choose among deals, but it's the market that's telling you which one of them is going to succeed. The banker makes the judgement, but he's not the maker of the prince. The power is in the borrower."

He can become almost euphoric when talking about international loans, pointing out that no country has ever gone bankrupt. "There is political and social upheaval in Central America, but it will get sorted out. Argentina is almost as rich as Canada. Poland has tremendous potential. Romania has suffered from mismanagement, but along with most of the Eastern Bloc countries, they're doing the right thing. I'm not cavalier, but I don't see any problems that can't be digested on the international side. Bankers are mortal. We make mistakes, but I don't think there have been excesses. Everybody talks about the size of Brazil's debt, but get on a plane and go to Rio. Isn't that economy worth $60 billion?" His optimism is tinged with realism, and he admits: "Bankers today are approaching the world more conservatively, but it's because the economy of the world is bloody awful."

Unless Ritchie dies before retirement age, Bell has gone as high as he will—one step short of where he hoped. When Bell was in Jamaica with the bank in the mid-1960s, Garfield Weston asked him to be president of Loblaws. Bell turned it down to see if he could make it to the top of the bank. He hasn't, but he's a loyal number two, even though Ritchie's tough style at their seven-thirty meeting every morning has been known to leave him shaken.

A tall, slender crane of a man, contender for the top spot Scott McDonald, forty-seven, is mild of manner and brilliant of mind. Withdrawn and almost studious, he is so shy that for years he resolutely refused to be interviewed for the standard pap of a profile in the bank's house organ. A University of Toronto and Harvard MBA graduate, he joined the bank in 1961 after working two summers with the Bank of Commerce and a summer with Scotiabank between years at Harvard. A training-orientation programme was developed for him when he joined permanently in 1961. Among the first areas he saw on this whirlwind campaign was the chief accountant's department, headed then by Ced Ritchie.

At the time, the Canadian Bankers' Association was preparing for the Bank Act revision by parcelling out various studies to different banks. Ritchie was to look into the question of inner reserves. (A bank has, say, $1,000 in loans and makes $100 in the year but thinks the next year will be worse. So the bank takes a reserve of $50, or half the profit, against the loan portfolio. Earnings are therefore debited by $50, net profit shows as $50, and the loan portfolio shows as $950. Only the bank officers know the real profit was $100 on $1,000.) McDonald was put to work on the CBA recommendation to retain inner reserves, which was not accepted under the revised Bank Act. His time under Ritchie stretched to six months before he was sent on, approvingly, to domestic credit, where he learned how to loan money by reviewing the work of others.

Then he took on a grooming job as a staff person, an assistant to Charlie Jameson, who in turn was an assistant to chairman Bill Nicks. McDonald, without a title himself, an assistant to an assistant, quickly dubbed himself the "assistant squared." There he became involved with international for the first time, specifically in selling shares to the public of the bank's holdings in Jamaica and Trinidad.

In 1966, McDonald was named executive assistant to Nicks, a man whom he regarded as "almost clairvoyant" for setting up the first consumer loan plan run by a chartered bank. "Every other bank in Canada thought [it] was, if not illegal, a licence to steal," says McDonald. It was at that time that McDonald made his sole trip to Nicks's house, the day the Consumers' Gas line on the street blew up and Nicks stayed home to supervise repairs. "There was an aloofness [in Nicks] that stemmed from an innate shyness," says McDonald. "He found it difficult to relate or relax even with people that he had known for a long, long time."

In 1970, when Ritchie was named chief general manager, McDonald replaced him in international, but as an indication he hadn't yet made the grade, Nicks called McDonald deputy chief general manager for international, even though there was no chief general manager there. It was his first major role, however, and he was in the right place at the right time just as international loans were beginning to take off. (The first syndicated Eurodollar loan was in 1969 for $80 million, to Iran.) McDonald rode the wave of change that saw the bank become more and more a wholesale operation, getting into the syndicated loans and corporate business in the U.S., moving away from the retail-oriented business in the Caribbean and the few branches in Europe that had been the offshore backbone of the bank a decade earlier. He also learned to become sanguine about critics of the bank who demand that loans to various countries be ended because of human rights violations. "A lot of the things that they are arguing are motherhood-type arguments. I'm not so sure that the banks are all that popular with the man in the street, simply because we're big business."

As the man with the prime responsibility for international, he is out of the country half his working year. Even so, since his appointment as a vice-chairman and director in 1982, he's become more involved in bank-wide policy-setting. Is his current position his last? "I would hope," he comments icily, "that given the age of Peter Godsoe and myself, that's not the thinking." Peter Godsoe used to report to him, but McDonald need not look over his shoulder any more: Godsoe has pulled even.

Short and cherubic, the forty-five-year-old Godsoe was two years behind McDonald at Harvard, joined Price Waterhouse in the U.S. as a mathematician, earned his CA degree, and in 1966, at twenty-seven, decided to return to Canada for what he terms "nationalistic" reasons. His father, Gerald Godsoe, a well-connected Halifax lawyer, opened the door for his son to be interviewed by each of the Big Five bank chairmen of the day. The Scotiabank interview began with Nicks saying, "Well, what the hell can you do?" "That's what I'm here to prove," Godsoe shot back. "What I want to do is give you a practical answer by working for you." All the banks offered him a job, but Godsoe was drawn to the gruff Nicks and signed on for $10,000 a year. He was dispatched to an Ottawa branch where he ran various departments in turn, to gain experience. Because he was a university graduate and they assumed he could spell, he says, he was sent to evening Parliamentary committee hearings on the Bank Act and wrote reports on proceedings for various members of the executive.

The following year he was transferred to main branch in Montreal as an assistant manager. As the first accelerated trainee going through the branch system, he faced hostility and was kept at the smallest desk for four months. He won his colleagues over by helping them write reports, and after eight months was given the same loan limit as the manager — $100,000 — an unheard-of accolade. "You've got all the education, now let's see if you're big enough to handle it," his manager told him. "Go out and make some money." Among his first loans, one, for $5,000, went sour. "I got sweet-talked into giving the bank's money," he recalled. The borrower didn't have the security he claimed, so Godsoe camped on his doorstep until he retrieved the money.

Offered a posting in idyllic Nassau, he turned it down because he knew that all the Commonwealth's decisions were made in Toronto. Instead, he chose New York, where he knew he could learn from American bankers; he steeped himself in foreign-exchange operations and the mechanics of the reserve system, and brushed up against Chase Manhattan's David Rockefeller and Citibank's Walter Wriston. It was a sharing experience that formed his method of operation, so that today he regularly calls up Warren Moysey at the Commerce or Joe Regan at the Royal for help in solving problems in operations or methods.

The time in New York also positioned him to return to Toronto under McDonald to co-ordinate U.S. activities before taking on a larger bailiwick in 1975 that included Latin America, the U.S., and international treasury operations. This vast chunk of the bank, some 20 per cent of assets, was still under McDonald, but Godsoe was given a free hand to set it up the way he wanted to. He named the new organization Western Hemisphere International Regional Office (WHIRO) and spent six months planning it. Part of its success was due to the almost folkloric appeal it had as an élite fraternity that exuded fun. There were books, cartoons, jackets, WHIRO hero awards, WHIRO hero awards with bar, a crest with a bull on it, and a Latin motto that translated: "If you don't have a hernia, you're not pulling your weight."

In addition to the foolishness, however, WHIRO was carefully crafted on the matrix organization system Godsoe had learned at Harvard. The theory worked and the results came. During the four years from 1975 to 1979 when Godsoe headed WHIRO, as the international division of the bank expanded to become more than 50 per cent of assets, WHIRO doubled from contributing an initial 35 per cent of international's profits to producing 65 per cent. As a reward, he was made an executive vice-president, WHIRO was divided into several pieces under others, and Godsoe was sent on to do large corporate credits, to pinch-hit whenever senior people were away, and to travel extensively internationally.

By 1982, when they were both named vice-chairmen, he had pulled even with McDonald. As they continue to sort out duties and plan policy, Godsoe is growing outside the bank as well. As the only golfer and tennis player left among the senior executive after Robert MacIntosh departed for the CBA, Godsoe admits: "I'm the only gadabout left." In 1982–83 he also served as president of the Canadian Club, a high-profile position that meant he gave an introductory speech at each weekly meeting and carried out public duties unlike any other Scotiabanker at his level in the institution's more than 150 years. When Godsoe was appointed vice-chairman at forty-three, his first question was a joke: "What are the pension benefits?" He went around telling friends he would retire soon. He didn't. And when he does, it could well be with the title of chairman.

THE TORONTO-DOMINION

At fifty, Dick Thomson still has another fifteen years to go before normal retirement age. While no one would suggest that the aggressive, interventionist Thomson is doing a bad job, his long stay cannot help engendering dissatisfaction among eager pretenders to the throne. There is little meaningful upward movement in the ranks.

Thomson's current number two, president Robin Korthals, is two months older than Thomson and has been president since 1981. He was chosen for the job by a committee of four including Thomson, former chairman Allen Lambert, former deputy chairman Sam Paton, and former president Ben Boyle. That selection process measured chemistry and compatibility as well as achievement and talent. As a result, Thomson finds it difficult to explain what it was about Korthals that set him apart from the other candidates, but points to Korthals's financial capabilities and his technical orientation, announcing: "He loves how things work."

Korthals is the perfect man to run the bank's internal operations, the one with whom Thomson could form the classic Mr. Inside, Mr. Outside combination. Korthals can mind the store, Thomson can walk the streets pushing his wares as the high-profile salesman for the bank. Further, Thomson and Korthals are both graduate engineers and fitness buffs. When Korthals was chosen, two other men were passed over and have now gone as high as they can: Ted McDowell, fifty-four, who was made a vice-chairman in charge of domestic operations, and Bob Dickson, fifty-four, who became a vice-chairman for international. Thomson is unlikely to retire early or depart for another job, so only severely failing health would bring Korthals into Thomson's chair. Long banking reigns are becoming commonplace at the TD. Lambert ran the bank for eighteen years; Thomson could be in charge until 1998.

Where Thomson is smooth, Korthals is almost saucy. A ski-jump nose, front teeth that protrude like those of a cartoon mouse, and a tuneless hum that emanates from his throat for no apparent reason simply reinforce his image as an unusual banker—even "strange," in the word of director Monte Black. It is an image he almost curries by regularly wheeling his ten-speed Polish commuter bicycle the three miles he travels to work, jogging every morning, sporting brown suede shoes in place of the regulation black oxfords of his peers, and sipping beer, rather than martinis, at bank receptions.

He was born in Venezuela in 1933, where his father worked for Royal Dutch Shell. Korthals's mother, a woman of Scots descent, wanted to christen him Robin. The registrar at Maracaibo could come no closer than Roberto, however, so his official name remains Roberto Willem Korthals. All bank documents refer to him as Robert, however, and the whole thing is further confused by the fact that he is universally known as Robin. When he was five, Korthals's family moved to Curaçao, where his father was managing director of the refinery. Curaçao had so little crime that as a boy he could wander anywhere on his own, tramp the beautiful beaches, learn to sail in the gentle trade winds, and bring his dog to school.

About the time Robin was ready for high school, ten years later, his father was transferred to Argentina, and boarding schools in Australia, South Africa, and Canada were sifted. Canada was chosen because of what Korthals's father saw as a frontier entrepreneurial spirit, although he had never visited the country. Initially, however, Robin's time at Ridley, a private boys' school, was a shock as well as unwelcome regimentation. "I'll not forget getting off the train on a February morning in St. Catharines with the wind blowing across the vineyards. It was like Siberia." His English was poor and the school did not offer the sports he'd played at home or the personal freedom he'd enjoyed. The three years there, 1947 to 1950, were rites of passage, toughening times when he was forced to adjust: "The greatest value I got out of Ridley was surviving."

From there he went to U of T for chemical engineering; he graduated in 1955 and went to work for Electric Reduction Co. of Canada Ltd., selling inorganic phosphorus-based chemicals to various corporate buyers. He travelled thirty-six thousand miles a year, did not enjoy it, and was not a particularly good salesman: "The job wasn't taking me anywhere except improving my driving." He'd made some money in the stock market and, still unmarried, decided to drift around Europe.

Before he left he was overcome by pangs of guilt, however, and applied to Harvard, vaguely hoping that he wouldn't be accepted. He was. The six hundred or so students in the two-year MBA programme were divided into seven sections. His group produced no scholars but no failures, either. He finished in the top half, partied actively, skied in Vermont regularly, and suffered his first marketing and production failure. He and two other students set up a brewery in the residence washroom. Even with a snappy name, the Old Hummingbird Brewery, and sporting its own logo, no one would buy the stuff. The three were forced to drink all their output themselves. At Harvard he learned that three or four people could offer the "key values" for the rest, a lesson he later applied in the bank.

Before he joined the bank, he worked from 1961 to 1967 for the investment firm Nesbitt, Thomson. There he soaked up analysis skills and negotiated corporate financing such as the $50-million Rio Algom underwriting that was the biggest of that era. He also learned humility fast. On the first day on the job, June 10, 1961, he sat ensconced behind his desk in the thirteenth-floor walnut-panelled office with a secretary on call and two phones at hand, waiting for the deals to roll in. His phone buzzed with the first call. It was his boss, senior vice-president Ian Crookston: "Mr. Korthals, could you come down here a moment, please?" Down the hall, up to the desk, ready for action, only to hear: "I wonder if you could go downstairs and get me a chicken sandwich on white?"

Recruited by Allen Lambert and Dick Thomson into TD, Korthals, with Thomson as his mentor, moved through term financing to national accounts, a new and aggressive corporate credit department. It was there he made his name as a tough and skilful negotiator, and became general manager in 1972; he was elevated to the level of vice-president for administration later that same year. There he was involved in the bank's television campaign with an ad that used Russian dialogue during the Canada–Soviet Union hockey series. He was the golden boy who could do no wrong, and in 1978 he was appointed executive vice-president and chief general manager. Not every one of his peers was impressed. It was an appointment that precipitated the departure of five officers, who could see that their chances were slim in a place that rewarded such johnny-come-latelies who had been with the bank only a decade. After all, the whispers went, he hadn't spent time in the branches, he hadn't gone through the upheaval of countless family moves around the country. And then there was his attitude—so unconcerned, so unnatural. "Having a senior job brings satisfaction," he admits. "I'm lucky in the sense that it's happened, but I wouldn't have sacrificed very much to achieve it. I'm not consumed by ambition."

He *is* consumed by fitness; he has completed the hundred-mile Canadian Ski Marathon from Montreal to Ottawa and calls himself a "mildly compulsive" jogger. At one point he was doing a bone-rattling eight miles every morning, then dragging himself in to work. By two o'clock all he wanted to do was steal an afternoon nap. He knew he had to reduce his running, and his duties as president have also meant that he has cut back on his sailing. Before becoming president, he could slip away on a Tuesday afternoon to the Royal Canadian Yacht Club on the Toronto Islands. There he'd sail his blue-hulled $60,000 thirty-four-foot C&C racer-cruiser, called the *Rangeley* after the swift blue land-locked salmon found in Maine, where he and his wife, Judy, honeymooned.

Now that he's made it to the top in a job that pays $300,000, he has gained something else, the freedom to be honest about himself: "I've always been lazy, I've always had trouble psyching myself up. I don't have a high energy level. I kind of like taking it easy." He knows, too, that failure is possible. "The penalties for not getting psyched up are fairly great in terms of public embarrassment or very serious error. And fear is a great motivator. In your heart, you know if you've failed, even if it's not obvious immediately to all those around you."

In private he can be a severe critic of the bank. Once, a mix-up at the Chargex Centre meant that when the wife of a prominent individual used her TD Chargex card at an exclusive shop, she was suspected of fraud because the name on her card was the same as that of a delinquent card user. The card was seized on the spot. Korthals was irate at the mistake and told the story to others with this opening line: "Did you hear what the Gestapo at Chargex did?" Another time, after a management foul-up, Korthals could only shake his head and wail: "If I was a teller in this bank, I'd be in the god-damned union so fast."

And there are those who see him quite differently, as a very powerful man who uses his position to disregard the rules that apply to ordinary folk, such as the regulation prohibiting animals on the loose at the RCYC. The Korthalses persist in bringing their two Siamese cats to the island, letting them run about when they spend time on the boat, much to the chagrin of neighbouring craft owners. Complaints to the club go nowhere; Korthals has too much clout. And for all the family closeness (Korthals built one of his three children a sailboat in the garage), there are still times when the job stands in the way of good marital relations. Judy has been known to phone her husband at work and announce herself by saying: "This is your doormat speaking."

Korthals's unorthodox behaviour often amazes those who watch him, but old friend Monty Gordon, chairman of Gordon, Lloyd-Price Investments, sees the advantages that his unique qualities bring to the bank: "A lot of senior bankers are like trained seals. You wonder how they got there; they don't seem very bright. I think of Robin as an *American* businessman. He can pick the meat off the bones faster than most." Says Paul Morton, president of Global Communications, whose television network was saved from oblivion in the mid-1970s by Korthals's efforts: "I don't think he tries to create the impression — as some senior bankers do — that he is God Almighty Himself."

After two years on the job, Korthals has lost some steam. The times have turned sour and his hair is going grey. Friends wonder if he will last the fifteen years to retirement or whether he will be wooed elsewhere, not content to while away his remaining productive years in Dick Thomson's shadow. He misses the creativity of deal-making; the vicarious pleasure he receives from watching others have all the fun may soon pall. Certainly there are those around the bank who wish he'd never come and would be glad to see him gone. His disappearance would open up that upward-bound slot again. But Korthals dearly loves to win and might not give them the opportunity to beat him, even by taking the top spot at another company. When he bought a Mirror Dinghy for one of his children, he and the seller dickered about the price for a while and were $100 apart. Korthals finally agreed to pay the asking price — but only if the seller agreed to deposit the proceeds in a TD bank account. It is in his nature to want to win — and he hasn't got it all. Not yet.

Among those who might benefit from his departure are executive vice-presidents Don Carman and Alan Hockin. Carman, fifty-nine, however, could be judged to have insufficient operational experience, having functioned in more or less a staff job as Korthals's executive assistant. Not a launching pad for the top. Nor is Hockin, at sixty, likely to get the nod. His time has all been with the investment department. Both are simply too old for the top. Senior vice-president Ernest Mercier, fifty, has a slim shot, but only if Korthals or Thomson were to leave soon. His divorce and subsequent remarriage to a former underling twenty years his junior may not have done his career any harm, but it didn't help, either.

There are also three others within the bank whose meteoric careers have made them comers, although another decade would be a long time for any of them to wait. At 250 pounds, Bill Brock is a portly Santa Claus figure who looks older than his forty-seven years. Another MBA, he's paid his dues by working in Hong Kong and Singapore and he's had two postings in England. As a graduate of the Ontario Agricultural College, he's also been involved in less romantic operations, including food airlifts for starving farm herds in Newfoundland seized by the bank one snowbound winter. As the number two man today in international under Bob Dickson, Brock makes most day-to-day decisions. Thomson and Korthals often defer to him as well. An articulate spokesman in public, he is also known as a hard-nosed negotiator. Of the three comers, he alone has an office on the executive floor.

S. R. (Bud) McMorran is a 1963 graduate from the University of Western Ontario, but his career path has been all in Canada. He moved swiftly through various credit positions in Montreal and Toronto and was named a vice-president in 1977. He then became senior vice-president for commercial development, in a move often compared around the bank to Dick Thomson's own fast track. Now senior vice-president for operations at forty-four, his domestic background and familiarity with commercial deals — rather than the country risks that Brock works with — may give him a leg up when the job of president comes open.

At forty-three and a Harvard MBA, Charles Baillie is a personable and soft-spoken man who married into the Roland Michener family. A cosmopolitan banker, he can talk freely about any number of topics from sailing to U.S. politics. He loves to do deals and is well positioned for personal plaudits during the bank's current push for growth in the U.S. markets.

In fact, succession at the TD is more than stalled, it is stopped. The heirs already identified are in their forties and if Thomson follows his own pattern, the next chairman and chief executive officer may well be someone who is now in his thirties and as yet unidentified — or it could even be someone not now with the bank.

The crop of bosses before the current Big Five chairmen were authoritarian and reclusive. They ran their banks solo, in the days when the world and its money could afford to move a little more slowly. Today, with electronic funds transfer, automated tellers, complex international economics, and the need for wider horizons, the man at the top has been forced to share some responsibilities while shoring up his hushed, wainscotted office with security systems, support staff, and high-priced help. The next wave at the top will bring another change, for the time has passed when a bank could simply promote someone who joined as a teller thirty-five years ago. Says Doug Peters, Toronto-Dominion senior vice-president: "It used to be that you joined the bank at sixteen and took all the crap, and you finally might get what you wanted. If you ever left — ha! — and if you ever joined another bank, that was the end of it. Things are different now." What does matter these days is not how many cities someone has served in, but education, outside experience, political savvy, communications skills, and issue awareness.

But no matter how different the breed becomes, or how the financial system they devise may change in our electronic age, the focus of the function will never alter. In whatever form society decides to exchange goods, amass wealth, or wield power, the moneyspinners will be its high priests. They will continue to serve and to be worshipped, but they will be loved neither more nor less than they have ever been — or deserve to be.

Index